# Ramblin' Boy

# Ramblin' Boy

## The Letters of Steve Hoyt

*Edited with commentary by*

## DANIEL LEEN

# Contents

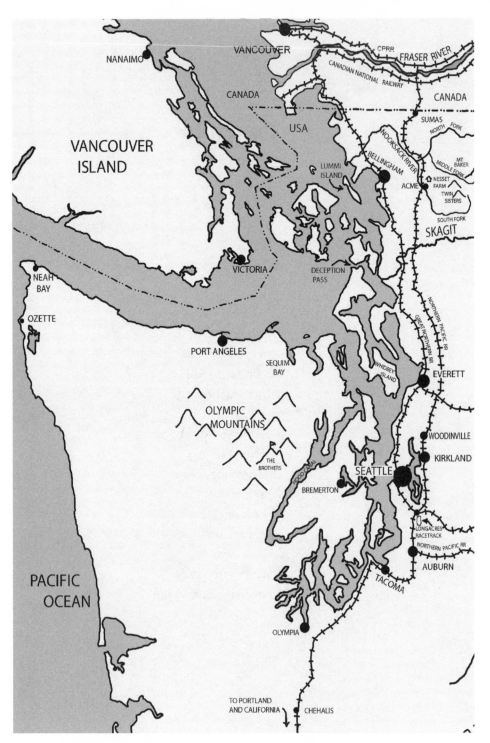

Steve's world, 1972. Western Washington, railroads, rivers, and mountains.

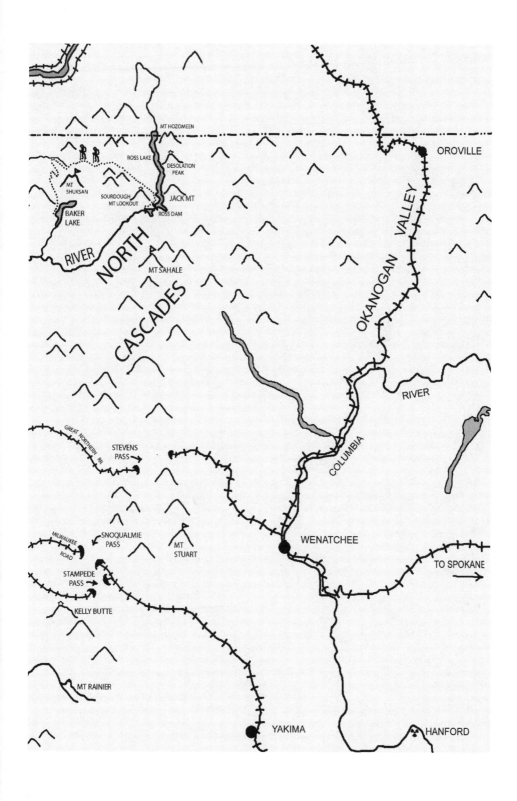

# Author's Note

**D**URING the winter of 2010–11 I had occasion to spend a couple of months in Calgary, Alberta, and while the snow fell and the temperature dropped I needed a project to keep busy with. I had accordingly brought with me a packet of letters and postcards I had saved for about 45 years, letters from a young man by the name of Steve Hoyt dating from the time he went to Europe in the summer of 1965. I thought they would make an interesting present to give to his brothers, two of whom I knew were still living in the Pacific Northwest. While transcribing the letters what I had not anticipated was how I would be slowly drawn back to the time I had received them, and how much they would affect me. I naturally began reminiscing about what I had been thinking and doing at that time and I was not yet finished with the transcription when the idea of filling in the gaps between the letters inspired me to begin a more ambitious project; for the next few years I attempted to reconstruct what three friends, Steve, Doug, and I had been doing between 1960 and 1972. This book is the result. Although it contains first hand accounts of our youthful adventures during a pivotal time in America—hopping freight trains, climbing mountains, working on fishing boats, hitch hiking across America, even experimenting with psychedelic drugs—it is not intended to read like the page turning plot of a best seller but an accurate description of the era it covers. All of the individuals in this account are real people, and at least to the extent that memories can be accurate after forty plus years, all the events depicted actually happened. Also, to protect the guilty and innocent alike, some minor modifications have been editorially exercised. In filling in the gaps between letters, memory has the advantage of hindsight and the perspective of considerable maturity (at least as measured in years) while it may also suffer from inaccuracies due to the passage of time. As historical documents, Steve's letters have the opposite strengths and weaknesses. Perhaps combining these two versions of our personal histories will at least partially balance out some of the imperfections that would otherwise result from relying on only one of these approaches. The few readers who knew Steve personally will have no difficulty understanding why I have taken the time to produce this history. For those who are meeting him for the first time on the printed page, I only regret that my literary skills may not have done him justice. Steve's letters, never written with the idea that anyone but their recipients would read them, will however, offer more than occasional hints of his true character and thus repay the reader for any effort involved in reading this story of an unusual individual and an unusual time.

Daniel Leen
*Seattle*
*October 2015*

# Foreword
## Russ Pfeiffer-Hoyt

THIS is a story that begins at the end of an era and the end of adolescence. These letters illustrate the development of a sensitive young man's thoughts as they are caught up in the increasingly frantic pace of change of the late 1960s. The slow pace of freighthopping and fishing described in the first half of the story gives way a more rapid evolution of thought, with huge leaps between letters as the story approaches its end. We meet Steve Hoyt at 17, just out of high school, driven by a fierce sense of adventure to experience the world. His letters detail his romantic journey to a small fishing village in Norway, revealing his roots and at the same time beginning to create his future. Later, upon his return to America, we see him change from "Steve" to "Sven" as he takes charge of creating himself. Through Sven's eyes we watch the escalation of the Vietnam War and its accompanying draft as it yanks each young man willy-nilly out of their youth, the deathly specter of the war hanging over their heads. This generation, driven together by this threat, creates an unprecedented episode of cultural change. We see Sven drawn into this maelstrom, changing but still retaining a sense of identity as he evolves.

The other major theme of these letters is the story of friendship and its impact on who we become. The friendship between Sven and Dan is of great importance for both. Even when distance and differences of direction separate them they are always bound together by their love of travel, embodied in freighthopping and at the same time a mutual drive to become more than they are as they attempt to find their place in the world. By telling their stories to each other, the stories finally become real.

The tragedy of early loss of such a creative spirit leaves us to ponder who Sven would have become with all his promise and intensity. We live in a time when few see a clear pathway to a hopeful, positive future. Sven's letters hearken back to a time when the future looked brighter and love could prevail over evil in spite of their being written in the era of the Cold War, with human technology poised to destroy all life momentarily. Perhaps today we could use more of the faith and hope that shines through these letters.

Russ Pfeiffer-Hoyt
*October 4, 2012*

# Preface
## Steve Hoyt, 1947–1972

STEVE HOYT was born in Seattle in 1947 and spent his first nine years living in a West Seattle neighborhood before moving to Kirkland in 1956. An early anecdote related by his brother Daryl tells of Steve asking his mother Inez if he could walk around their block when he was three years of age. He completed his first solo trip with no negative experiences, and the encouraging attitude of his mother fostered his independent spirit and love of traveling which runs through all of the letters included in this book. Steve died just before his 25th birthday, but during his short life he experienced more than many of his contemporaries still living.

I first met Steve in Kirkland, Washington, when we both began seventh grade at Kirkland Junior High School. Kirkland at that time was still a fairly small town, with plenty of woods and fields surrounding it, not yet growing like neighboring Bellevue had after the first floating bridge across Lake Washington was completed in 1940. I did not get to know him well until the last year or two of high school, when we formed the Railroad Club. The Railroad Club—one day a bunch of us were sitting around shooting the breeze and someone suggested that since there were so many other clubs at our high school, we ought to have our own club. This was met with gales of laughter, but to continue the joke I typed up a hokey constitution for the club and showed it to

From our slideshow

the rest of the guys. We soon browbeat our Physics teacher into agreeing to be our advisor, and then got a friend to introduce the subject to student council. I remember attending the student council meeting as the subject was broached; it was quite evident that most of the council had the impression we were a group of model train geeks. Instinctively flying under the radar, I did nothing to correct this misapprehension; calling the club the Hobo Club would of course have made this part of the joke impossible to pull off. Since we were already quite active with our field trips, the real purpose of creating the club was merely to have a joke on the rest of the school, especially those who would disapprove of our admittedly illegal and dangerous activities. Our so called field trips consisted of sneaking out of the house at night, catching a local freight train in Woodinville, and riding an empty boxcar down to the old Longacres race track near Renton. There we would jump off the slow moving freight and shiver in the dark, waiting for hours for a northbound freight to take us back to Woodinville, just as dawn was breaking. Then we would sneak back home to spend the rest of the day catching up on sleep. These short trips involving sleep deprivation and

Doug filled with elation as we begin rolling north
from Woodinville to Sumas, March 1965

long boring waits eventually palled on us, and we became more ambitious, deciding instead to catch the same northbound freight when it arrived in Woodinville in the morning. Well fortified with food, we soon began taking an entire day to ride the old N.P. (Northern Pacific Railroad) from Woodinville up to the Canadian border. In the spring of 1965, one outing was particularly memorable. My companions were my friends Doug and Kim, another club member who was new to the experience but nonetheless an eager would-be adventurer. On the train we met a homeward bound Canadian hobo (who, interestingly, was promptly arrested when we reached the border town of Sumas). The crisp, sunny weather with a backdrop of the snow covered Cascade Mountains inspired me to shoot a couple of rolls of slide film. After I got the slides back from the lab I showed them to my fellow travelers, and it seemed perfectly reasonable to us that we should have a slide show at school so everyone else could see what they were missing. One budding hobo swiped a few mimeograph blanks from the office and created a series of eye-catching posters, advertising our upcoming media sensation: "Thrill to the clatter of the wheels... Gasp at

Viewing The Sisters and Mt. Baker as we roll along the Nooksack River, March 1965

live action hobo techniques... See a live Canadian hobo!!!" Along with
the florid prose, he adorned them with a crude drawing of a steam
locomotive, and much underlining and stars. We promptly ran off a
few dozen copies when the office staff wasn't looking and distributed
them around the school, tucking some into the locked glass trophy
cases where they couldn't be easily removed, thus thwarting the Vice
Principal, who was tearing them off bulletin boards as soon as he saw
them. The day of the big show arrived and our unorthodox travelogue
was well received by the students, but such deliberate flaunting of our
activities led to our club promptly losing its official status by fiat of
the Principal. High school as we experienced it in those days involved
more than a little tedium, so it is not surprising that a lot of my classmates found our theatrical prank more than a little funny. I suddenly
found myself being congratulated by many students I barely knew;
although I studiously carried a briefcase and had gotten a straight-A

Documenting railroad culture at Sumas in the spring of 1965. The US-Canadian border can be seen as a vertical white streak on the distant ridge line.

report card for the mid term that year, I was now no longer seen as a mere high school nerd. From that time on, my closest friends were guys like Steve, who hopped freights and climbed mountains to satisfy their craving for fun and adventure.

Although I had been riding freights for a couple of years by this time, Steve's first trip by freight train was with me when we caught one out of Woodinville in May of 1965 on the northbound NP and rode up to the Canadian border. As we waited by the tracks to catch out we encountered an older fellow who told us he was walking to Alaska. He was carrying a good sized pack with a small sign proclaiming: "Visit Alaska, that's where I'm heading" and another adding: "no riders". A spare pair of hiking boots dangled from the back. With his salt and pepper hair and a grizzled three day stubble beard he was to us the epitome of an old time sourdough from Alaska. We naturally urged him to catch out with us, but he refused, insisting that he would walk all the way. When we

COMING SOON!

TO A THEATRE NEAR <u>YOU</u>

THE

# RAILROAD CLUB

MODESTLY PRESENTS

A PROGRAM OF SLIDES AND COMMENTARY

OF ITS LATEST TRIP TO <u>SUMAS</u> ON

THE

# CANADIAN

BORDER

★ <u>SEE</u> THE <u>BIG</u> <u>CITY</u> OF SUMAS!

★ <u>THRILL</u> TO THE CLATTER OF THE WHEELS!

★ <u>SEE</u> LIVE ACTION TECHNIQUES OF FREIGHT-HOPPING

From our slideshow

Steve, hobo and scholar, reading poetry as the train rolls past Sumas Mountain, 1965

questioned him on how long he thought it would take him to get there he succinctly replied, "as long as it takes." We then wished him well and he continued up the road, following State Route 9. We caught our train shortly, and as we rolled up Clearview hill just north of Woodinville we waved to him as he sat resting by an overpass. Although watching the houses and farms of the lowlands roll by with the snow covered Cascade Mountains in the distance was reason enough to enjoy this trip, our meeting with a free spirit who intended to walk more than two thousand miles north was the sort of inspiration that stoked the fires of our wanderlust.

A few weeks later, just after finishing high school, we caught an eastbound Great Northern (later merged with the NP and CB&Q into Burlington Northern) riding a chip car (imagine a giant shoebox filled to the top with green, aromatic wood chips) over Stevens Pass to Wenatchee, "the apple capitol of the world" as it then styled itself. Here we first encountered the fruit tramp in his own element and Steve, who was an avid photographer, took many color slides of the tramps in the yards, inspiring me in turn to want to capture on film this world of the hobo as it then existed. Most of them were alcoholics but quite

Rolling uphill over the Cascade Mountains, June 1965, another Railroad Club outing

Steve rolling into Wenatchee, Washington, June 1965

harmless when sober as I was later to learn. At that time the apple orchards up and down the length of the Okanogan Valley required this seasonal labor to maintain and prune the trees, and later to pick the apples. They were mostly older white guys, who showed up during the spring and summer, riding into Wenatchee on freight trains. We did not know it then, but they were the last of their breed. Our trip back across the mountains the next day was equally inspiring as we took in the same scenery from a different angle, and when we finally got off the train at InterbayYard we immediately repaired to the men's room at nearby Fisherman's Terminal. After copious use of soap and water, we wiped the grime of diesel smoke off our faces and hands, onto the continuous roll of cotton towel, which Steve then autographed: "This dirt courtesy of Great Northern RR".

Riding the freights was thus a new experience for Steve at the time he left for Europe, and I can see how our two trips—one through a rural landscape of western Washington, and the other over a scenic mountain pass to eastern Washington—left an indelible impression on that part of him that yearned to ramble. By early July he had gone

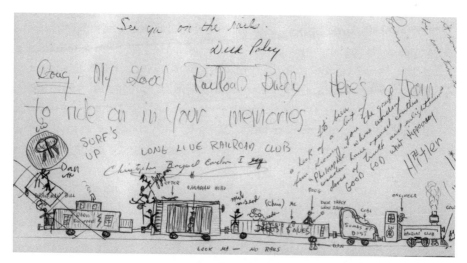

Doug's yearbook

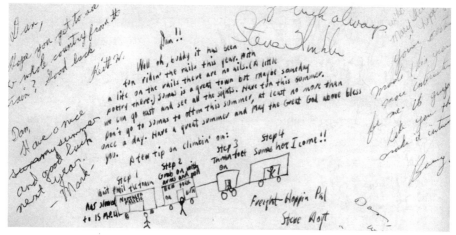

The only part of my high school yearbook I have saved

to Europe with his family, and although he was able to hitch-hike and travel by bicycle, he would have to return to America to satisfy his desire to travel by boxcar.

From the moment I first met him, Steve impressed me as being soft spoken almost to the point of seeming shy. He was, however, athletic as well as being handsome and charismatic and I couldn't imagine him ever having an enemy even in the social jungle of our teenage years at school. In spite of being somewhat straight-laced, he never came across as being anything but a regular guy. He had been a member of the Loyal Temperance Legion, the youth wing of the Women's Christian Temperance Union, and had taken the pledge not to drink, smoke, or take the Lord's name in vain, yet he never made an issue of his beliefs and had no trouble fitting in with those he spent time with. If I were to characterize him now, he exemplified the adage "Still waters run deep." A friend who worked closely with Steve to create the CO-OP garden in Bellingham during the early 70s referred to him as..."somewhat quiet, but visionary in nature. He had strong ideals that he adhered to. He was principled, spiritual, modest, and I don't remember conversations about things like drugs or sex. It was mainly about nature, preserving the earth, gardening, and Aquarian or new age thinking. We connected to spirituality through gardening and discussing poetry, for example. He was not materialistic and camped out a lot in the tent at the garden on 32nd street." After high school he went off to Norway, while I attended Beloit College, a small liberal arts college in the upper Midwest. We corresponded fairly regularly from that time until his death in 1972, seven years later. Most of Steve's letters to me are reproduced here. I have only a couple of letters that I wrote to Steve, but it was his thoughts and dreams that I felt were worth saving, and the loss of my side of the correspondence seems negligible.

I have grouped the letters into five periods: Norway, Traveling, Bremerton, Alaska, and Bellingham, but I see the evolution of Steve's thoughts and worldview in three stages. In the first, he is fresh out of high school, and chooses to experience the world directly, riding a bicycle across Europe, working all winter on a fishing boat in Norway, and then hitting the road again in the spring on his way home. His letters at this time are filled with the immediacy of direct experience and any reflections on their meaning comes more from his heart than from any formal philosophical framework. In the second period, Steve is back in western Washington, surrounded by forests, the mountains, and Puget Sound, studying English Literature and Composition, Botany, Geology, and Russian, as well as reading books in Norwegian which he then spoke fluently. His summer job with a marine biologist and a visit to the 1967 Montreal Expo provide a break from academia, but I believe that his extensive reading of diverse authors (Dostoyevsky, Whitman, Kerouac, Wordsworth, Camus, Twain, Conrad, Bellow, Mishima, Burns, Service, Farrell, Dreiser, Carlyle, Huxley, Plato, Kazantzakis) greatly influences the development of his worldview at this time. While still in Bremerton he mentions plans for building things out of wood, but it is in Bellingham where he moves on to the third stage. After a summer working on a salmon boat near Kodiak Steve enrolls at "Western" (now Western Washington State University), continuing his studies in English Literature and still reading voraciously (Tolstoy, Snyder, Watts, Lorca, Emerson, Thoreau, Updike, Kesey, Hesse, Gide, Kafka) but eventually drops out of college just a few credits short of a degree. Tiring of what he termed "four walls education", Steve moved into a more hands-on approach, connecting with the Puget Sound area by building and sailing wooden boats, fishing in the sound, scuba diving, and gardening. His interest in Oceanography and Marine Biology appears to be of a more practical nature, directly connected with his increasing involvement in local political and environmental issues; he also begins writing articles for the *Northwest Passage* (a counter-culture newspaper published in Bellingham), and helps to found the CO-OP garden in south Bellingham.

One theme runs through all of Steve's letters: a kind of innocence; while he obviously knew that there was evil in the world, his focus was always on the positive. There were strange lands and friendly people just over the horizon; the stalemate of the Cold War which effectively kept large portions of the world off limits to would-be travelers such as he seemed fundamentally pointless to Steve, who enjoyed meeting and conversing with Russian seamen on the docks of any large port. The mystery of life lay buried in the ocean depths, drifting in the breeze of alpine meadows in the high Cascades, and he wanted to experience and understand it all. As enamored as he was of the call of the open road, Steve also had a deep connection with the place he came from, spending significant amounts of time and energy trying to protect it from the worst ravages of an inadequately regulated industrial system. In these times of virtual reality and digital connectivity, going on line might now seem an easier way for young people to satisfy their intellectual curiosity about the world they are in the process of inheriting. Like Steve, I hope that they will also want to learn from the "school of the road", keeping alive the taste for adventure that made life so exhilarating for our generation's "rucksack revolution".

Ramblin' Boy

*. . . here's to you my ramblin' boy*
*May all your rambles bring you joy*

# Introduction

## Coming of Age and
## the Myth of the '60s

**A**s I began to consider the idea of creating this book, I gradually realized that it would also have to be partly my memoir; Steve's letters were a significant influence on my own process of finding my path in life. Of course in the 1960s and early 70s there were no social media such as smart phones and the internet—just radio, TV, newspapers and magazines for information and entertainment, and people regularly exchanged letters when far apart; long distance telephone rates cost serious money in those days. It is somewhat amusing to realize I am now old enough to have to explain to younger readers what the world was like for us as we came of age; my youth is now history. When we were beginning grade school the words "under God" were added to the Pledge of Allegiance as Joseph McCarthy managed to cow an entire country with his anti-communistic witch hunt. By the time we were in our sixth grade year the world had (probably more than once) narrowly avoided a nuclear exchange between Russia and the USA, and about the time we graduated from high school, Viet Nam and the draft were looming over the horizon. At the same time, first marijuana and then more powerful psychedelics made their appearance on college campuses and throughout the "Great Society". While the mostly white labor union movement complacently reveled in its own successes, the civil rights movement was just getting into high gear. Likewise the environmental movement and criticism of the military-industrial complex were only in their beginning stages compared to where they would be by the end of the decade. After being repeatedly told that we lived in the best political system in the world, after being thoroughly indoctrinated as to the clear superiority of what was termed the "free" market economic system, we left home, soon to encounter the bewildering complexity of all these and many related issues. Is it a surprise that some of us began to question various aspects of the world we were confronting?

Perhaps the first thing to mention here is that unless one was inordinately precocious, the early '60s were really an extension of the '50s. As depicted in the well known documentary *American Graffiti*, in high school the cool things were still cars, booze, and James Bond movies, and it was only in the mid '60s that cracks began appearing in the dike of '50s squareness. One seemingly innocuous symbol of the changes happening in America was the character of Maynard G. Krebs, the beatnik high school student on the Dobie Gillis TV show. While appearing in a non-threatening context, a Hollywood version of the beat movement which had already made its mark on the American psyche, it is not stretching things too far to say that he paved the way for many of us to discover and read beat literature a few years later.

But a small, low wattage FM station that began transmitting in December of 1962 in north Seattle was perhaps even more important in this regard. KRAB FM was one of the first community radio stations in the country, and as it grew it began to spread a subtle, unconscious message that things could be done differently. It spread this message not so much in its programming (mainly consisting of music that could not be heard on the commercial stations), but simply by not being like the other stations, not having commercials, not trying to extract dollars from consumers' pockets, not being part of the big machine. While the regular rock & roll stations continued to play the usual fare, the folk music revival had its beginnings at this time as well. At first it was the rather homogenized and sanitized versions by mainstream groups, epitomized by the song *Tom Dooley* as sung by the Kingston Trio in 1958. It was only when I left home to attend college that I encountered Alan Lomax's scratchy Library of Congress recordings of old black men singing their traditional blues, the source material drawn upon by the people we heard on mainstream radio. But the dike was giving way, and even on the rock and roll stations we soon began to hear protest songs by the likes of Tom Paxton, Joan Baez and Bob Dylan. The times they were a changin'.

Those of us who enjoyed hiking and camping as kids later became serious mountain climbers as our experience and mobility allowed, but by the time we were in high school such activities were generally considered rather dorky. At a time when having your own set of wheels was the benchmark by which all versions of cool were judged, merely to be seen riding a bicycle was a terrible *faux pas* and touring the Puget Sound area by bicycle was the height of uncool. Although I regularly attended Explorer Scout meetings throughout high school I wouldn't have been caught dead wearing the uniform at school. The party line from adults (then as now) was to keep away from alcohol and cigarettes, and of course the more adventuresome of us experimented with them. While very few in my high school senior class had smoked a joint, those who had were certainly smart enough not to mention it to the rest of us. For the overwhelming majority of us the idea of taking drugs to "expand one's consciousness" was unheard of. For those of us interested in getting some bread together to buy and fix up an old car, jobs were available, but a minimum wage of $1.25/hr. made such pursuits seem to me rather like an entry level position for joining the rat race. Like Steve, I might occasionally try to earn a few bucks, but only enough to buy gas for the next trip into the mountains or the army surplus back pack and hiking boots that would make the trip possible. Small wonder then that freighthopping seemed too good to be true; we could now aspire to longer trips at virtually no cost, the perfect version of adventure travel. Our transportation options were greatly expanded, and very little specialized gear would be required.

There are three main characters in this book: Steve, myself, and Doug, although other friends were also involved in the experiences described here. We spent a lot of time together between 1964 and 1972, the year Steve died. Mostly we hopped freight trains, hitch-hiked, went back-packing and mountain climbing, mostly in the Pacific Northwest. Because Steve's letters form the skeleton of the book, Doug and I have diminished roles, but I have tried to fill in our parts where it seemed that it would shed light on the ethos of the time or otherwise round out the general picture. In the fall of 1965, about the time I began classes at Beloit College, I read *On the Road* (Kerouac, 1957) for the first time and was thereby inspired, beginning with a hitch-hiking trip from there to northern Wisconsin that Thanksgiving, to keep a journal of my trips by freight train and hitch-hiking. Thus I am able to recount some of those experiences in detail even where my own memories have faded. Along with Steve's and Doug's letters, I have included some fairly detailed accounts of my trips as neither of them described much of their trips in their letters. There are not many of Doug's letters reproduced here (he was not as prolific a letter writer as Steve), but those that I have included vividly depict a third perspective on this time period. Because I knew Doug for a few years before I met Steve, I also want to describe here a bit of our earlier activities in order to give the reader an idea of how it all began.

I had met Doug in fifth grade, about the time we turned eleven. Our first outing together was to explore the gravel pit where Juanita High School now stands, and our first summit achieved was the old water tower which stood at the east side of Finn Hill. From there we were able to survey all of the Juanita Creek drainage, with the new housing developments just beginning to alter an otherwise bucolic landscape of fields and fir trees, harbingers of the changes to our community that Steve later so deplored. The following year we joined the Boy Scouts and at about the same time, we began an instinctive guerrilla campaign against the housing developments, sneaking into the vast swaths of bare earth where once stood "our" woods, moving the surveyors' grading stakes, vandalizing bulldozers, and stealing lumber and nails to build tree-houses in the woods not yet destroyed. Almost as an extension of our camping and hiking activities, we also began going on bike-hikes to a remote beach on the southern tip of Whidbey Island, around Hood Canal, and over the hills to the Snoqualmie Valley during the next few years. By the time we were in high school we had gone through the fairly rigorous Explorer Search and Rescue training near Mount Pilchuck (under the aegis of the Boy Scouts of America and the local Mountain Rescue Council). Search and Rescue training was as demanding as any activity I have pursued as an adult. Long before the advent of GPS we were required to navigate through rough country, following compass bearings from hand held compasses, using topographic maps, counting our paces to determine our progress through areas devoid of trails, all this in cold rain or wet snow as the winter weather dictated in the foothills of the Cascade Mountains. I realize now that I joined the organization for the adventure, not because of any inner streak of altruism. But once I started going on searches, I did take pride in helping to carry injured hikers out to a road and helping to locate lost children by tramping through the dripping woods for an entire night. In the summer of 1963 (just before our Search and Rescue training) Doug and I caught our first freight train out of Woodinville, down to Black River Junction next to the Longacres racetrack. At first our outings by rail were very short (actually night) trips, but eventually we succumbed to full blown dromomania.

Our most ambitious backpacking trip was also that summer when at the age of 15 we crossed about 90 miles of wild country up near the Canadian border. At the road's end we were dropped off in the upper reaches of the Skagit Valley at the base of Diablo Dam and from there began hiking farther up the valley until we could turn west and continue across the North Cascades Primitive Area. This US Forest Service designation could have been translated at the time as "We'll log these trees later, when we get around to them", but the area now constitutes the northern portion of the North Cascades National Park. We hiked through this wilderness for a bit over a week, skirting the north side of the Pickett Range, eventually reaching the end of the road following the north fork of the Nooksack River to Mt. Baker. We saw no one on the trail for the first five days, and then only a few people as we neared the end of the trip. Doug's folks drove up to Baker Lake where they found us hiking down the road toward our rendezvous campground, out of food but otherwise none the worse for wear. On that hike, we had minimal emergency gear, good compasses and a USFS map that was ½ inch to the mile with fairly detailed creeks delineated, but without topographic lines. We ate a lot of dried food, were generally hungry, and even surprised a black bear at one point, but our greatest danger was when we found some old dynamite sticks in one of the Adirondack shelters, which we foolishly (and unsuccessfully) tried to ignite with a firecracker we had had the foresight to bring with us. I have however never forgotten the vastness of that stretch of wilderness, especially as we looked across the peaks and valleys from the high passes, reconnoitering the probable route that the very faint and poorly marked trail might take.

The following year, we spread our wings a bit more, wanting to see just how far we could get by rail and thumb in the two weeks we had left until the beginning of our senior year of high school. I don't believe we even bothered to tell our folks exactly where we were going to go "hiking", but I do remember telling them we were going by bicycle to the Olympic Mountains. We loaded up our gear and rode over to Woodinville where we cached the bikes and caught the southbound NP freight that night, heading for California. To us California was a magical, almost mythical place—surfers and sunshine, palm trees, and warm nights. We found a loaded lumber car and rolled out sleeping bags on top of the aromatic green timber, watching the starry sky slowly rotate as we rumbled around the curves past Auburn and Tacoma. We scarcely slept all the way to Portland as we watched the hypnotic sweep of the engine's headlight against a dark backdrop of trees and sky. Once in Portland, we caught a ride into town as the sun came up, feeling tired and dirty. Sitting in back with our packs, I happened to look down on the floor of the car and saw a $50 bill. I picked it up in amazement and gave it to our benefactor who was so pleased to have the money (which he had lost earlier) that he said he would take us anywhere in Portland, which certainly pleased us. He drove us over to Brooklyn Yards where we caught out on the fly (boarding a moving freight train), riding a gondola down to Eugene. We spent half the day sitting in Albany however, waiting for clearance to continue south, and while there we made the acquaintance of some fruit tramps who were passing around a jug of Mogen David (a sweet fortified grape wine termed "Mad Dog" by those who drank it). One of them jokingly offered us a drink. Doug declined, but I wanted to know what it tasted like, and bravely took a sip while the other tramps laughed. It tasted pretty bad, but at least I would have something to brag about when I got back home.

Our freight rolled into Eugene around midnight and we began hitch-hiking. We caught our first ride with a GI who had just returned from a hitch overseas and was driving an old car which he couldn't get out of second gear. I sat in the front and talked while Doug snoozed in the back seat. We rolled slowly down Highway 99 and sections of the incomplete Interstate 5, which was then in the process of being built. In the morning we caught another ride with a couple of guys not much older than us, driving a souped-up car with a cut-out on the exhaust pipe. Once we were well out of a town, they would pull a small wire cable on the floor to let the exhaust bypass the muffler (thus the term "cut-out"), which resulted in a most satisfying throaty roar from the old V-8 engine. Although they were a little vague about their own situation, we realized that they too had flown the coop, not telling their parents that they were driving down to LA before they had left town. We gave them a couple of bucks for gas and they dropped us off in Sausalito, where we crashed with Doug's aunt and uncle. Once in California, we called our folks to notify them of our change of plans, knowing that they couldn't do much about it at that point. We hung around the Bay Area for a few days, essentially mooching off of Doug's relatives, and then continued hitching south to Anaheim where we crashed with another aunt and uncle. We spent a day visiting Disneyland and Knott's Berry farm, spending almost no money, but did have one small adventure on a train. The steam train at Knott's Berry Farm proved too much of a temptation for us, and when it left the station, we swung on board on the side opposite the paying passengers and briefly enjoyed our ride. Part of the steam train experience however, involved two "train robbers" coming through the train to "rob" the passengers, and after performing this bit of theater they encountered us in our adjacent and hitherto private car. They asked us what we were doing there and were not amused when we told them we were hobos. We were then turned over to a supervisor, who lectured us and kicked us out of the amusement park. Our brief ride did have one rather obscure symbolic consequence however. Among all the hobos, only those who have ridden steam trains can be called "bridgers" (because their careers bridge the periods of steam and diesel power), and now Doug and I could claim that august status.

After our brush with the law, we continued hitch-hiking south to Carlsbad (California), where my grandparents lived. We stayed there just a day or two, and then started towards home, having run out of excuses to go any farther south. As we started back north, we had one of our best rides, in a semi, sitting high above the rest of the cars as we barreled down the highway, asking the truck driver questions and learning the lore of the big rigs. They had no CB radios, instead communicating with flashing headlights and hand signals as they passed each other in opposite directions. We also learned that there was an informal traffic in nudist magazines carried on by some long haul truckers; this guy had a dozen of them sitting in his small berth directly behind the cab. One of us reclined there, looking at pictures of sun worshippers at work and play while the other rode shotgun and took in the highway experience. Although at this point having little cash, we took in a side trip to Reno and Lake Tahoe with a guy who picked us up and offered to give us a place to stay while he was in town trying to organize a church camp. Then we continued north catching a series of shorter rides until we were eventually let off in front of the Jockey Shop, a restaurant at Longacres racetrack just south of Seattle. This happened to be next to the NP tracks at Black River Junction where we had so often waited all night to catch the northbound freight back to Woodinville, and we felt we were almost home. Nevertheless, our main concern at the moment was eating. We pooled our last few coins and a waitress took pity on us, saying she'd give us a long stack for the short stack price. We were just about to dig into our stacks of waffles topped with ice cream and strawberries when we heard the whistle of a northbound freight. Without a word spoken between us we dropped our utensils, put all our money on the table, grabbed our packs, and headed for that freight, running across an open field and up a steep bank to catch it on the fly. Soon we were sitting atop a boxcar (at that time all boxcars had ladders to the top with a metal catwalk running down the center of the roof, providing a relatively safe place to sit when riding on top), Doug playing a Jew's harp and I a harmonica. As we rolled past a grade crossing near Kirkland we were spotted by a guy we knew who worked with Doug's dad; we were busted. When we got back to our respective homes later in the day we were told how wrong our trip had been, especially hitch-hiking and hopping freights, but do you think we really believed it?

At this point I will include a bit of historical context regarding the construction of the interstate highway system. Passed by congress as a defense program, it would tie the country together in terms of speed and convenience, making long haul trucking much more efficient and thereby starting a slow decline of the passenger railroad system it largely supplanted. When Doug and I hitched south to California in 1964 however, there were only scattered sections of I-5 completed, with islands of the old US Route 99 in between. These sections of two lane road not only slowed traffic significantly, but they embodied a different mentality concerning hitch-hiking. On Highway 99, one could stick out his thumb wherever it was convenient for a motorist to pull over with little hassle from the cops. Thus we always asked a prospective ride if they were going as far as the next stretch of the older, two lane highway so we wouldn't be stranded on the newer interstate, where hitch-hiking was not only more difficult, but also prohibited. On old Highway 99, there were usually stoplights in the larger towns it passed through, which made hitching even more convenient. Although we didn't think much about it at the time, it would be only a few short years until we would be fenced out of the interstates and hitch-hiking there would be a ticketable offence, making the hitch south to California a continual game of cat-and-mouse with the California state bulls. By the time we were out of high school in the summer of 1965, it seemed that everybody and his brother was hitch-hiking; the freeway onramps then had as many hitch-hikers as they now have the home guard flying the sign. Many older men who picked us up would gratuitously comment that we should be careful about who we got a ride with, because, while hitch-hiking had been safe when they were young, "now there were a lot of crazy people out there." I remember hearing this in the late '50s, hitch-hiking home from town. I also heard it during the '60s, the '70s, and the '80s. I have no doubt that this caution is still given today when drivers pick up hitch-hikers.

Aside from hiking, mountain climbing, and freighthopping, Doug and I also spent a little time sailing his folks' small sailboat on Lake Washington, just enough to give us a taste of the nautical life and want more, neither of us then guessing just how much time we would both be spending on sailboats in the future. Whenever the opportunity presented itself, we also engaged in many of the usual teenage male risk-taking activities: climbing the 250' local radio tower one night in Kirkland, climbing the Space Needle from the basement up to the top of the roof (where Doug stole a small bronze fitting off the very top) and other such "harmless pranks". There were older guys in the area who engaged in even more dramatic and illegal behavior, such as burning down derelict barns and condemned houses, letting the air out of all the bus tires for the entire (Lake Washington 414) school district one night when they couldn't find their scout meeting location, and detonating the contents of a certain case of stumping dynamite that disappeared from a small logging outfit up by Granite Falls. But although these latter mentioned activities were talked about among my peers, they were generally perpetrated by others and it may well be that they made our own choices seem quite reasonable and restrained by comparison. Most of this restlessness was, I think, a reaction to the tedium of our somewhat regimented lives at school, where it seemed we were hectored daily about the importance of getting a good education so we wouldn't end up as "bums".

During my senior year of high school my brother returned home one weekend from Wenatchee Community College, telling me about a book he had recently come across: "It's all about a guy who hops freights and climbs mountains!" He was of course describing Kerouac's *The Dharma Bums*. In my first year of college I would be reading *On the Road*, which made me want to find and read Kerouac's later book, but *The Dharma Bums* was by this time out of print, its rarity making it a sort of sacred text to those of us who were serious about hitting the road and "seeing the elephant". The main character in this *roman a clef* was Gary Snyder, a west coast poet who was part of the San Francisco Poetry Renaissance in the mid 50s. I was soon to find and read Snyder's essays and poetry about the Northwest landscape, native culture, labor history, and Zen Buddhism. Although Kerouac's novel was hastily written and rife with the author's particular hang-ups, meeting Snyder had greatly impressed Kerouac, just as his book had in turn awakened so many of my generation to Snyder's "rucksack revolution". This was the Northwest that I knew and understood, and here was a blueprint for the lifestyle I was yearning for. Snyder's voluntary poverty as a graduate student at Berkeley was a modern exemplification of Thoreau's ideals:

> [Gary] and I were kind of outlandish-looking on the campus in our old clothes in fact [Gary] was considered an eccentric around the campus, which is the usual thing for campuses and college people to think whenever a real man appears on the scene—colleges being nothing but grooming schools for the middleclass non-identity which usually finds its perfect expression on the outskirts of the campus in rows of well-to-do houses with lawns and television sets in each living room with everybody looking at the same thing and thinking the same thing at the same time while the [Garys] of the world go prowling in the wilderness to hear the voice crying in the wilderness, to find the ecstasy of the stars, to find the dark mysterious secret of the origin of faceless wonderless crapulous civilization. "All these people," said [Gary], "they all got white-tiled toilets and take big dirty craps like bears in the mountains, but it's all washed away to convenient supervised sewers and nobody thinks of crap any more or realizes that their origin is shit and civit and scum of the sea. They spend all day washing their hands with creamy soaps they secretly wanta eat in the bathroom." He had a million ideas, he had 'em all.
>
> "I've been reading Whitman, know what he says, *Cheer up slaves, and horrify foreign despots*, he means that's the attitude for the Bard,

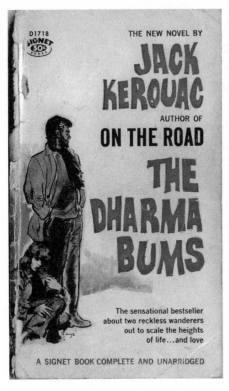

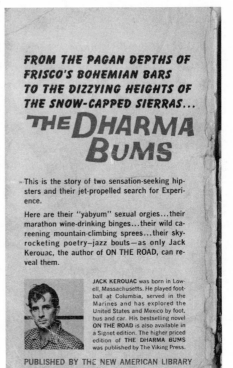

the Zen Lunacy bard of old desert paths, see the whole thing is a world full of rucksack wanderers, Dharma Bums refusing to subscribe to the general demand that they consume production and therefore have to work for the privilege of consuming, all that crap they didn't really want anyway such as refrigerators, TV sets, cars, at least new fancy cars, certain hair oils and deodorants and general junk you finally always see a week later in the garbage anyway, all of them imprisoned in a system of work, produce, consume, work, produce, consume, I see a vision of a great rucksack revolution thousands or even millions of young Americans wandering around with rucksacks, going up to mountains to pray, making children laugh and old men glad, making young girls happy and old girls happier, all of 'em Zen Lunatics who go about writing poems that happen to appear in their heads for no reason and also by being kind and also by strange unexpected acts keep giving visions of eternal freedom to everybody and to all living creatures, . . .

Like many of my friends, I had been camping out and hitch-hiking locally since about the time I was in sixth grade. Now we had discovered a world where this was a cool thing, almost a revolutionary act. The rest of the story about how the Beat Generation slowly evolved into the Hippy Generation is too long to retail here, but it is clear that the beat literature of the '50s had a significant role in awakening our hippie consciousness of the '60s. Along with Henry David Thoreau, we also read Alan Watts on Zen and LSD, as well as Ferlinghetti, Ginsberg, Burroughs, and many other beat writers as the mid '60s turned into the decade of the hippies. Eleven years after Kerouac immortalized a lonely ridgetop in two of his novels I found myself climbing the trail to Desolation Peak where I spent the summer of 1967 as a fire lookout, watching for the distant smoke of forest fires and contemplating the "void of Hozomeen" just as Kerouac had. As indicated in many of his letters, Steve's impressive ability to live on very little money was clearly inspired by Thoreau as well as Kerouac's depiction of Snyder's acetic lifestyle, but it was also grounded in his experiences hiking and riding the freights, as it was for Doug and me.

It is difficult to find any discussion of the '60s without frequent references to psychedelic drugs. Marijuana ("pot", "dope", "weed", &c.) was of course the first and most common of these, smoked by everyone who was going to try anything at all. In 1966 it was being talked about and experimented with by the adventurous, and by 1967 it was quite common on most college campuses. Before further descriptions of reckless and illegal behavior are provided however, perhaps I should stress here that in the narrative that follows, I have attempted to present events as they happened and the thoughts I had at that time (insofar as I can remember them) regarding the use of psychedelics and alcohol. Not surprisingly, with the perspective of age my attitudes have undergone significant changes, and a description of my own occasional reckless behavior then is not intended to glorify it or encourage anyone to imitate it now. "The fool who persists in his folly will become wise." At that time however, my first experience with marijuana produced a change in my perception of the world which seemed at once profound and intriguing while at the same time very hard to explain to straights (as non-dopers were termed at the time) such as Steve. These early experiences also made me want to read Zen Buddhist texts; the paradoxical riddle-like Zen koan seemed to resonate with the altered states of consciousness produced by marijuana and thus seemed to be a potential key to the philosophical questions I was then beginning to grapple with. After a few months of smoking pot occasionally, I also became interested in the indole group of hallucinogens: LSD, Mescalin, Peyote cactus, Psylocybin, and psilocybe or "magic mushrooms" and I began reading whatever I could find regarding their effects on one's consciousness. (At that time, LSD was still a legal substance, only becoming outlawed in the US in October of 1968.) A number of psychiatrists had conducted studies on its effects on healthy people, and out of these experiences an underground cult developed. Individuals who had profound experiences while under its influence "turned on" their friends, who in turn turned on more friends and acquaintances. It was common to prepare a quiet place where the people taking the trip, a trip into another world, another consciousness, would not be disturbed, and an individual who had previously experienced the drug would often act as a guide. Doug had taken LSD before me, and thus acted as my guide, just as I was a guide to others when I later introduced it to them. Through a contact of Doug's in San Francisco, I was able to score about a dozen fresh peyote buttons in early 1967 and back at Beloit College later that spring I shared them with a few friends, choking the nausea inducing cacti down with the help of some Dramamine. This experience was again intriguing but fell short of being definitive, and most of us resolved to seek further, which we did after our classes ended that spring. From Beloit we had hopped a freight out to Seattle, scored some LSD from our erstwhile Railroad Club member Kim (who later became a big time drug dealer) and then caught a southbound freight, heading for the Bay Area. After an inconvenient delay in the Portland "Crowbar Hotel" due to getting busted by an unsympathetic yard bull, we finally found ourselves sitting on a grassy slope in the hills above Berkeley, surrounded by eucalyptus trees, basking in the mild sunny weather of California's endless summer. We all dropped (took) acid together, and in about an hour our existential questions about what it was all about were answered, but try as we might, we could not seem to put the experience into words, and continually collapsed into gales of laughter as we tried. We all remarked that we finally understood the koan in *Zen Flesh, Zen Bones*, a collection of cryptic zen stories and proverbs we had all been reading during the winter term at Beloit. But perhaps this was merely because we had been focusing on Zen koan, perhaps some other spiritual discipline would have yielded analogous results. The main point I am trying to make here however, is that for Doug and me, taking psychedelic drugs was fundamentally a spiritual quest. Although I took LSD a few more times during the next year or so, eventually I realized that while one can experience the enlightenment that it can produce, one cannot retain that kind of satori, and eventually one has to take what he has learned and simply go on living. I had one friend from college who never learned that lesson, and having taken acid (LSD) a few too many times ended up in a psychiatric ward, later dying of an overdose, possibly suicidal. When taking drugs as an end in itself, this was a possibility and we were quite aware that we were playing with fire. At that time our desire to understand how we fitted into the cosmos made the risks seem acceptable; for us psychedelics were merely the means to an end. Although Doug was an early adopter of marijuana and LSD and I followed his lead not too much later, we both eventually quit using them when the experiences no longer seemed useful. Steve's innate caution in this area served him well however, as he avoided all drugs and alcohol for most of the time that I knew him. I do not remember even smoking a joint with Steve, and although he did smoke pot occasionally by the early 70s, consciousness expanding drugs just weren't his thing. I believe however, that any psychedelics he may have taken would only have enhanced his inspiration from the ideas in books he read, the people he interacted with, and the mystical connection he felt with the Pacific Northwest and the road.

My original interest in Buddhism was sparked by reading *The Dharma Bums*, but it was Doug who introduced me to the writings of Gary Snyder and D. T. Suzuki as I was beginning to develop my own personal philosophy. As a philosophy, Buddhism stresses awareness of our relationships with one another, how we treat all living things and (in modern neo-Buddhist thought) the earth itself. The struggle to attain right behavior in these two areas were exemplified by my generation's attitudes toward the environment and by our reaction to the draft and the Viet Nam War.

While strands of the philosophical tradition can be traced back to Emerson, Thoreau, and more recently via John Muir, Aldo Leopold, and Rachel Carson, Carson's *Silent Spring* (1962) is credited by many as the seed that sprouted into the modern environmental movement. By the end of the '60s the word had spread and politicians such as Wisconsin senator Gaylord Nelson were sponsoring a national event, the first Earth Day. I remember hitching down from Fairbanks, Alaska, arriving in Seattle on the first Earth Day in April of 1970. A bunch of freaks (as long haired hippies were termed in those days) picked me up around Wenatchee and told me they were headed to Seattle to help "turn things around". There were stories around this time about an early "monkeywrencher" in the Chicago area who bricked up the outfalls from factories which were dumping poison directly into the nearby Fox River. He was thus dubbed "the Fox" and his actions were championed by Mike Royko, a well known newspaper columnist based in Chicago. While attending Beloit College, surrounded mostly by suburban Midwesterners and city kids from the east coast, I had initially been perceived as some kind of nature nut because of my continued praises of the beauty of Washington's Cascade Range, but once the environmental movement caught on I didn't feel quite so nutty. The hip popularity of Kerouac's and Snyder's writings describing their experiences on fire lookouts also helped to make such ideas more mainstream. Once I was out of college and finally doing what I wanted to, I found myself surrounded by other dharma bums for the most part. I hitch-hiked to Alaska, built a log cabin, worked two more summers on a fire lookout in western Montana, and then moved to the British Columbia coast to build a sailboat. Like Steve, I realized that this was my home ground, and I wanted to make a deeper connection with the land of salmon and cedar. The importance of the environment to Steve is evident in almost all of his letters. His love of the "mountains and rivers without end" of his home state and his deep attachment to the waters of Puget Sound were rivaled only by his admiration for the majesty of Kodiak's wild landscapes and the rugged coasts of Norway and Scotland.

Our attitudes towards the draft and the war in Viet Nam evolved swiftly during this period. At the time I graduated high school I was politically naïve, generally of a libertarian or conservative bent. I believed that communism was evil and should be resisted and fought against, and that our country best epitomized the concept of human freedom, although I knew that it had a few imperfections here and there. During the next year or two I encountered a number of students who had very different views of why "we" were in Viet Nam, and as I learned some of the historical facts that had led up to our military commitment I began to harbor doubts as to the validity of the American position. It didn't help that many guys who picked me up hitch-hiking during my college years were returned veterans who spoke very candidly about the futility of the military situation, some of them bluntly telling me that our guys were dying for nothing. Although I eventually came to feel that it was morally wrong to go to Viet Nam, I also understood that each draftee had his own story leading him to put on the uniform, and I felt nothing but compassion for all of them. With the exception of the rare psychopath, they were no more inclined to kill people than I was. These comments however, are not intended to argue for or against any point of view regarding that war or any war. My intent here is to illustrate what a lot of young people in America were thinking at the time. Of course I would never have wanted to live under a government like that of North Viet Nam, "Red" China (as it was designated at the time), or Soviet Russia. But here in America, the idea that if you didn't toe the line on the Viet Nam war you were unpatriotic seemed then as it seems to me today to be a false dichotomy. Those of us who questioned the war were admittedly idealistic; we wanted America to live up to its stated ideals and values, values that we had been indoctrinated with since early childhood. We wanted an end to America's support of client states, an end to neo-colonialist domination of small, third world countries and the creation of puppet regimes enabling an opportunistic few to steal from the citizens of their countries while the USA sat back and let the capitalist system do its thing. It is immaterial that in 1995 Robert McNamara admitted he had known that the war was unwinnable and yet continued to send the young men of my generation to their deaths. The point here is that we already sensed that this was going on by the late '60s. "You don't need a weatherman to know which way the wind blows…" The comments in our letters to one another in the late '60s clearly reflect an awareness of the wrongness of the war, but I do not think that Steve, Doug or I were in any way unpatriotic to have felt that way. Another example of how I felt let down by my parents' generation in this regard occurred when my mother had encouraged me to meet the youth pastor at our local church, the Congregational Church of Kirkland. I remember discussing religious topics with him, but when I professed a belief that going to Viet Nam to kill the Viet Cong was wrong and asked for his help to get conscientious objector status, I was pretty much given the brush off. Evidently my church didn't believe in such a radical doctrine. We felt that our parents' generation, which had done so well during the great depression and World War II, had badly botched things by the time the old colonial empires were disintegrating as the 1950s turned into the 1960s. We wanted America to do better. We didn't think supporting corrupt regimes and killing Vietnamese was the way to go about it. Steve's comments in his letters about "sharing bread instead of bombs" and his desire to visit places like Russia and Eastern Europe when the Cold War was still going strong aptly illustrate his openness to individuals from other countries and political systems. Such ideas may seem hopelessly naïve and idealistic to some, but Steve truly believed that world peace is only possible when people from different cultures get to know each other as individuals.

In 1960 Gary Snyder published a collection of poems titled *Myths and Texts*. The memories in this book are my myth of the '60s; the letters and photographs are the text.

*[A note on the text: Steve's letters (and other sources) are in normal typeface, with my comments italicized. I have corrected Steve's spelling errors, added brief explanatory additions in brackets, rephrased a few of his awkward constructions, and occasionally omitted brief sections in a few of the letters that seemed out of place. Numerically written dates from Europe are read "day-month-year".]*

Steve with family in Säffle, Sweden, May 1966
(Steve at far left). Photo courtesy Daryl Hoyt.

# The Letters

*Soon after graduation, probably in late June or early July of 1965, Steve and his three brothers went to Europe with their mother Inez. They toured many iconic cultural sights, but after a couple of weeks Steve began to get itchy feet and decided to strike out on his own. He bought a bicycle in Germany and told the rest of the family that he would see them down the road a bit. He first pedaled south to Innsbruck, Austria, and then back north through Germany, Denmark, Sweden, and on to his family's ancestral home in southern Norway. Although he never mentioned it to me, his desire to visit the town of Egersund, Norway may have had something to do with meeting a distant cousin there about five years earlier, when he was 13.*

## NORWAY

*Letter fragment addressed to the Hoyt family—June 1960*

---

...the place I like best in Norway, Egersund. I haven't told you much about it, but it's the place where my 5th cousins live and I've been spending most of my time there. I have a Norwegian girlfriend and she is a very nice girl. Her name is Ingerid T. and is my 5th cousin. Mom, how would you like to have a girl in the house for about two months next summer? Ingerid might fly to Seattle sometime next summer, you never can tell she might be with me this summer maybe. She's a real nice girl and is real good looking.

---

*But Steve's first postcard to me only mentioned his immediate plans to pedal north:*

*Postcard- postmark OBERAMMERGAU-summer 1965*
*[picture of cows grazing below mountains with legend*
*"Karwendelgebirge b. Mittenwald (2385 m)]*

---

Dear Dan, How is the olde Sumas Kid now days? I miss the olde run. I suppose most of your summer has been spent down at the P-X [a local mini mall where I was working at a garden store]. In about 4 weeks I start working myself. I'm just about out of money and I'm on my way to Norway to see if I can get a job on a fishing boat. I've got a cousin who works on one and I'm hoping through him I'll find a job. I'll spend my winter in Norway and then see if I can find a ship going to Nova Scotia next year about June. I've met a lot of anti-Americans and in general some real characters here. My address, if you would like to write is: Steve Hoyt C/O Eric T. Asheim, Eigersund, Norway. Your Pal, Steve

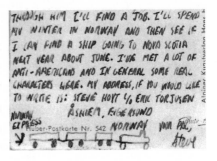

---

*My job at the "PX" ended in early July; there was little business, so there would be no need for me. As soon as I got home I loaded my pack for the road. Steve had left for Europe, and Doug was working pretty steadily, unable to get free enough to go on even a three day hike. Milo and "Sunny" Jim (other friends from high school) however, were over in Oroville, in the Okanogan Valley, thinning apples with the fruit tramps and winos, and sent the following letter to Doug and me:*

Dear Mr. Daniel G. Leen and the Distinguished D.A. Wilde

Upon having arrived at our present quarters we find them rustic yet homey. It is a beautiful place surrounded by majestic mountains and long clear lakes. There are many moments of creative thought, ah! for my notebook. Tis truly paradise. Below us there is the 15 mile long Lake Osoyoos. We are three miles from the Canadian border. Earlier this evening we ventured across and Jim discovered Canada didn't have snow all over the ground and Mounties on white horsies.

The natives here are very friendly and there is a lot of local color, oh, such dialogue.

We went through Brewster, about thirty miles south of Oroville here, and the Great Northern RR tracks go to Oroville from there.

We are really set for a great time swimming, fishing, boating, motor bike riding, and some work. We really hit a good deal here. Finished for now, will report in later, Milo and Jim (the migrant workers)

PS Why don't you come up and see us. Drop us a line, our mailing address is: Milo and Jim c/o Linger Longer Motel, Oroville, Washington

---

*I had no idea what thinning apples involved, but figured if winos could do it, so could I, and best of all, I could go by freight. Doug and I had heard from older hobos we had met that the Okanogan Valley had "thousands" of hobos, and in one town there was a hobo jungle with its own hobo "mayor" so I was eager to finally experience this world first hand; I would not only be riding freights with the hobos, I would be working with them. I rolled my sleeping bag inside my poncho to keep it dry if it rained, rigged a carrying strap, and filled an old army surplus musette bag with a towel, a change of clothes, a razor, and a copy of Camus' The Stranger. (I neither knew nor cared anything about existentialism, but the book was on the reading list for Beloit College). I grabbed some fig bars, baking chocolate, a loaf of bread, and some cheese, and told Mom I was heading over to the Okanogan to find work there since I was laid off. She asked a few nervous questions about where I would be staying and how did I plan to get there, but by this* time she had pretty much given up trying to keep me from riding the rails. I tried to make it sound routine, normal, and safe, and reassured her that I could always take a bus if I got stuck. I hitched around the north end of the lake, my last ride dropping me off by the Ballard Bridge near Interbay Yards, where I discreetly walked into the roundhouse to check the board (a small chalkboard that had the train numbers, track numbers, and the time the engines were called for) learning that the 82 wouldn't be leaving before 11 or so; I had enough time to scope out the strings of boxcars which were going to Wenatchee and find the best ride. When it was dark enough to pass unnoticed across the tracks, I found a nice clean empty boxcar, tossed in my gear, hopped inside and retired to the upwind end where I made myself comfortable and waited for the highball. I remember the trip mainly in that I slept quite well, waking up as we were rolling down the east side of Stevens Pass through Chumstick Canyon. For breakfast I had 7-UP and fig bars, and was packed up and ready to jump as we neared Wenatchee. A series of rides took me up the Okanogan Valley and I got to Oroville around 4 that afternoon. I asked around a bit for the orchard I was looking for, caught one more ride along the river and then found myself walking up a dusty road towards a group of shacks standing in a neat row on the downhill side of a very large orchard.

Milo and Sunny Jim were glad to see me, and immediately introduced me to an older guy who was sitting on the front steps of the shack that they lived in, a gentleman by the name of Red Helton, from Mountain Home, Arkansas. I had never met anyone from that far away, with such a different accent, and found Red quite exotic. He had a great sense of humor and was nobody's fool, at least to the eyes of this 17 year old. He drove out to the Okanogan Valley every year with his wife, and sometimes his kids, working steadily all summer, first thinning, and then picking. This was at a time when almost all the apples from the valley were Washington red delicious, a very popular apple that sold all over the world, and except for a few locals, almost all the "apple knockers" were older white guys, basically fruit tramps who came and went by rail. The next day I went down to a labor office to ask about finding work at any of the orchards in the area, and was immediately hired at an orchard near Milo and Sunny Jim's cabin, so I arranged to bunk and cook with them. Our food was mostly out of cans, store bought bread kept in an old fridge, things like Dinty Moore stew, pork & beans, and maybe instant coffee or Kool-Ade to drink. The weather was at least in the low 90s, with very low humidity, and we had outhouses and cold running water only, but hot water seemed unnecessary in such hot weather. We chopped wood for the woodstove, and had a small hotplate as well. After work we would go down to the big lake just north of town for a swim in order to wash off a day's worth of dust and sweat. I did learn that thinning apples was indeed a kind of black art; it took me quite a while to get the hang of which apples to remove and which to leave, and I discovered that schlepping a tripod ladder and climbing up and down a tree all day long in the heat was real work. After I had been there about a week or so, Milo and Jim headed back to Kirkland, leaving me to bach it on my own. I was making $1.00/hr plus two bits more for each tree that I finished, and was actually saving most of it, as my only expense was food. I had however begun to sneeze almost continuously, and after a few days of this realized that I must have an allergy, perhaps to one of the chemicals that was sprayed on the apples. By the end of about three weeks I was mostly just bored from doing nothing but thinning apples, cooking for myself, and reading books on chess. In my naivete, I still didn't understand why people were always talking about how difficult it was to find a job, as here I was, able to get one right away. I did not consider the kind of work I was doing, the seasonality of it, the relative wages being paid, that it would never support someone beyond the most basic sort of existence. I also did not question the possible health problems I might be exposed to from the various sprays being used in the orchards. I did not see the bigger picture.

When my job ended at that orchard, my boredom inclined me to head back home myself. I packed up my kit, told the Canadian border guards that I was going to visit a friend up in Osoyoos in order to get into Canada, and then hitched back to the west over the Hope-Princeton Highway, following the Similkameen River. I crossed back into the US at Sumas and walked down to the small railroad yards to inquire when the 676 would be heading south. I rode home from there in a nice empty, hitching and walking the last six miles from Woodinville to the house. Thus did I describe my summer travels to Steve, feeling that they were rather paltry compared to his *more exotic trip across half of Europe. Although a mere three weeks of apple knocking scarcely qualified me as one, I thought he might enjoy hearing about my experience as a fruit tramp that summer.*

*Postcard- postmark GUTERSLOH -13 7 65*
*[picture of St. Pauli Landungsbrucken in Hamburg]*

Dear Dan, How are you doing old buddy? Have you taken any trips on the two-o-clock hotshot? Oh, what a train!!! I'm now visiting in Hamburg, Germany. It's raining almost every day. It seems like winter. For an hour or so it is sunny and then it rains and then it's nice again for an hour. Not very good for ridin' the rails. Speaking of trains, here in Germany there are freight trains going everywhere at almost anytime. I talked to a boy from Germany who spoke English and he says nobody rides the freights here. Apparently there are strict rules concerning freights and all the trains are government controlled. Most everybody hitch-hikes because there is no law against it. The trains here are quite a bit smaller but with the same track span. Concerning Canada: I talked to several trainmen in Canada and they said it was against the law, but I'm sure it could be done quite easily. Even in the big yards I saw maybe four men at once in the yards. Canada is beautiful and the mountains are very sheer. Your Pal, Steve

*Postcard- Swedish postmark- 21 8 65*
*[picture of "Varbergs Fastning", a fort or castle on the sea coast.]*

Dear Dan, I'm now in Sweden, and moving up the west coast toward Oslo, Norway. I'm still using a bicycle for transportation and besides having three flats and a broken seat cover everything has been goin' just peachy-keen. And guess what? In Sweden I saw several trains with hoboes on them. Swedish hoboes look about the same as the American boys, with a sack or box to carry their belongings and an old dirty suit, for some of the more wealthy ones. I was attempting to ditch my bike and jump on. While I was in Gotenborg, Sweden's largest seaport town, I went bumming around the ship yards and two old Swedes, drunk as skunks, came up and asked for some money, for lord knows what!! Sweden's great!! Your Pal, Steve

*Another letter fragment addressed to his family describing his trip:*

---

As I rode toward Säffle and saw the trees and the logging trucks I thought about a man who many years ago left this land for something he knew nothing of. He struck out blindly into a new world far from his homeland. All he had was a will to work hard and an honest heart. That was all he needed. Men like him made America. We can certainly be proud of him when we think of all he gave up for a new and strange way of life. It means a lot to me. Although I knew him very little I can imagine some of the questions he had to answer.

Today we are going out to where he lived and our cousin Kent, who is 15 and Signe's grandson, and I will pick more blueberries for his mother and Signe. I'll be leaving here on Sunday and will travel toward Oslo and then Egersund and Nesset.

If you could, would you please send my tennis shoes and my red sweater. My boots are slowly falling apart and at the moment I have not enough to buy new shoes. I haven't signed up for the draft yet, but when I arrive in Oslo I'll look up the American Consulate and sign up. Please send any letters I receive to Egersund. I hope all is well with you. I'm fine and at the moment very glad I came to Säffle, but anxious to get to Norway. Aunt Signe is a wonderful person, but when you come, bring some food for they are not wealthy. Goodbye for now and good traveling in Yugoslavia and Greece. Your Son and Brother, Steve

---

*It seems that by the time he got to Norway, Steve was low in funds and looking a little tattered overall. Apparently romance did not blossom in Egersund, and he soon began looking for work in the area, working here and there at a few short term jobs before eventually finding a berth on a fishing boat owned by two brothers, based out of Egersund.*

Dear Dan, Thanks so much for your letter and card. I've finally made my way to Eigersund, but for a time, while I was on the road, I began to wonder if the place really existed. No, really I had a great trip, sleeping in everything from barns to mansions, eating cheese and bread with a can of fish mixed in, and meeting some real characters. I met one fellow in Oslo, who was born and raised in New Mexico and when he was 17 he took to travelin' and he hasn't been back home since. He said he was now 23 and that he'd been from Viet-Nam to the Rock of Gibraltar working from place to place. Most of the guys I met were travelin' just for the summer, many of them students. I met a number of English blokes, as they call themselves, and almost everyone was using his thumb for transportation. I liked the English fellows I met better than the Germans, mainly because they all seemed to have a real spirit about them and that English accent was just too much!!

As far as costs go, I'm sure a person could make it by with no more than $2.50 a day, and that is living high on the hog!! I slept in youth hostels most of the time, and the most I paid was about 75 cents a night. Most of them are around 50 cents in Danmark, Sweden and Norway, and in Germany they are all 25 cents. Germany is a very beautiful country in places, but it is very crowded and all the water tastes like it's been pumped right out of the local sewer plant. Sixty million people live in Germany, which is only the size of the state of Oregon. Life here in Norway is much cruder and so much healthier. Egersund where I'm staying now is about 70 kilometers south of Stavanger, right on the coast. Don't be confused about the two spellings of the town, Egersund or Eigersund, like I first was. For those who live in the town it's Egersund, and for us farmers it's Eigersund.

I haven't seen Jon L yet [an exchange student at our high school the year before], but I know where he lives and there is a chance I might be going up near his home at the end of this month. He lives about 250 miles north of here near Bergen.

At present I'm working as a common laborer in the harbor here at Egersund. Cleaning the dock, hauling crates of fish, mending and drying nets. Keeps me busy most of the day. The fishing season will soon be over, but by next spring I'm sure I can find work on a boat. There are many small freighters coming in and out all the time and if I find any work openings, I think I'll ship out to sea as soon as I can. I would like to work on a Norwegian boat that transports goods up and down the coast. There are many of those here. Although the work is not the cleanest and tiring, I love to be around the Norwegian fishermen. They work hard and they're not like so many of the fancy dandies that you see in America, all dressed up and making a lot of money. You probably experienced much the same thing when you were pickin' apples.

Did you go across to Beloit on the train or with your father? When I come back to the states, perhaps late next summer, I'm going to see if I can take the train via Canada from Halifax, or perhaps hitch-hike to St. Paul and climb on there. Did you find anything out about the Canadian trains or the hot-shot run to St. Paul? And by the way, did you hear from Kim Conners [Another classmate from high school who was hitch-hiking around the country that summer] and how he made out?

At the present, I can't give you much info on the Norwegian trains, but they do have freight service all the way up to Hammerfest, which is about as far north as one can go. I'm learning Norsk as fast as I can and maybe before the winter sets in I'll take a trip up to Stavanger on the train. The tracks lie only about a mile from where I live, but I don't know the schedule as yet, and the trains don't run as regularly here as they do in Germany. But I'm going to give it a try on one of my days off.

The weather here is starting to get a little colder and darker, but the sun does manage to peep through now and then. The coast about Eigersund is very rocky, much like Maine's coast, with little bays and inlets and small rock islands all over. Sometimes on a sunny day, the rocks, right at the water level have a real reddish appearance, due to the high iodide content in the water. I did learn something in chemistry!!

I got those pictures back from our trip from Seattle to Wenatchee and back. I'm sending all the ones I have of you to add to the main collection. If I take a trip to Stavanger, I'll send you some of those. I know you're really busy at school, but drop me a line when you have time and good luck on your studies!! I'm trying to read a few books myself, but you know how things go. Your olde freight-hoppin' fisherman, Steve

*I had been planning my trip to college by freight trains as soon as I learned that I had been accepted by Beloit College in southern Wisconsin. Since Steve and I had gone as far as Wenatchee that same spring, the obvious next step was to catch the same train and keep going, especially now that I had a convenient destination another 1500 miles farther east. By the end of summer I had daydreamed my trip into gigantic, heroic proportions, something like a cross between On the Road and Bound for Glory. Mom however, had other plans for the initiation of my college career, and decreed in no uncertain terms that Dad would be driving "back east" (as we then perceived Wisconsin) to visit his cousin Connie in Spooner, and that we would drop off my luggage in Beloit before backtracking to northern Wisconsin. The trip across the Rockies and the Great Plains was mostly forgettable. When I wasn't taking my turn at driving, I read some of the assigned readings for my impending classes and also The Catcher in the Rye. We did stop to see the faces of four dead presidents at Mt Rushmore, and also some very tacky nonsense at Wall Drugs, in Wall, SD, but the high plains were not to my taste, being rather flat and too much the same compared to mountainous country. We sped through the plains on the interstate, stopped for meals at small family restaurants that I did not appreciate until years later when they had all but disappeared, and stayed at cheap motels. My dad, being the Norsky side of the family, was not terribly talkative, and of course was over 50 and just not seeing the world the way I was trying to.*

As we cruised for hours at 60mph, the subtle transition from the Great Plains to something else gradually accelerated and soon we were traversing a lusher, greener landscape of undulating hills and trees. We were in the upper Midwest now (although I did not know it then by that name). There were no more of the wide open spaces, raggedy-assed, broken down out-buildings, abandoned, rusting vehicles, with trees a rarity. The cause of this change was rather prosaic; around those parts there was enough rain to make a living farming—farther west there generally was not. We stopped for breakfast at a diner in Baraboo and Dad tried to point out to me that we were seeing an institution which was becoming increasingly endangered with every McDonalds and Howard Johnsons being built. We finally rolled into Beloit and unloaded my trunks, mostly full of clothes that I would never wear, but again, I didn't know that at the time. I took in the campus, then devoid of students, and thought it looked like a set for the Ricky Nelson Show on TV or maybe the movie "Andy Hardy Goes to College", and I wondered what it would be like when populated with my fellow students. Then back on the road to the hills of northern Wisconsin, another long day's drive, me mostly thinking that the landscape of northern Wisconsin seemed a great deal more interesting than the flat land around Beloit. I saw signs along the old two lane highways for Leinenkugel Beer, and wondered what it tasted like. We got to Spooner, I was a bit shy around my (second) cousin, a stunningly attractive girl who was just beginning her last year of high school. She quickly put me at ease however, talking about school and her college plans, so the visit wasn't too dull, but I was itchy to get out on my own, and told Dad that I was going to hitch up to Winnipeg to visit a friend I had met the summer before in Sea Cadets (a program similar to Sea Scouts, but sponsored by the Navy League, connected with the US and Canadian navies). Before I left, I was asked to help a neighbor bring in some hay, and spent a hot and sweaty day bucking hay as it came off a baler while we slowly chugged around a large hayfield. As it was both hot and quite humid, I was wearing cut off jeans, and it wasn't long before the hay had poked more than a few holes in my shins. Toward the end of the day I got to drive the large tractor. It had a rather long stick shift which had to be double clutched, and it took a little grinding before I got the hang of it. The guy gave me five bucks, which I protested I didn't need, but he insisted so I took it. The next day my cousin dropped me off just north of town, and I stuck out my thumb, heading for Duluth and points north. Coming out of Duluth I caught a ride with a guy driving a big flatbed semi hauling bricks. After Bemiji, he doubled back to Blackduck, and then took the county roads across northern Minnesota, rolling past the Indian reservations along Upper and Lower Red Lakes. As we barreled down the road Indian kids came running out of their houses and stood by the side of the road, pumping their arms up and down like pistons, which I didn't understand until the driver reached out his window and pulled down on a rope, sounding the air horn. This was no doubt the high point of their day. The trucker dropped me off in Hallock, and in the morning I hitched up to and across the border, and once again I noticed that the landscape was as flat as a pancake. Nearing each small town as we approached Winnipeg I noticed the commanding presence of massive grain elevators and realized that I had seen this somewhere before. When I later looked on the back of the Canadian one dollar bill I had kept for a souvenir, I realized whence my deja vu had come. My friend in Winnipeg had an Ariel motorcycle so we tooled around town on that, much to my amazement. I wasn't exactly frightened riding in back, but wondered if I had ought to be. (Of course in those days, no one wore a helmet). We talked about our parents' expectations regarding school, played pool, and listened to the Beatles on the jukebox at the pool joints, and after a couple of days I headed back south. I got dropped off on the south side of Winnipeg and followed some railroad tracks, eventually finding an old French Canadian switchman, but when I tried to get information from him regarding a train heading down to the Twin Cities I began wishing that I had studied French instead of Spanish in high school. The best I could get out of him in English was something like, "The tren, she come up, she go in, then back, t'ree time, then hook up, then you go." All this was accompanied with much gesticulation. I was pretty much buffaloed, but after thanking the man profusely I reasoned that the best thing for me to do was to stick around, keep my gear packed up, and wait for my opportunity to show itself. Another couple of hours and a train did indeed show, it switched a bit, and when I saw what looked like a string that might roll south I got on a rideable car and eventually was taken to the American border. When I got there, there was more switching, and I did get snookered at that point. A single switcher came

Sketches made by me in class at Beloit, bored with Economics 100.

*rolling around a giant semicircle with a radius of about a half mile, hooked onto the string which had been deposited by the Canadian power (locomotives), and appeared to be backing up in preparation for more work, but to my surprise it just kept chugging back around the loop, the engine at the back pushing the string of cars with no caboose, ending up at Emerson, Minnesota while I was left cooling my heels about a mile west at Emerson Junction, Manitoba. I walked the mile loop, but had already seen my train depart for points south long before I was even close, so I took my time. At the border the American border guards tried to give me a hard time about coming back into the country, which made me a little mad. I told them where I lived and where I was going and that they better not try to stop me or they would hear about it, but I suspect that they were merely bored and having a little fun with me. I slept in an empty on the American side that night, but in the morning I learned that there was one freight per day, the same one I had missed the day before, so rather than waiting all day for it, I began hitching south. I got a series of rides on Route 75 leading down to Fargo, usually with people who had a ways to go and were in enough of a hurry that they would pass any slow pokes. I was not quite used to the wide open plains, the straight roads, and not much to slow you down when it wasn't snowing. That morning I had the novel experience of having a Greyhound pass me four times, and each time overtaking it soon thereafter with one of my faster rides. By the third time he passed my outstretched thumb I had the driver waving at me and shaking his head. Once in the Twin Cities it took me the rest of the day to hitch my way across town to the "Q" yards (the Chicago, Burlington & Quincy, or CB&Q) which were located next to the river at the east end of town. By late afternoon I was walking the tracks below high bluffs overlooking the yards and the river, and had no trouble finding a friendly and informative clerk in the dispatch office to give me my train number, track numbers, and departure time. I decided on the fast one leaving the following morning, the 82Q, double checked the information with a couple of car knockers and then headed up the hill to a small cafe for dinner; with my wages made bucking hay I felt I could afford a restaurant meal. After supper I hiked over to the top of the bluffs and was rewarded with what was to me a rather uninspiring view: a big curving Mississippi River bordered by sprawling industry with dirty scrub willow growing here* and there along the many scars in the earth. There were some larger trees off in the distance, perhaps oaks I thought, but aside from the bluffs facing the river the entire landscape was so unbelievably flat that I again wondered how I was going to like living in the upper Midwest for the next few years. This feeling of spiritual desolation stayed with me until the following spring, by which time I had slowly developed an appreciation of the unique and subtle beauty of the Midwest on its own terms. In the meantime I would occasionally catch myself gazing off to the west, subconsciously expecting to see "the mountains". I would catch myself, thinking ruefully that it would take a mighty high hill....

At the suggestion of the railroad workers, I slept in the last caboose in a line of eight, had a leisurely breakfast of Ryecrisp with peanut butter and jam, some cheese and salami, and washed it all down with the hard Midwestern water, which I still was not used to. To go with the last of my Ryecrisp I saved my sardines and a can of pork-less beans for whatever the evening would bring me. I stepped out of the crummy (caboose) at around 9 AM, rechecked my "ticket" information once more and then checked out the two strings that were already made up. A yard donkey honked and rang its bell as it shoved together the cars of the final string. There were a few empties, but I chose a grainer for the view as it looked to be another hot and sunny day. Once the power hooked up to the first string I got on board and stashed my gear in the cubbyhole (a small compartment at the end of the car). I knew that I was OK where I was, but I had been warned of the "pussyfoot" (railroad detective) who hung out about a mile down the main line near the yard office. I read a bit until we got up air (for the pressurized air brake system—an indication of imminent departure), and then hid in the cubbyhole until we were well past the yard limits and beginning to really roll. Once out of town, I climbed up on the corrugated steel catwalk and enjoyed the view, watching the river go by; this was all new to me, and I didn't want to miss anything.

As the day wore on, I finally got used to seeing the river, alluvial islands, even occasionally boats. I read when I got bored with the scenery, and then climbed up top when I got tired of reading. The train turned east and left the river when we came to Savanna, and soon it began to get dark as the train began traversing northern Illinois. I was anxious to get off of the train *before it pulled into Chicago proper, as I had heard tales of the yard workers having a different attitude towards riders compared to points west, but the train continued to barrel through the night, seeming as if it would never stop. Once off the train, I figured that all I would have to do was hitch west to US Route 51 and then follow it north to Beloit, but I was pretty much into Chicago before I was able to bail. As the train gradually slowed, my eyes were now eagerly devouring the scenery and it seemed to me that I was very tangibly moving into a new period of my life. After I hit the cinders, I staggered around a while and then walked about a mile back down the tracks where I found a small bridge with a level place beneath it suitable for rolling out my sleeping bag. In the morning I rubbed the sleep out of my eyes but it was probably just as well that I couldn't see the railroad grime on my face. I finally got to a gas station, slapped some water on my face, breakfasted on peanuts and root beer, and was ready to face the day. I asked the pump jockey which way to highway 51 and then began hitching my way north and west towards my destination. I appreciated the low hills and groves of hardwoods of northern Illinois, hoping against hope that Beloit would have places like these where one could get out and explore a little when book-learning grew tiresome. My last ride took the old road along the Rock River, and before I had mentally prepared myself I was being let off next to a bunch of aging dirty brick buildings just a block from the campus. I ceased my musings about the age and purpose of the old buildings I was seeing and forgot about analyzing the landscape for potential escape from academia. Here I was, wearing an old U.S. Navy chambray shirt with my name over the left pocket, cut off jeans, nondescript black plastic Buddy Holly glasses, a three day stubble beard, vibram soled hiking boots, and mud spattered up to my knees, contrasting with the wounds of my recent hay baling adventure. I thanked my ride, shouldered my gear, and walked up toward the dormitory, a very green 17 year old westerner, excited but wary, about to begin college. In spite of my mother's plans for me, I had after all been able to achieve my daydream of going to college by freight train.*

*My first term at college was novel for me—new friends and an on campus dormitory living situation, but as the weather turned colder my enthusiasm waned and I missed the northwest. I spent most of my time studying, as I knew almost no one there and was not the gregarious party animal that some of the more sophisticated kids from the East Coast seemed to be. A postcard from Doug in late September didn't help:*

---

Decided to come down to Frisco to relax my over worked body before I face the stress of college. Got a ride at Olympia with three beatniks, one a girl with long black hair. They took me all the way to Sausalito. We discussed Bob Dylan and society. I stayed in the North Beach Area of town which is the beatnik area. Now I am on the road to becoming a beatnik. I am getting a good look at the conditions in Frisco and understand even better what makes people like Don Anthony White [a black convict about whom a documentary movie was made in the early 60s]. Your buddy Doug

---

*[I was just beginning to study German at Beloit, and at my suggestion Steve wrote the following letter half in German and half in English. Fortunately this experiment was not repeated. I have mercifully re-translated it back into English for the reader's convenience but that also has resulted in slightly stilted constructions in places].*

*Aerogram- postmark STAVANGER- 4 10 65*

---

Dear Dan, I got your letter yesterday and it sounds like you got in some good travelin' before school. I have been doing a bit myself, but it was not with trains just hitch hiking up through the mountains, for a bit of a visit of my cousins. They live in a little village named Nesset. Nesset lies about 75 miles back in the mountains from Egersund. Fifteen people live in Nesset and all work as farmers. I was in Nesset for 14 days and worked pulling potatoes and cutting wood. At night it was very cold but they have a good woodstove.

I am now in Egersund and I have a job on a fish boat. I live on the boat and we fish every day but Sunday. At 2:30 in the morning we start out to sea and we travel almost 150 miles out to the North Sea. The name of the boat is Havblikk, which means in English "Quiet Sea". Only two other men work on the boat and I got the job by asking every fisherman that came into Egersund. I work loading the fish into crates and sorting them. During the week we start work usually at 2:30 in the morning and don't finish loading the fish off at the freezer in Egersund until 8 at night. Sunday is the only day I can write letters. But I like the men I work for and on the fifteenth of October they will go back to Bergen where they live, and I will go with them. Perhaps I will stay with them in Bergen, or find another fish boat, I don't know. I might even stay here in Egersund if I find another boat that is good. There are so many boats that it isn't hard to find one, if you're willing to work for only a little money. We're fishing for mackerel. Instead of one hook each line has 50 hooks. Sometimes when we hit a big school almost every hook has a fish on it.

You asked about the youth hostels and whether they serve meals. In Germany every youth hostel serves breakfast and dinner. It is very cheap and tastes good, two marks for dinner and one mark for breakfast.

You asked for some stories I have written. Here is one I wrote on my travels through Germany, Danmark and Norway:

AN OLD MAN REFLECTING

There was a lad I saw going down by the way that's near the tracks. He was going as if something was comin' after him, although I saw nothing as I stood and watched him plod out of sight. He had a torn coat and his face needed some warm water mixed with our old Boraxo. He was slowed a bit, for he had an old sack slung over his back. It looked as if all he cared about was contained in that meager sack. He had the look of sadness, as if he'd lost his last friend and had to now face the world alone. "Where are you wanderin', young lad?" I said to myself as he reached the crest of the hill and disappeared down the other side. I wonder now where he was bound? Perhaps he'll find a friend down the road. Perhaps he doesn't want another. Maybe he's just a lonely rover and feels content to roam alone. It's hard to say for he passed so quickly and now is like a dream in my mind. As if it was all contained only from here within. Perhaps it was. Perhaps it was.

Well Dan, tomorrow is Monday and that means out to sea again. Write when you have time and if you have any news about trains going west from the Twin Cities in Canada or the U.S. I'm planning when I come back to hitch hike part of the way across and then jump on a train. I'm almost guaranteed a job on a boat across the Atlantic, there's one leaving Norway almost everyday. But it's a long time until next summer and there is lots of work here in Norway to keep me busy. Hey! When do you get out of school? Maybe I could leave Norway near the end of May and meet you in Beloit and we could make the trip together. And we wouldn't have to go right home to Kirkland. Maybe we could head north into Canada and go to Halifax and up into Labrador. Or maybe we could go south and stir up a little dust down in Mississippi. What do you think? If you think you could I'll plan on it. If not going north or south, at least we could make the trip west. Well, I guess that's all for now.

Your RR Club Vice President and General Manager in charge of Photo,

Steve

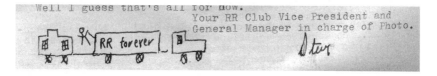

Well I guess that's all for now. Your RR Club Vice President and General Manager in charge of Photo.

RR forever

---

*Aerogram- postmark- BERGEN- 3 11 1965*

---

Dear Dan, I'm here in Bergen today, and tomorrow plan on thumbing up to Odda to visit Jon. Odda lies about 120 miles southeast of Bergen and is on the main road from Bergen to Oslo so I shouldn't have too much trouble.

I came up to Bergen on the small fishing boat I was working on just off the coast, south from Egersund. I think I told you in my last letter that I found work on a mackerel fishing boat, whose owners live here in Bergen. Perhaps you would like some information about my work and things I picked up from the other seamen and fishermen.

Well, to begin with I found my job by just asking and saying that I was willing to work for very little. It's hard for a novice to sign on at regular wages, for most of the young Norsk boys that work on the fishing boats, work for their father. Quite often I'd meet father and son combinations or even more often father, uncle, brother, son, well an entire family. That's just the way it is, if your father is a fisherman 99 times out of 100 you'll be one too. I found the father-son type boats were hard to find work on, but where two brothers or an uncle-nephew are working it's easy to find work. Perhaps the greatest reward I got was seeing the entire southern coast from Bergen to Kristiansand. I don't think there is a more rugged coast in the world than Norway's. The rocks are gigantic and the little fishing towns built in between them are small because they have nowhere else to grow. Actually just seeing and being around the coast is reward enough for me. Well, the mackerel season starts in June and runs through October, with the best months, August and September. The work itself is hard, but one stays busy most of the time so the time goes fast. My main duties were steering, sorting the fish into 60 lb. crates, and cooking. As far as pay goes, in all, for a month's work, I netted about $20 which worked out on an hourly basis comes to about 10 cents an hour. I know that [low paid] immigrants make more than that, but I have no ambition to become a millionaire.

I came here to Bergen with the hope of finding work on a larger boat, preferably a coastal freighter or regular trade route boat from Hull, England to Bergen. I was told by all the white collar boys who control or think they control everything that until December 1st things were all filled up and because my pocket book is not the fullest in the world, my stay here comes to an abrupt end tomorrow. They did say though that after Christmas and along into March I'd have little problem finding a boat. I half suspect if I continued to pester them I could find a boat before December, but I know of several fishing boats in Egersund, who I think will take me on, so I thought I'd save what I did make and go back down south. During the winter most of the boats fish for shrimp and lie in pretty close to the coast. The North Sea can be pretty cruel sometimes; I was in two nice storms myself. You know that's one thing about the sea, when there is no wind it can be the most quiet, peaceful thing in the world. But it, mixed with a strong wind, can be the loudest, most terrible thing imaginable.

Now, as far as freight trains here in Norway, they are controlled very strictly. Even in the small Egersund yards there are two watchmen at either end of the yards. The trains are small, the most with about 40 cars, and instead of diesel they're all electric so you have to get on them when they are at a dead stop, for when they leave it's not a slow roll, but a quick shot, like one of those old electric buses in Seattle. But I think at night it could be done, the controls are naturally more lax then. How is the Beloit branch coming? Keep the information coming about trains going west from St. Paul, or Canadian trains too. I haven't been in Egersund for more than two weeks, but should be there within the next four or five days. How is school going and have you heard from Doug lately? If you have his address I'd like to drop him a line.

I'm in the process of finishing a roll of film which includes some shots of the Egersund Yards, that might add color to the collection. You know, a sort of RR Club international!! Your Pal, Steve

*Letter, no postmark*

---

No maa du lese Norsk. [No need to read Norwegian.] Odda den 6 November 65

Dear Doug, I'm here in Odda today, visiting with Jon. He, of course, has been very hospitable and although I've only been here for two days, and plan to leave tomorrow, I'm sort of sad that I have to leave and plan to stop by and see Jon again before I return to the States.

Before I say anything about Odda, you might be interested in work conditions here in Norway and especially concerning the fishing. I don't know if you plan to kick up any dust here in Norway (or should I say snow), but if you do I know you'll want to stay longer than the three months of summer. And I've found working with the Norwegians is the only way you get to know them. The many tourists that come to

Norway in the summer see only the front stage, so to speak, and not what is involved behind the scenes. Before I started fishing I was more or less a plain old tourist who thought I knew just about all I needed to know about fishing here in Norway. But now after two months of fishing can I even begin to become knowledgeable about it? And of course fishing is not the only thing done here in Norway, but it is the biggest industry and employs more Norwegians than any other occupation. Norway exports tons of fish each year. Along the coast, I think there are more fishing boats than houses. Many of the fishermen live on their boats year around. They are all the jolliest fellows you have ever seen and are a different brand of people than even the rest of the Norwegians. Sort of like the freight train bums at home, except for one thing, they all work much harder.

I was employed with a small fishing boat named the "Havblikk", which in English means "Quiet Sea". She was only about 45 feet long and 20 feet in width. I worked with two other men and they did most of the fishing while I was kept busy loadin' up the fish in 60 lb. cases. The mackerel fishing in the North Sea is the best in the world and mackerel is eaten by all the Norwegians. When the fishing was good just two men could catch up to 7000 lbs. of mackerel in one day. The mackerel swim in schools and never any deeper than 60 feet. Well, my day when I was fishing began at about 3 in the morning and went until about 9 at night, so I can't say the hours were the best, but I'd usually catch up on my sleep during the day when the fish weren't hittin'. When we climbed out of the sack at 3 we would motor out into the sea for about 5 hours , or about a quarter of the way to Scotland and then begin fishing. After about 7 hours of fishing we would bring the poles up and start home. The fish are all deposited at a large freezer at about 8 and after supper we hit the sack. I guess days could be spent more pleasantly, but just being out on the sea and breathin' cold sea air is worth more than anything you can buy on land. And the Norwegian coast is so rugged and rocky that you can't compare it with anything else. The thing that interests me most about the coast are the many lighthouses. I think there are more than 50 along the entire coast and more than 30 from Bergen around to Oslo.

Here in Odda life is much different from that found on the coast. The mountains take the place of the sea. I've been goin' with Jon to school and during the evening a bunch of his classmates get together and dance the old folk dances of Hardangerfjord. They are fun to watch and hard to do, but Jon tells me that many of the dancers have been dancing for 6 or 7 years. They even do the one the Russians are best known for, where you kick your feet out while almost sitting on the floor. Man, have you tried that?

There's snow all over in the mountains around Odda but none in the town as yet. But it is cold enough to snow, for the ponds are covered with ice in the mornings. It is sort of strange to see Jon in his own surroundings, only knowing him from last year. Instead of him being the Norwegian, it's me the American, at school. Many of the students are interested in America and all can speak pretty good English, most have had it for 4 years. The mountains are so beautiful here. Jon lives high on the side of the mountain's base on a small farm. His house was built in 1918, but has been remodeled and is now quite modern. He has about 10 sheep and used to have some cows but sold them. They grow lots of apples and pears and have a large garden of potatoes and carrots. When they want some hay for the sheep they go up into the mountains and cut it and then instead of carrying it down, they have these long wire lines that go up the side of the mountain, and they shoot everything down on those, even firewood. They usually kill a couple of sheep in the fall and smoke the meat. All the farmers have large smoke houses and even make their own sausages. The mountain climbing around here looks good and Jon says there are trails all through the hills.

Well, I have to go now, but write when you have a chance. How is school and have you been up to Sumas lately? That's one thing I miss, the "olde run". When I return next summer I'm hoping I can meet Dan in Beloit and come home on the hotshot. When does your school end? I'm hopin' we can bring the RR Club back to life next summer. Maybe even give the Canadian trains a try. I'll try to write more often and see if we can't plan at least one good trip during the summer. I'll probably have to work most of the summer, but maybe we can do it pickin' apples.

Your buddy, Steve

P.S. Jon says he was sorry he didn't see you just before he left and you are welcome here anytime.

*Aerogram- postmark STAVANGER-EGERSUND-16 11 65*

---

sender: General Manager in Charge of Freight-Hoppin' in Norway

Hobo Dan, Sounds like you plan on doin' some good "toe and heel", "rod and rail" travelin' during your vacations. Man sometimes I get to missin' the old rumble of the Sumas-Black River run as she used to shoot by about 10 in the evenin', and shake every log in my old cabin down by the tracks. All the trains here are electric and pretty quiet and their whistles sound more like a joke, than anything else. I got some fair shots with my camera of work around the yards here in Egersund and the general set up.

When I was down takin' 'em all the trainmen kept lookin' at me as if I was some sort of spy, but no questions asked. You can keep all the ones of the trains, when they come, but I'd like all the others.

I guess I'd better answer your questions before I run out of space. I'm not an expert but here's what I've found. (1) You asked where I'm stayin' at present. I'm here in Egersund and should be in and out until after Christmas. By "in and out" I mean out to sea for a couple days and then back in. Mainly fishing for shrimp. (2) My Norwegian isn't the best, but I can be understood, mostly by the fishermen, almost 3/4 of the Norwegian know English, so I use more English when I'm on land than I do Norwegian. But only some of the fishermen know English, mostly younger ones who have been seamen. (3) I came to Norway by myself, on a bicycle from Innsbruck, Austria. It took me 20 days. (4) You asked me if I plan workin' back to the states on a boat. Yes, I'm hoping to, but while I was in Bergen I found out that most of the big ship companies here in Norway that trade with the U.S. like to hire only full-time seamen. By that I mean if I started workin' on a regular trade route boat tomorrow, maybe by next summer I could leave the boat. But you know how to solve that problem, although your name would be "mud" with the shipping companies. As far as finding

Railroad lanterns at the Egersund Yard

a boat back to America next spring; little problem. There is at least one a week leaving from somewhere in Norway to America. (5) A good 3-speed bicycle and basket can be had for $50. The best place to buy them is Germany. (6) Gasoline is between 50 and 60 cents per gallon, down right expensive!! [about double the price in the US at that time] (7) You can hitch-hike here in Norway and it's not bad, but it takes time. It took me two full days to go from Bergen to Egersund. (8) Now, as far as work, if you want to get rich you can't go fishing. Oh, the fishermen make a lot but they don't hire anyone at full wages who hasn't had at least a year or 2 of fishing before hand. Just last Friday and Saturday I was workin' at one of the herring meal factories here in Egersund. It was just a two day job loading 100 lb. sacks of herring meal on to a Danish cargo boat. But just for those two days I received $35. [Minimum wage in the US at the time was around $1.25/hour] Of course the work is only off and on and I just happened to be at the right place at the right time to hear about it. If you want to really earn the money in the summertime, the herring meal factories are the best place to work, but I'd never trade fishing for the money I could earn there. When you're fishing you can see the land and its people at the same time. But summertime is the best time to find work here. By next spring I'll be able to give you a better idea of working conditions here. All I can say now is, on the whole there's lots of work to be done and during the summer is the best time. I guess that's all your questions answered for now.

As far as next summer: man I want to do some hard travelin', but mainly in Canada. What do you plan to do for work next summer? I'm thinking about Wenatchee apples and then just before school a week or two exploring around up in B.C. or along the Pacific Crest Trail in Washington. I will have to work and I know you will too, but school isn't free. When I went through Canada on the train on my way over here I saw just enough to make me want to see more, B.C. and Alberta especially.

It's been pretty cold and blowin' the last few days, but we are all hoping the weather will improve soon. Thermometer reads about 10 degrees above tonight. That's as close as I can figure it. Here in Norway they use celseaus (Norsk spelling) instead of degrees Fahrenheit. Write when you can and good travelin' to you. Study "good". Your fellow hobo, Steve

*Letter- 27 November 1965*

---

Hobo Dan, Received your letter a couple days back. As far as my mileage on the freights, it's a big fat 0. I'm down right ashamed of myself, but when it's snowin' and blowin' out it ain't such good ridin'. Believe me, I intend to redeem myself, next summer, when I return to the States.

It looks like your school president don't believe in much time off. [Beloit College was then experimenting with its "new plan", which ran three terms of three and a half months each per year, with only about two weeks off between terms.] At least that's what I gather after looking over your itinerary. Guess we'll have to make the best of it though, and actually it might work out pretty good. Here's what I'm a thinkin': You get off during August, right! Well I'm plannin' on still seeing Quebec, Nova Scotia, and Labrador which I could do during July and then meet you at Beloit on the 1st of August. I say this because conditions here in Egersund for fishing are poor and I've decided to work pretty steadily through the winter at the herring factory. If I just fish, we can only go out when the weather is good and in the winter that's about once every two weeks. Most of the fishermen just call it quits until the end of February. But there's lots of work at the factory so I can earn my money for school now.

My mom and brothers are in Sweden now and will be in Egersund for Christmas. They'll be stayin' here until the 1st of February and then go south to Spain and Portugal. I may go with them, if they have enough room for me, and if not I plan on workin' on a coastal freighter until the middle of June. By then I'm sure I'll be homesick enough and will see if I can catch a freighter home. A one way crossin' costs about $135 and by then that shouldn't be any problem. Well, as I said before, I could meet you in Beloit and we could go home on the hotshot. You would still have about 2 1/2 to 3 weeks left in which we could, I'm sure, find something to do. Your suggestion about the "Ptarmigan Traverse" sounds good, but I'm not a real experienced mountain climber and I've learned the hard way that the mountains can be cruel. Not that I only like the trails, because I don't, but somethin' a little easier I think is better. I've been to E.C. Manning Provincial Park and really liked the whole settin', so maybe we could start there and go back down into Washington on the Pacific Crest trail. Of course there's lots of time until next August. Save your pennies!!

You asked about my bicycle trip from Innsbruck to Egersund. As close as I can figure the distance between the two, it is about 1,550 miles, by the route I took. As far as cost, the whole thing was about $70. I think, in Germany you can get by for $1.50 a day, but here in Norway and all of Scandinavia it takes almost $2.50, but could be done for $2.00. Most hostels here are over 75 cents a night.

If you can find out about some of the Canadian train routes it would sure help. I'll probably have to be hitch-hikin' most of the time.

I don't know if everything will go as planned, but I'm hopin' we can <u>bum</u> around during August together, at least.

We got about 6 inches of snow here in Egersund today and the sea has been real rough the last few days. Just two days ago 12 fishermen almost lost their lives in one of the storms. It's no fun!

How is school? and the Beloit RR Club comin'? Well I should be goin', but in closin' I'd like you to read a free verse poem I wrote not long ago.

MOVING
When I walked the streets of a populous city.
When I saw a thousand faces, all hurriedly moving
When life was controlled by the clock and pleasure
sought after in the tavern or dance hall.
Oh, when I saw friendship founded upon wealth
and destroyed because of its foundation.
Oh, then is when my feet forced my body onward.
Out from the hard buildings, away from the geometrically
laid streets. To a place where nothing lay changed
by man, where the meadow thrush sang and the
whip-poor-will hummed and I slowly plodded on,
moving, as the earth.

Your best Pal, Steve

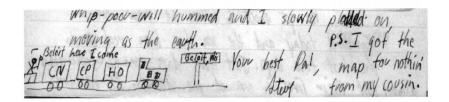

*Letter-postmark EGERSUND- 5 December 1965*

Dear Dan

It was good to hear from you again. Sounds like you had a good trip up to Spooner. Most of my travelin' lately has been out on the sea. I'm still fishing, but man I'm lookin' forward to the spring and warmer weather. If you've ever had fingers that feel like frozen rocks, you know what I mean. I'm more used to it now, but for a while I didn't know whether I was alive or not.

I liked your poems and I'll send you the one I read while waitin' for the 12-0-1 as soon as I get it, in the mail, from home. You mentioned you were collectin' maps, pictures, etc for your room. If you have any more space I'm pretty sure I can get some good pictures of some of the lighthouses along the coast and maybe a detailed map of the area around Egersund where we go fishin'.

Now, as far as next summer it's really hard to say right now... You mentioned about wanting someday to go down the Nooksack River in a canoe. I have two cousins who live right on the river and who have surveyed most of it by canoe. I sure wish you could travel back home on the hotshot in August, but it's true your stay at home would have to be short. It's best we wait and see. Write soon. Your fisherman friend, Steve

*Aerogram- postmark EGERSUND-11 12 65*

Dear Dan

I returned to Egersund and found your letter waiting for me...

Speaking of Odda I did stop and see Jon and he insisted on me staying for several days. Odda is a beautiful little place, surrounded with high mountains. Jon lives on a small farm overlooking the town. He has about 10 sheep and grows almost all his own food. That's the one big difference between most Norwegians and Americans. Where the American goes down to the local shopping center, most Norwegians make and grow most of their food. Jon had just killed several of his sheep and was smoking the meat for the winter. They make their own flatbread and in Jon's house he has a small room completely filled with it. He has one smaller brother and another brother studying in Oslo and two older sisters one living in Odda and the other in Bergen. His mom is the nicest Norwegian mother anybody could have. Man can

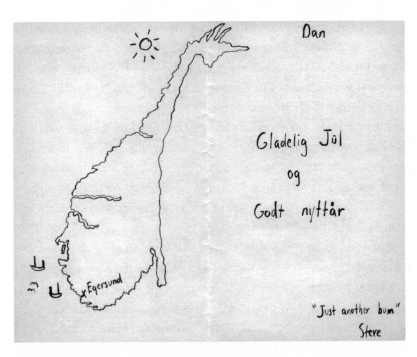

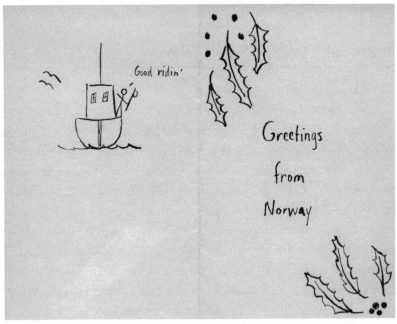

Steve's Christmas card from Norway, 1965

she cook!! While I visited with Jon he had to go to school so I tagged along just to see what it would be like. Really wasn't much different than the old Alma Mater. It was a brand new school and seemed to be pretty crowded. There was snow all over the mountain tops in Odda, but none in the town as yet. Jon said it usually comes early in December. I left Odda on Sunday morning and Jon gave me a lift almost 1/4 of the way to Haugesund. I'm hoping I can go back next spring before I come home. He's a real Norsk, through and through. He asked me to greet you for him.

How is school coming? I'm sorry I'm not writing in German, but man, speaking Norsk all the time I've just plain forgot most of it. I could write in Norsk, but I don't know how much you would understand. Really it is a lot like German and sounds, to my ear, much nicer. Here in Norway the language is spoken differently all up and down the coast. Jon speaks much differently than my cousins here in Egersund and up in Bodo and Tromso in the north it's different again. You asked how I liked Danmark. It was a nice little place with a beautiful coastline. Sweden has beautiful trees and is just like Washington, but with areas, especially in the north, that have never been explored. Miles and miles of just wilderness. I plan to make it back to Sweden someday!!

Well, I guess it's goodbye for now, but write when you can.

Your buddy, Steve

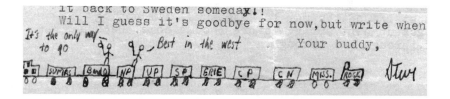

*a letter excerpt from Jon L. to Doug, Odda 18/12/65*

Dear Doug! I guess you have got the letter Steve Hoyt wrote you when he was visiting me this fall. It was really nice to have him visiting me here, and I hope that you can do the same? I have not heard from him since he went back to Egersund, his folks is coming for Christmas. My

English at school is much better, but the teacher always tells me to talk English, not American. I have been showing the slides and the films for many of the students at school. Steve followed me at school every day when he was here, and he was round in many classes and told them about America. They asked him questions about the schools, about politics, KKK, and the discrimination of the negroes, and like that. He got paid for it too, and I guess Steve needed the money because he did not earn too much on the fishing boat. God Jul, Godt nyttår! Jon

---

*A letter from Doug at this time also made me more than ready to spend some time on the road during the Christmas break. He mentioned the situation of our Search & Rescue group, offered to send me some enlargements of our summer trip climbing The Brothers in the Olympic Mountains, and mentioned the view to the east from Everett Junior College:* "...the mountains look quite close from Everett—Whitehorse, Pilchuck, Index, Glacier Peak, &c...." *perhaps not realizing how much I missed such sights— but most intriguing was the more detailed description of his earlier trip to California:*

---

Dan- I ought to tell you about my trip to California. I decided to quit work a week early and go to Frisco so I packed my bag and took off. After a series of rides I got to south of Tacoma. I stood on the freeway with my thumb waving in the air when a cop pulled over, and not to give me a ride. I was very nice and friendly as always and told him I had no money and had to get to college in Oregon. He said "sorry, no soliciting rides or pedestrians on the freeway." He said, "but you can stand on the side of that road over there and hope someone will stop. But if I catch you hitchhiking you'll have to spend the night in jail." So I said cheerfully "goodbye" and trotted over to the road, after about 5 minutes of standing there I cautiously stuck out my thumb, and after about 30 cars of suspenseful thumbing I got a ride in a cool sports car. He took me almost to Olympia and that was where I got my golden ride. Three beatniks pulled over in their car and motioned me to come, so I leaped in the back seat and off we went. The driver was an ex-Shakespearean actor and opera singer- and while reciting lengthy lines of Shakespeare he sped the 56 Merc 70 miles an hour down the freeway [well over the limit in those days]. We had four flats on the way and one we had repaired and pealed out without paying. The other two in the car were husband and wife (legally- I don't know), she had long black hair and was a progressive painter her husband a poet. We had a great time discussing the beatnik movement, and I got them started on the evils of hunting, and man's killing greed. We pulled into a small Oregon town and everyone was gone up in the hills hunting, it was opening day, we went into a restaurant and they began shouting out the evils of society and deploring all the insensitive hunters. We lived on peanut butter sandwiches and coffee for a day and a half and finally we reached Sausalito- where else would they live but Sausalito- the thinkers of America come from Sausalito and Greenwich Village, the only <u>true</u> people. I didn't want to stay at my cousins' in Sausalito that night, I wanted to see Frisco. I got a ride to Frisco with a guy that had a sailboat (bear class, 24') moored at Berkeley where he lived. He asked me to stay at his place later in the week and we would go sailing. I stayed in Frisco and North Beach (beatnik area of Frisco) that night and the next night went to see my sailor friend. He wasn't home and on my way back to the Berkeley bus station I got nabbed on a prowling charge, and after several hours of intensive questioning I was freed, the police got me into the Y.M.C.A. for the night for nothing, because I tried to get a bed in the police station. I went to see my cousin at Cal. State and returned her Bob Dylan songs. .....I got a job washing dishes in a small cafe, the owner was a little Greek, about half out of his mind. Getting home was no problem, I rode with truckers most of the way. I would wait at the truck stop cafes and ask. I asked all the Washington trucks. The trouble is that most of them can't take riders, like those Los Angeles-Seattle express trucks, the drivers say "man, you can't even look inside this truck". Then there's those Vancouver (BC)-Mexicali express trucks. I got a ride from northern California to Tacoma from a trucker. It was such a thrill riding in them, it's so much like riding the freight train, well I guess you know. When I got to Seattle late at night I was getting a $1 room on First Avenue when who should drive by in a T bird but Hank S. and Juicy Johnson [guys we knew from high school]. They were looking for girls. They gave me a ride home. I haven't yet calmed down from that trip—the urge to travel has almost reached a boiling point in me, I've got such an urge to go I'm doing everything I can to hold it back. I don't know how long I can resist it though Dan. Kim and I were going to go to Denver for Thanksgiving but four days is just enough to get us there. We got to talking about traveling and we lost all sense of reality. I might come with you through the South. I don't know for sure yet. Milo is coming up for Christmas, by bus- I think there's something wrong with that kid, or could it be me, no surely not.....Concerning my political leaning- even more liberal but the influence of liberalism, conservatism & beatnikism is molding a different philosophy from before. Oh, I almost forgot I got a letter from Steve Hoyt yesterday. I'm almost tempted to go over and see him but I've got to go to school. Oh, well...."

---

*At this time I certainly did not see my experiences at Beloit as worthy of recording in a journal, but I did make a few notes of my trip home at Christmas time. Between Steve's letters and those from Doug I was more than ready to hit the road by the time classes were out. I got a ride to the west coast via a bulletin board notice, but it was to LA, not Seattle. Still, I figured I could hitch-hike once I was in sunny California, and the west coast would probably not be too cold compared to Wisconsin. Our drive across Route 66, five students packed in an old '54 Plymouth Savoy, was memorable, but my trip up the west coast even more so. On Christmas morning I managed to hitch-hike up to Santa Barbara, getting out there after a hair-raising ride in the back of a station wagon driven by some Mexicans. The instant he got his feet back on the ground the old hobo who had also gotten a ride with them said that the one thing he needed at that moment was a drink. Not having acquired that habit yet, I instead tried hitching at a traffic light right in town. I stood there with my thumb stretched out for a couple of hours until a stranger came over and told me that a northbound freight train was sitting over by the main line and I could probably get a ride on it. (It was likely* stranded there without a crew because it was Christmas day, but neither did it seem like a good day to hitch-hike so I was willing to take my chances waiting for a train crew). I walked over to the tracks and spotted a car in transit, essentially an empty caboose that was being delivered to another division. As I stepped in the door a gravelly voice demanded, "Where's yr ticket?" Taken by surprise, I nervously stammered out, "I ain't got one..." which greatly amused the dozen odd hobos already on board. With this as my initiation I took an empty seat and listened to the old fruit tramps talking shop, wishing I had an invisible tape recorder to document the arcane details of their conversations. We pulled around midnight and I was in the Bay Area by the next morning. I caught a city bus to my uncle's house in Berkeley where he gave me a bag of beef jerky to keep me going on my trip north, and then was also given a ride out to the Carquinez Narrows Bridge where I began hitch-hiking again. Only one ride from that trip sticks in my memory: The rattley old car was probably something like a Ford Falcon, straining to stay at 70 or 75 mph and shimmying when it didn't. The Okie girl who was driving may have been a little short on common sense, but she attempted to compensate for this with sheer determination when passing. After creeping up on a car doing less than 70 mph, she pulled out to pass on one of the straight stretches that are as flat as a pancake south of Willows. Our speed was only marginally faster than the car we were overtaking, and an approaching car (initially well over a mile away) was coming at us at about the same speed. We ended up passing between them, straddling the center line while abreast of the car we were gradually passing, all of us hitting about 70 mph, the approaching driver leaning on his horn, with the Okie girl swearing at the other two vehicles for not being more reasonable about her need to pass the slower vehicle. We did pass the car and I did live to tell the tale, but this was one of those experiences that I never told my parents about, as I didn't want them to worry about me when I was on the road.

I eventually made it home and spent some time hanging out with Doug, realizing how much I was missing by not going to college somewhere near the Cascade Mountains. While at home, a girl I had known since first grade came by one evening to tell me of an event that I wouldn't have wanted to miss. It seemed that the house of some friends had been condemned due to being in the way of progress, namely, the widening of I-405. It also seemed that one of the guys who grew up in that house had come by her place to have a little heart to heart talk with her dad, who just happened to be the Assistant Fire Chief of an adjoining fire district. He had supposedly asked "Hypothetically, if one wanted to burn down an old house, how would one go about making it burn quickly?", and had been answered, "Well, hypothetically, one would pour some accelerant around the base of...." Just as all this was being related to me, my mother walked into the room and asked us where we were going. Thinking fast, I quipped, "to a weenie roast". It was a grand fire, the house far from any other combustibles, the heat keeping us warm from a distance of over a hundred yards.

After the short break between terms it was time to head back to Beloit. Although it could be said that I left town with a bang, I will save the details of that story for another time. Suffice it to say that the last of the dynamite originally liberated by friends of my brother was disposed of with no injuries aside from the dignity of the local cops at the Kirkland police station. Aside from this, my trip back to Beloit was much the same as the trip out, hitch-hiking and freight hopping down the coast to LA as opportunity beckoned, and then a long ride across Route 66 in the old Plymouth with my fellow Beloiters. I was not overly thrilled to be back in the Midwest, but I plugged away all term, waiting for the spring break. Recently out of the navy, my brother had come out to Beloit to finish his undergraduate degree, and being eager to hit the road and see new sights, I soon talked him and a friend from Hawaii into hitch-hiking down to New Orleans when the warm weather came at the end of the term.

*Letter- postmark EGERSUND- early January 1966*

---

Dear Dan, Well, the new year is here and the days are slowly increasing. Man, I'm all for summer, but I guess we can't have summer if we don't have winter too.

How was California? and did ya find your way back to Beloit on the freights? How are Doug and Kim?

We finally got a break in the weather and went down the coast, out from Flekkefjiord. In all, we were out for only two days, but we had a uren, Catherine, 5, and Billy, 10.

# Big boom 'shakes up' area Mon.

It has been concluded a loud explosion which shook parts of the Kirkland area early Monday was a sonic boom.

Off-duty Kirkland policemen were called out after the blast "shook up" the city hall, downtown Kirkland and some outlying areas about 1:49 a.m. They were pressed into duty to help scour the area for the explosion site, believed at first in downtown.

The search turned up nothing.

Calls received by police indicate the blast was heard in Kirkland north and town to 132

*Eastside Journal* article of January 3, 1966

fine catch of shrimp (300 lbs.) along with 200 lbs. of cod. We just came in about an hour ago and tuned in on the weather report which said "full storm". I could feel the wind pickin' up on the way in. Just down the way I can see the East German and Polish boats tying up. I think today there are more of them than there are of us.

Speaking of weather, which affects all of us, I enjoy listening to the Norwegian radio and the weather reports, which come on four times daily. In all of Norway there is only one main station. When they begin the report they start in Oslo, as soon as the report is completed there they switch over to Bergen and then later to Tromso. In Oslo they give the report for the southeast coast from Kristiansand on up to Oslo and then the mountain regions of Telemark, Hedmark, and East Hardangerfjord. In Bergen they cover the coast from Kristiansand up to Trondheim. In Norway it's known as "West land". The report from Bergen includes us, Rogaland and the fishing banks just outside, known as Jaeren. After the report from Bergen has completed the coastal waters, they give a complete report of the North Sea including the Fluden banks just out from Aberdeen, Scotland; Dogger banks between Danmark and England down into the English Channel; and Shetlands bank out off the Shetland Islands. Along in the spring and summer a lot of the fishermen here fish on those banks. Then the report switches to Tromso and in that report is included the northern coast from Trondheim to Vadso; and Spitsbergen Island. Spitsbergen belongs to Norway, but I'm told it's mostly populated with Russian fur traders and trappers. The only other industry up there is coal mining in the summer and early fall. After listening so often to the weather reports you get to know the names by heart.

New Year's Eve was really somethin' here in Egersund. About 15 minutes before 12 almost everyone in the town gathered in the main square. A lot of guys were pretty well out of the picture, if you know what I mean. It was pretty stormy out at sea that night and the Polish boats were carrying more Russian Vodka than fish. From what I hear, at about 7 or 8 that evening there was quite a line-up down in the dark end of the harbor. You said in one of your letters that you got a ride home from Spooner with a guy who was pretty high. As far as I feel, a man is much better off without it. Some of the young kids were in pretty poor shape around 12:00 that night.

My mother and brothers are here for Christmas and January. After talking with them it looks as if I might be passin' through Beloit around the 15th of July. I plan to continue fishing until the 1st of May. Along about the 1st it'll be road work, maybe up north. As far as the East Coast and Canada this August, it should be A-OK. I'm hoping I can be home at the end of July and then meet you back east in August. Save those nickels, the trip might cost one or two!!

Write soon. Your Christmas card was great. Obey all hobo laws, and may the God above bless you, as he does all good bums! Your best fish friend, Steve

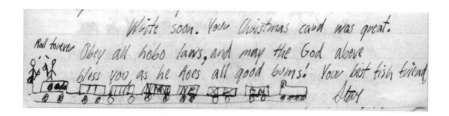

[*For my Christmas card I recall sending Steve a map of Wisconsin with a railroad line drawn from Beloit to Spooner, although I had hitch-hiked there on my Thanksgiving trip rather than riding a freight train.*]

*Letter-postmark EGERSUND- late January 1966*

Fellow Bum, It's a rainy Saturday afternoon here, we've been stormed in for the past four days- and the fish supply from last catch is runnin' down, so I'm hoping for pretty weather Monday.

I think I mentioned in my last letter that I hope to stay here in Egersund and fish until May. The boat I'm on is not a bad one at all. The fellow I work with is a young Danish man, but he's settled down now, here in Egersund. He just bought his boat, right before Christmas, from a fellow up in Tromso, so we're both learning together. The fishing so far has been all we could have hoped for, with our best catch: 160 kilo of shrimp and 100 kilo of cod. John (the Danish man) says the best months are usually February and March, so we can now only wait and see.

Sometimes my feet start yearnin' to move on; I'm startin' to feel I've been here and around Egersund much too long. Actually you can travel over here on about 20 cents a day; some guys can do it for less, but by that time one's livin' completely off the land, and in the winter time she can be pretty cruel. I've often wondered what the professional bums do in the winter; where they go and what sort of work they have. Although it's not much of a life in society's eyes, I think it can be just as rewarding or fulfilling (for actually aren't we all looking for something that we feel gives our lives purpose and fulfills an inner yearnin'?) Society smiles on the college grad, but to my way of thinking some of those bums have just as much upstairs as the big boys who run our government or the big, important industrial companies!! A lot have had tough going, partly their own fault, but when a guy is down and hasn't anything to pick him up but alcohol, he can't do anything but decline. I can see that here with the seamen who come in on the cargo boats. (During storms I've been doin' longshore-man's work along the harbor). When you read books or hear stories about the sea, they always tell you about the exciting sea (and true, it is full of excitement), but the picture painted isn't the complete one, I'm a thinkin'. Sometimes I even see guys takin' sips right on the job, drink controls 'em.

Well now I'm gettin' too religious, and one of the last men I'd want to be is the one I see walkin' around town with his white lacy collar and long black robe, the <u>humble</u>, <u>meek</u> Lutheran minister.

I was talking about college earlier. I do plan on going this coming fall, only because I feel it's the lesser of two evils: college or the service. The service can be a good thing, but with everything good there's the evil side too. I figure if America doesn't get off her material throne she's pretty well doomed anyhow. No! I haven't been talkin' to any anti-Americans, just what I've seen with my own eyes is convincing enough. I've heard about student riots there, or should I say did hear (for I'm a thinkin' most of the young rioters are walkin' 20 miles a day in some boot camp right now!) Freedom is tough thing to keep in this world, individually, but also on a wider scale, nationally. I'd rather be laying in a hole of mud than bein' told by some Chinese dictator that his men would shoot me if I moved out of my two foot square assigned piece of land. But instead of sharin' bombs with 'em, it's best we share bread. Stay a bum forever!! Your comrade, Steve

*At about this time, Doug sent me a clipping from the EJC student paper which although it now seems hopelessly naïve, struck a chord with me, naïve and romantic as I then was:*

---

Ever get the urge to hop the nearest freight train out of town? Doug Wilde, a bright-eyed freshman from Juanita, has done just that... [He] helped found a recognized club at Lake Washington High for youths attracted to the romance of the clickity-click and the adventure of riding atop high boxcars...A hopper, girls included, wears old clothes, but carries a night sack with a change for hitch-hiking between trains.—Carrying just a night pack, a sleeping bag, a little food, a light mountain stove, and $30, [Doug] traveled to San Francisco and Berkeley last summer and again at Christmas.—'I lived with the beatniks in Berkeley and in the slums in Frisco,' he said. 'That's the only way to see a place, especially on a dollar a day.'—'And the people were very nice to me. One would invite me to stay at his place, and I'd stay there for a week before moving on. While hitch-hiking and at bus stops I'd also receive invitations to dinner, but beatniks and people in slums were especially considerate.'—'There's a whole different outlook on life in a beatnik community, ' he said. 'They're very sincere and like to exchange ideas and philosophies.'—Lately, when he hears that train whistle, he thinks of trips he plans for this summer to California and Mexico, where he hopes to hop a steam-train, which he calls 'the ultimate.' He also plans a rally to start a club here.

---

*Largely because I was on a different academic schedule, Doug and I never managed to take another epic trip together such as the one we pulled off in 1963, but I passed the article on to Steve when I told him of my spring travel plans.*

*Letter- postmark EGERSUND- 21 Feb, 1966*
*[PHOTOS of Egersund docks and a Danish trawler enclosed]*

Hobo Doug, It's a snowy, overcast Sunday afternoon here in Egersund. Every once in a while a gust of wind comes down over the hill and sends all the boats gliding farther out into the harbor, and then as it decreases the ropes slacken again, and peace is restored.

There are close to 500 boats in today. Most of them Swedish, but there's also Danish, East and West German, a couple from Poland, and two large herring trawlers from Iceland.

We all have one thing in common even if we don't speak the same language. We are fishermen and hoping for good weather tomorrow.

What have ya been doin' lately?, besides blowin' up Kirkland. I'm hopin' on returning there someday so leave a few of the outlying houses standing, but as for most of the downtown area, I guess it could use a little remodelin'. I never much cared for that right angle turn just below the junior high. Maybe if the new telephone company were switched around there on the corner you could reduce the turn to no more than a 45 degree one. But perhaps it's best to go down to City Hall and speak

*Left*: Egersund, Norway,
winter of 1965–66

*Right*: Scenes from the docks
at Egersund, Norway

with the city planners first. [About the time (1:49 AM) Doug had driven me over to Seattle to catch the southbound Greyhound an unexplained blast was heard in downtown Kirkland. No damage was reported.]

Well, I haven't been doing much mischief lately. I've sort of settled down here in Egersund trying to learn as much as I can about being a fisherman. You know, as I look back at my days at the olde Alma Mater, and then try to associate them with today it's sort of hard to do. There's very little in common, so it's sort of foolish to look back, and I find it much better to look ahead. You mentioned in your letter that the yearning to travel hits you so hard sometimes that you have to ride the train home from school to keep from bustin' at the seams. Man, sometimes I get to feelin' like I could roam around 40 lifetimes in northern China or along the northern shores of Australia, or live in a freight car for 10 years. The only limiting thing is time. While I'm still on the subject of travelin', what are you planning to do this summer? I've been writin' to Dan now and then to see about a trip along the east coast, mostly in Canada (fewer worries there). In his last letter he says he plans to see Mexico this summer. With spring comin' on I don't plan on being in Egersund much longer than the 1st of May, and

A COUPLE OF "NORWIES"

hope to be home about the 1st of August. I'm hoping Dan will change his mind about Mexico and if he does is there a chance you could get the month of August pretty much free and come with us? Or maybe we could all go to Mexico, I don't know. But man, I say plan now and hope for the good weather, &c.... Write and tell me what you think.

If things don't work out and time is too short for a long trip I'd have some time for a trip along the Pacific Crest Trail, but now I'm jumpin' too far ahead, yet it's something to keep in mind.

Perhaps you'd like to know what I've been doing since I last saw you eight months ago, and more about the time since I wrote to you from Odda.

I've been in Norway six out of the eight months. And most of the six months have been spent working, trying to get completely on my own... &c. Since last November when I was in Odda, I left there and returned to Egersund where I've been ever since. During November I worked at a herring meal factory, loading herring meal bags onto cargo boats. Then along the 1st of December I saw an ad in the Egersund newspaper: "Wanted 2 men for work on a shrimp trawler". Well, I filled half the ad and now my work is also my home and meals. Oh, I don't eat fish all the time, but pretty much of it. The weather here in the winter is not always the best, so fishing has been sort of a touch and go occupation. But I really enjoy it. The Norwegians here along the harbor work hard. If you ever have a free Saturday, go over to Lake Union and especially the Ballard area. Some of the fishermen here have relatives fishing out of Seattle. Seattle is pretty well known by all those along the harbor. Some of the men have been there, as seamen, while others have friends and relatives there.

On the boat I'm on, we fish mainly for shrimp, but catch a lot of cod, some halibut and herring. We, as a crew, are three. The boat is just under 60 ft. and goes by the name of "Havglimt" ("Hav" meaning "sea" and "glimt" meaning "glimmer"). If the weather report is good tonight we'll be leaving on our first long trip this year. Since December we've been fishing about four hours off the coast from Flekkefjord (S.West from Egersund), but tomorrow we're heading for the northern coast of Scotland on a bank called "Fladengrund". It takes a day to get over there, and the whole trip takes a week, with 2 days of travel and 4 days of fishing. I think it's safe to say that there are more shrimp on that bank than any other sea bank in the world.

You asked about mountain climbing here. I would say "real good", with probably the best right up around where Jon lives. The price of a Bergen pack I was not able to learn. They are probably sold here in Norway in the large towns, for most of the mountain people make almost everything they own, from hats to shoes. Norway exports so very much: fish, clothes, skis, &c.

You mentioned that you had discovered some more routes on the freights. Do you know anything about the connections between St. Paul and Seattle? Does the hotshot still go every day? If it does I'm hoping to come home on it, instead of thumbin'. How far did Kim ride the hotshot last summer? And did he have any switching troubles? I got a nice letter from Dan not long ago tellin' all about his ridin' with the California lemon pickers and how the S.P. treated it's boys "real good", seats and a water fountain.

Yes, I am learnin' some Norwegian and can tell most of the good language from the bad. Aside from life around the harbor most of the ladies are content to spend their time gossipin' and such, while the latest fashion with the men is the Russian style winter hat; looks something like this: [a sketch of a head with a hat on]. I guess society exists everywhere!!

Doug, you should see some of the salty characters that call themselves Norwegian fishermen. There is one guy here who fishes alone and sort of just crawls around his boat like a bear. The ones in the harbor today are from all over Norway. Many from the southeast coast from places like Artendal, Kragerø, and Larvik, but I think today there are more from Kristiansand than from anywhere else. The Egersund fleet (if you could call it that) consists of about 15 boats. There are dozens of Swedish boats, mostly from Götenborg. The three pictures might give you a little better idea of life around and on the sea. Could you send them on to Dan when you've seen them. Well, I'll close for now, but hope to be hearing from you in the near future. (It's really nice to get a letter with stamps on it from home.)

Keep ridin' and hold on tight!!
Your Norwegian comrade, Steve

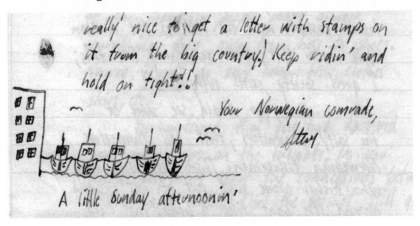

*A little Sunday afternoonin'*

*Post mark- EGERSUND-22 2 66*

---

Dear Dan, Thank you so much for your last letter. It's a stormy Monday afternoon here today, so we're laying in, just sittin' around talkin', and drinkin' coffee. The weather really has been quite good, though this February, but there haven't been many shrimp caught by any of the fishermen. It's been the coldest winter here since 1942 and the sea temperature has been below normal. Whether that's the reason for a lack of shrimp I can't say. Last week, for three days it was right around -5 degrees. That may not sound real bad (it probably gets that cold in Beloit) but for one thing, Egersund is on the coast and there's a lot more moisture in the air. Along the edges of the harbor I found some ice a good 10" thick. I heard over the radio that in Oslo Fjord, ice right in the middle was over a foot and a half thick. But now the cold air seems to have gone home for it's raining today some. First we've had in a long time. If the wind settles down we're all ready for Fladengrund, 3500 liters of gas, 200 large fish crates, two full tanks of water, and 30 lbs. of potatoes.

I'll say more about fishing later but I want to have my say about some of the things you wrote about: Viet Nam and the draft, and college, travelin', &c. [At this time I was likely in favor of US military intervention in Viet Nam.] First of all I agree with you that we shouldn't just pull out of Viet Nam completely and really we never could <u>now</u> anyway. True the South Vietnamese are going to have to help themselves if they are going to proudly call themselves a nation. At present it's quite apparent they are pretty helpless and do need assistance. I heard Dean Rusk talking over the TV here not long ago. He kept stressing that the US was trying very hard to meet with the Northerners at the conference table instead of out in the fields, which I'm sure you yourself have heard a thousand times there at home. Just <u>how</u> hard they are trying neither you nor I know. Being from America I naturally have a love for the country, but whether I should completely believe and trust in those who are running things is another thing. Look at the people in North Viet Nam. They've put complete trust in their government, never questioning only because they are forced to, yes. But I'm sure most, if not all, believe that South Viet Nam only naturally belongs to them. Now back in the days of guns there wasn't too much inter-questioning. Everyone banded together and fought for all they were worth. But both you and I know that mankind has reached a point where there could be not just a war, but complete destruction. Whether this is the plan of the universe that man was made merely in the end to destroy himself, I don't know, and then again that he really could seems to me impossible. Well, it's a pretty puzzling discussion. Naturally each of us likes to think we play an important part in life, we have to. Otherwise life would have no meaning for anyone. What do you think? Well, back to this subject of complete faith in the government. Just what do you think about government, anyway? I feel the less the better. That, I feel should be the goal each person should push toward. Instead of fighting, country against country; if mankind is to live in peace all governments, borders will have to be dissolved.

But you know Dan, in the back of my mind I keep thinking that no matter what finally happens, whether changing times are ahead, that in the end a good fulfillment of what life is really for will prevail. As long as men search for universal truth, something worthwhile will become of it. In my spare time I've been trying to finish *The Agony and the Ecstasy*. I think it's got some real thoughts behind it. I never have been a real avid reader, but it's certainly the best book I've seen. And the way Walt Whitman writes, as if he had become part of the "open road". He was satisfied with what he saw. It wasn't probably always pleasant, but he said he found just as much evil in good as he found good in evil. That in the end things weighed out, that the scales were exactly even. And what more do we really want than that?

I'm glad you're planning to see so many places in this old world. And even more your idea of getting to know as many different ways of life as possible. That's why I have a basic dislike of governments controlling people's lives. Until man is free to travel where he wants, when he wants, without himself abusing other's rights, he still seems to me more like a slave. Lately I've been thinking about staying here another year. But, Uncle Sam thinks it's best I be back at home getting smart in some institution for higher learning rather than just remaining a stupid North Sea fisherman. [Unless Steve enrolled at an accredited college or university he would have been drafted.] You know Dan, I remember all through my school days and especially in high school how everyone (teachers, counselors, administration, and now finally the government) kept saying that without a college education a fellow was doomed to a life in the poorhouse. But I believe that the best education one can receive is not behind college doors but on the open road. But don't get me wrong, it's certainly not a waste of time unless when one leaves he feels he's become completely educated. I think you're smart staying in school because there's a lot of <u>good</u> knowledge there. The open road isn't just the only nor always the best way for learning. But I believe it's better than college, yet a combination would be an ultimate. What do you think?

You wrote that you hope to go to Mexico this summer. Man, I've been wanderin' around by myself for what will be more than a year by the time I see you again. It's up to you but I'd give my left arm (I'm left handed) to travel with you along the east coast and up into Canada. I wrote to Doug to see if he could find time during August to come too. (Oh, I did get a nice letter from him tellin' all about the little remodelin' job and how he enjoys ridin' home from school sometimes on the train.) I remember when we came home from Wenatchee how nice that stretch from Everett to Interbay was. Well, anyway if your plans don't work out for your trip to Mexico, I'll be wanderin' around in Canada during August.

There are a lot of boats here today from the southeast coast of Norway. All fishing for shrimp, the same as we are. Perhaps you would like to know how we do it (catch shrimp that is). We use a long tapering net that looks something like this when in the water: [two rudimentary sketches of a conical dragging net] The shrimp, being small, sort themselves out in the very end of the net, while the bigger fish build up in front of them. We have a big winch that pulls the net up. We usually fish for about 5 hours and then bring the net up, and then fish another 5 and pull again, until the weather turns bad or we've seen the sun rise and fall three times. Then we come back to Egersund and sell the shrimp and fish to a factory, which in turn exports them to England.

It was nice to hear about your days spent with the California lemon pickers. As worthy an occupation as there is, lemon pickin'. OK, I'll agree that a bums' life isn't always a happy one, but I've met a lot of unhappy people who were far from being bums.

I got the poem I read to you while we were waiting for the 12-0-1.


HOMELAND (FREE VERSE)

There was a south wind.
It blew within the trees and made them rustle.
It was a warm wind, yet it cooled me parched body.
It was a movin' wind, a steady wind.
Blowin' north, towards the northlands, the uplands
The land I love.
As I wandered over the hills, I stopped to feel the wind.
The south wind, that blew gently and with a wispin' stream.
It blew upon me face and caught within me hair.
It was a happy wind.
It was a south wind, blowin' north, towards the northlands, the
    uplands. The land I love.
Oh, it caught me by me sides and turned me lookin' north.

And a call came out, from within the air.

"Go north, my boy. Go north on the train.

Go north and nev'r come back again."

Said the south wind, blowin' north.

Towards the northlands, the uplands, the land I love.

And I saw within the valley, a caterpillar, that wandered slowly
toward the north.

And I heard it whistle, far, far below.

It was the north train, the lumber train.

That goes to the northlands, the uplands, the land I love.

I must hurry. I must run, for it will soon be too far north. I must
hurry for I hear it speeding on.

Towards the northlands, the uplands, the land I love.

Oh, not much further, will I make it? I hear the wheels a rollin'. I
hear the steel a grindin' on the

north train, the lumber train.

That goes towards the northlands, the uplands, that land I love.

I must run, I must jump, I must cling to the steel of the lumber
train. I am on, On my way to the

northlands, the sweet uplands, the land I love.

And I feel, feel the south wind blowin' on toward the northlands,
the sweet uplands, my

homeland.

Write soon   Your comrade Steve

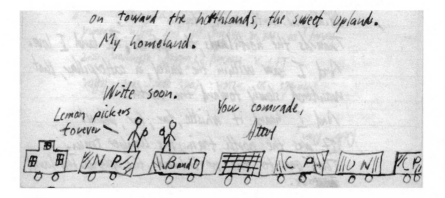

Hobo Dan, Well spring has arrived and I guess all hobos start smilin' a little more now that the crops will soon be wantin' some work done on 'em. Here along the harbor the fishermen are washin', mendin', tyin', hammerin': keepin' busy.

Since I last wrote we've been twice to Fladengrund and had good catches, both trips. It's pretty windy outside along the coast today, so most of the boats are in. Before I go any farther, you asked about your chances of workin' on the RR. To be truthful with ya, I'd say pretty slim. Most of the RR men are family men and the RR is on a much smaller scale here than in the US. The trouble with comin' in the winter is that it's so cold here you'd have to find a place to stay. Now I don't want to discourage ya from tryin'. But if you came all the way over here and then couldn't find work you could run into a little rough goin', but then again maybe that's when life's really the best. Oh, I might mention something else. About 3 weeks ago there were some Scottish fishermen here. I went down to talk to 'em and during the conversation I asked about work there in Scotland. They said there were good jobs to be had in Aberdeen and if not there, London can always use a couple extra dishwashers. Last summer I talked with about 4 or 5 guys who had worked in London. A lot of times it's being at the right place at the right time. If you do come, how do you plan on comin' over? If you work your way across and back on a boat that will take close to a month itself.

Well I'll say some more about college vs. the road. Really, maybe it could be described as education within four walls vs. education upon the open road. Now I'm not hopin' I have to argue with you about where a guy can get the better education. For I know that you find a real good feelin' just ridin' along in an old wood chip car and talkin' to the guys on the trains.

Now you said that you were glad you had learned how the economy works and some good insight into the problems that face the world today. And true, America is really controlled by the few; politicians who have a 4 walls education, as you said. But I feel that as long as we continue to have a growin' government our problems will grow in like fashion.

You said you enjoy seeking for the TRUTH, wherever it leads. I think there's a lot of truth to be found in the rollin' of the earth. Can we make this world a better place by learnin' and sharin' what we've learned between 4 walls or what we've learned in the open air? Isn't man a part of this earth, instead of his institutions, conformity built upon it? Doesn't the earth itself offer the real and never ending education?

You mentioned that you'd be headin' down south this spring so I hope this letter has reached you before you've gone. I should be here until the end of April and my address between May 1st to the 15th is: Steve Hoyt c/o Signe L-, PO box 198, Säffle, Sweden. This is in case you won't be back to Beloit until after the first of May. After my stop in Säffle I most likely won't have any other address over here. But I'll let you know when I hope to be passin' along your way. May the father of all hobos watch over you in your travelin' and provide for you.

Your best pal, Steve

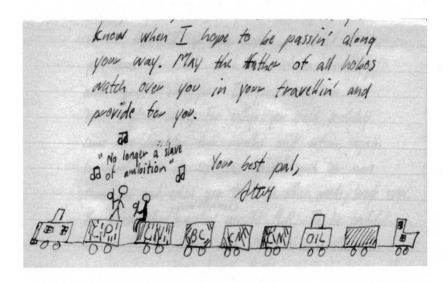

*from Steve's journal, May 1966- The journal had only a few pages of entries, these here, a couple of poems, and entries regarding riding freight trains across the US when he got back from Norway. At this point he was riding his bicycle.*

I'm on my way to Kvinesdal and have about 30 km more to Flekkefjord. It's a warm day and the snow and ice are breakin' up. The farmers are plantin', and seedin' their fields. After leaving Heskestad, tree growth is more frequent, more pine and firs. The hills are more rounded now. The road has a few ups and downs, but is paved most of the way with asphalt. And very little traffic, mostly salesmen and transport trucks. Veland, between Helland and Heskestad was a fine settlement. Good haying fields and even a monument erected for Ole Veland, an important man in the valley last century, 1799-1870. Lund is just up the road, so I best be movin' for I hope to make it to Kvinesdal before darkness sets in.

May 9th  My first camp north of Byglandfjord in the outskirts of Grendi, Norway. Setesdal when I entered it at Hovnnes was a broad valley covered with small but thick pines and firs. Now the valley is more distinct with more rocks, but still an abundance of pine. I hope to push north today and make Odda by tomorrow. Made 75 km yesterday.

Pushed on from byglandfjord at 5:30. Fine weather still and a gradual deepening of the valley. Scattered farms and log thinnin' kept the valley going. Valle had a very interesting style of church with curved outside walls. *[a small sketch of a church]* After Valle the road was gravel, but still easy goin' to Flateland. I saw the Flateland's Museum which consisted of an old Setesdal farm, house, barn, grain storage. Lots of precise work in the buildings. Off towards Bykle at dusk and camped 6 km south of it. Made 100 km.

Steve arriving in Odda by bicycle, photo courtesy Jon Låte

*Another letter fragment—May 1966*

Well, with May here I imagine it's pretty nice there in Washington. Today I'm visitin' an old cousin of mine who lives north, a few miles from Kristiansand (a town on the south coast). I rode down from Egersund almost a week ago and he and I have been slopping in cow manure and plantin' carrots and peas and dancin' around the burning pile in the evenings. I figure on turnin' farmer one of these years, so when I get a chance, over here, I've been askin' and gettin' in the way as much as possible. My cousin is about 60 now, but in his earlier years he mined gold in Alaska, so he's not hurtin' when it comes to tellin' the stories. You've never seen a funnier rascal in your life. I'll be pushin' on tomorrow toward Sweden. I hope to see my mom and brothers in Säffle.

I finally finished my winter term at Beloit and set out to see the South with a friend from college and my brother David, who had joined me at Beloit after getting out of the Navy. We caught a Kansas City bound freight out of the Beloit yards and rode into Iowa where we were switched off at a small town, but we soon caught another freight and eventually made it to KC, where $5 bought the three of us a room for the night at an old hotel. From there we hitched south into Arkansas, following Route 62 across the northern edge of the state through the Ozark Mountains. I didn't think that those hills merited the term "mountains", but the blossoming dogwoods were certainly beautiful and the locals who gave us rides were understandably proud of their home. We instinctively came to realize that by asking them about the area we not only would learn more about the landscape we were passing through, but also we might be given tours of various towns along the way. After a hot-rodding driver took a curve a little too fast we left the road at one point, but eventually arrived at Mountain Home where I looked up my apple picking friend from the Okanogan, Red Helton. We were taken in for a couple of days and given a tour of the backwoods across the White River which included a large limestone cave purported to have money from a large bank robbery hidden in it. From Mountain Home we continued hitching east, meeting the locals, who occasionally expressed curiosity about us. The three of us probably stood out like sore thumbs, as we weren't dressed quite like the locals, and my friend Gene was Nisei from Hawaii. Still, we were treated well, in spite of the then tense atmosphere in parts of the South generated by the growing urgency of the civil rights movement. A number of rides took us to Memphis and then straight south on Highway 61 through Mississippi. That evening, as we found ourselves standing beside the two lane highway in the waning twilight, an older man walked over from a nearby house and began to chat. He was an undertaker, and offered to let us sleep in his coffin warehouse, which was just a short walk from the highway. I remember my brother sleeping on a mattress that I presume was intended for the eventual repose of someone who would not care how narrow it was but Gene and I preferred the greater roominess of the concrete floor. In the morning we were invited into his house for breakfast and later given a tour of his embalming parlor. At one point he held out a bottle of fluid, telling us to take a whiff. I believe it was something like formaldehyde, as it hit our olfactory senses with the kick of concentrated ammonia while he let out a laugh. This alone made our visit hard to forget, but his parlor also belongs in a footnote on the civil rights struggle as he told us with a kind of modest pride that it was he who had embalmed Emmet Till in 1955 when no other white undertaker would do so. Once back on the road we joked about having slept with one eye open all night, but beggars can't be choosers; this had been a rather unusual place to spend the night. Continuing south we soon reached the town of Mound Bayou, where Beloit College had its tutoring center, intended to help the poorer, rural black people who lived in the area. By this time we were in the middle of the Delta, experiencing a bit of culture shock from encounters with some of the people who picked us up. Our rides were all with white folks, and some made a point of telling us that they weren't prejudiced and had grown up with black kids as playmates but they just weren't sure it was a good thing for outsiders to come down and stir things up. We told them that we were just hitch-hiking through the South to see it, as we had never been there before, and that we were not involved in the civil rights movement, which seemed to reassure those who expressed their concerns on the subject. As well, we were occasionally subjected to the "come to Jesus" talk, but we were usually able to deflect this well intended attention by saying that we were already saved. Our stay at the Red Shield Inn (the Salvation Army) in Vicksburg had a historic flavor to it, as we bunked in what had been a hospital for Confederate soldiers during the siege of Vicksburg. There Dave made a faux pas, by jokingly remarking to the Brigadier General on duty there that while "we may look dirty, we were respectable". This set the old guy off for quite a while, as it was apparently very important to him that we not think that he thought that we were in any way inferior to him. We were secretly amused by the inverted psychology of his blustering but, not wanting to have to find another place to sleep that night, we struggled to keep straight faces. One other experience would not have happened much further north was at a stop between rides when we were buying food at a root beer and burger stand. I innocently tried to order my food through the "wrong" window, not having seen the sign "COLORED", and thus caused a bit of confusion until someone pointed it out to me. Fortunately Gene was deemed to be "white" by everyone we met (presumably because he was not "black") thus appearing to them as being well behaved and non-threatening. Nevertheless, this particular aspect of the South seemed sort of crazy to me, as the food was coming out of the same kitchen, and the two ordering windows were about ten feet apart. I believe that this practice was soon to become only a memory in the South. I sometimes wonder when the last such sign was taken down.

From this small Mississippi town we got a ride with a guy who took us right downtown in New Orleans, dropping us off in front of Preservation Hall after presenting us with a six pack of beer. We sat there on the curb, drinking warm beer and listening to the jazz music emanating from within, too cheap to pay the dollar it cost to enter. We crashed in nearby Picayune with Doug's aunt and uncle, who had moved there from Anaheim, entertaining them with an account of our travels thus far. Then it was time to head back north, and we decided to split up to make it easier to get rides. Dave went first, and then Gene and I began hitching, heading up US Route 11 or Interstate 59, depending on the driver' destinations and the vagaries of the incomplete Interstate. A GI who had just returned from Viet Nam picked us up, and after talking a while I cautiously asked him a little about his experiences there, getting an earful in return. Although this was only one of a number of such encounters, the immediacy and undeniability of his commentary on the pointless stupidity of the Vietnam war influenced me far more than any of the more abstract political discussions I had with fellow students at Beloit. The driver let Gene and I take turns driving the powerful new muscle car, and also let us sleep in the spare bed in the motel room that night. Once we had left the deep South however, I felt a bit of the magic go out of the trip, but tried to convince myself that I was still having an adventure. Gene and I split up in Cleveland, he heading back to Beloit while I continued north to see Niagara Falls. I got a ride with a Pennsylvania hillbilly as he termed himself, hauling a semi full of barrel staves to Canada where they would soon be barrels containing Canadian Club. Although by this time down to my last few dollars, by virtue of riding shotgun in the semi I once again managed to get into Canada, and was able to treat myself to a view of the falls before hitching back west through southern Ontario to Detroit where I had hoped to see my girlfriend. She had just had all her wisdom teeth pulled and was in no mood to socialize, so I caught a bus back into town and, after surreptitiously sleeping on the garage floor directly *above the Greyhound bus station that night, I spent the next day walking the streets and at the Detroit Institute of Arts. My second night in the city I got a bed in the skid row area of downtown at the Red Shield Inn (paid for by sitting through a rookie preacher's rather incoherent sermon), and in the morning I began hitching west, shooting for Chicago and Beloit. With good rides I thought I should be able to make it back in a day, but I ran out of daylight somewhere near Joliet and managed to bum a bed by stopping at a church to ask for a place to sleep. The next day I got back to Beloit about two weeks after we had left. I was able to brag to Steve that I had spent less than a dollar a day, but of course that was due to the generosity of many of the people who picked us up and sometimes bought us lunch or dinner.*

*Aerogram- postmark ODDA - May 13, 1966*

---

Hobo Dan, Well, I hit the road about 15 days ago and am visitin' Jon today in Odda. It's been a nice spring in Norway this year and all over Norway the folks are getting' ready for the 17th of May (Norway's independence day). I've got to be in Sweden next week or else I probably would have spent the 17th here. Jon says they have folk dancing and traditional Norwegian games all day long and a big parade around noon.

I left Egersund in late April and rode down the coast to Kristiansand. On my way down I found some work on a farm just southeast of Flekkefjord and spent about a week there. (Got free room and board and $10). I left there about a week ago and rode from Kvinesdal Norway (small place) to Setesdal (Setes Valley) which cuts southern Norway in two parts and finally made it to Odda. I gotta be leavn' tomorrow for Oslo and then Säffle, Sweden (my aunt lives there). I figure on leavin' Säffle around the 20th, but to where I'll head from there I don't know, probably England to see if I can find work on a freighter, home. Even though Europe is OK it doesn't beat Washington by a long shot!!!!

Dan, I've been athinkin' some lately about comin' back to Norway after school and the military and not only Norway but quite a few of the other countries. You once wrote that you want to see a good part of this world before settlin' down. It's awful expensive travelin' if one isn't workin' at the same time, but let me throw out this idea. The <u>one</u> thing that is more dear than life is independence I feel. For without independence or the freedom to express one's self, life to me isn't worth a heck of a lot. But you know that better than I do. What I'd like to do when I get home is take the three year's course at Edison [now Seattle Central Community College] on boat building, and this is what I'm drivin' at: that within the next five years with a real concentrated effort we could set out on a real trip, working as fishermen around the entire world. I know it could be done. Just think about it these next few months. I should be in Beloit by the second week in July, if not sooner. I figure we'd need to find another fella if not two or three, and also it would be wise to find some coast land as sort of a home base. Land that could be cultivated and so forth. If we could find some land with oak and fir on it that would be all the better.

You said you'd planned on spendin' your vacation in Dixie. How'd it go? And have you been on any good train rides lately? I think the first thing I'll do when I get home is go on up to Wickersham, you know that little place before you get to Sumas?, and visit my Norwegian cousins who live on the Nooksack, and maybe work up there until school.

Whether I'll be drafted soon is hard to say, but I wrote and appealed to be given a chance to begin school. But it's really only a question of now or later, so perhaps it's better to have it completed.

Well, I'll spend the rest of this letter tellin' about life and such as I've observed it here in Norway and Sweden. First of all the Norwegians are for the most part followin' America's lead toward a high economic society. Slowly, yet surely Norway's industries are being run with machines and leavin' working men out on the limb. For example, the small coastal fishin' boats are becoming history, the fish are still there but most of the really good fishermen have died out and shiny new boats are the fashion. The car is getting' to be the big status symbol, &c. I'd describe Norway today as a nation of followers, waiting for the rest of the world to make a move, yet in a way they are forced to take that role. That's one side of the picture. But Norway is still a very peaceful place to live. That's especially true here in the valleys. Norwegians haven't forgotten their old history and customs.

Now as far as the land itself, the area I like best is along the west coast between Trondheim and south to Kristiansand. Northern Norway is very beautiful in the summer, but the winters are so long that living there is pretty tough unless a guy is a Lapp.

I mentioned before that I rode up Setesdal on my way to Odda. The valley is sparsely populated, with not much cultivated land but with vast forests of fir and pine. Many of the people living there work as loggers. I'm sendin' along a postcard I got there while passin' through. In the Folk Museum in Oslo many of the old things are from Setesdal. I saw quite a few old Setesdal homes and churches. The most interestin' places were Hylestad, Valle and Bykle. There was a pretty nice museum between Valle and Bykle.

Each valley here has its own customs and way of life, because in the old days there was very little travel between and over the mountains.

When I go on to Oslo I figure on goin' through Hallingsdal.

Well, I'll close for now. Keep your shoe soles bendin'!

See you soon, Greetings from Jon.

Your buddy, Steve

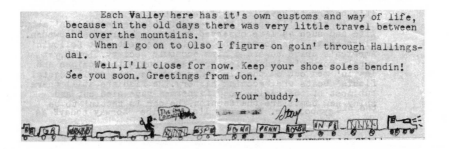

Each Valley here has it's own customs and way of life, because in the old days there was very little travel between and over the mountains.
When I go on to Olso I figure on goin' through Hallingsdal.
Well, I'll close for now. Keep your shoe soles bendin!
See you soon. Greetings from Jon.

Your buddy,

*Aerogram- postmark STAVANGER-6-6-66*

Hobo Dan, Well I'm spendin' one of my last days in Norway, figure on headin' for Scotland in about 3 days. Since I last wrote to you I've been over to Sweden and through almost every valley in southern Norway. I got your letter in Sweden. Sounds like your shoe soles haven't been layin' much in the corner of your room either.

Are you still plannin' on seein' Mexico this summer? If things don't work out for your trip down there let me know. You remember me mentionin' that I have two cousins who live on the Nooksack River? Well, both of them have started loggin' this spring on the hills around their place and wrote and said they would be keepin' busy at it all through the summer. It could be I'll be workin' there during August. Man, let me say that a couple a weeks up there and we'll both be as hard as nails. My cousin here in Kvinesdal, Norway, where I've been now for almost a week is loggin' too. So he and I have been pickin' 'em up and layin' 'em down like nobody's business (as he always says). Anyway think it over. There's a good chance they would pay us some too, if we worked hard. It looks like I probably won't get there to Beloit until the end of July, so if your vacation starts then and you decide to come to Washington, we could ride the trains home together. I don't blame you for wantin' to find new country to roam in so I'll understand if you can't make it. Just let me know where you'll be this summer.

So you've got yourself a girl have you? I guess they are OK. When I was in Oslo I met a girl from Aberdeen, Scotland and plan on stoppin' in when I get there. But, mind you, just passin' through. The Scottish girls are pretty nice and sorta natural lookin'. Not all painted as if they were goin' off to war. I guess they don't have to be freighthoppers to be OK, but let's only say that they gotta like the outdoors and can hold a little air in their lungs!!! Well I'll quit my gossip section for now. Good Luck.

After I spend a few days in Aberdeen I figure on goin' up on the Hebrides Islands, just off the west coast of Scotland and see if I can't find some work until the middle of July. There's a shippin' strike in England now so findin' a freighter there might not be so easy, but maybe it will be over soon. Last I heard there were 700 cargo boats layin' in England, just gettin' rusty because of the strike. If it breaks up soon the shop owners, I figure, will be yellin' all over the country for seamen.

How is school going? My mom had some East Side Journals with her in Sweden and you were on everything but the front page. I guess it's alright for bums to be smart too! Are you still takin' the same subjects and are you studyin' towards something? I've been readin' some of Rachel Carson's books on the sea, and after workin' out on it, they mean a lot more. I remember that trip we took up to Indian Head [Scatchet Head, s. Whidbey Island] to that old house. It's a pretty nice place up there.

I'll close up by tellin' you a little about my sole bendin' this last month. I bought an old bike in Egersund for $10 and the old baby has been holdin' together fine; I may even bring it home. In southern Norway there are about 8 large valleys between 50 and 150 miles long; that is, each of them. My favorite is Setesdal, but as far as real interestin' log cabins, saw mills, and churches, Hallingdal rates No. 1. Hallingdal is one of Norway's longest, beginnin' north of Oslo all the way to Kensarvik (which lies 30 miles north of Odda). Most of the people work as farmers and loggers in the interior of Norway. And life is pretty slow and deliberate. For example, I went into a country store and waited a half hour for the man to wait on two other customers. You just sorta get used to it that way. Most of the men have tractors, but I saw quite a few settin' their potatoes with the old horse and plow. In Rjukan, in Telemark there was a fine museum that displayed many different types of homes and water wheels all made of pine and fir, and I spent almost a whole day watchin' a fellow buildin' one there at the museum. I took a lot of pictures so when I get 'em back I'll send 'em on to you. This winter I spent some time in the library in Egersund readin' about old Norway and what the folks had to go through back then. Mighty interesting. A subject that could fill a thousand pages in a book and today still remains mostly untold is the story of the immigrants who left both Norway and Sweden in search of new land. Sure it's the story of America, but what compelled people to leave, what was life like in Norway in 1890? There's one Norwegian who wrote a trilogy about an immigrant farmer who settled in Alberta. The first book is the man's youth and desire to settle in Canada. The second about the first years, the hardest time. And the third a continuation of the second, his later years. I've met so many old Norwegians here in Kvinesdal who worked around Seattle and Tacoma in the woods. One fellow told me what Tacoma looked like in 1908. He said the trees grew right down to the Sound. Yesterday I went up to talk with an old man

(87) who spent 10 years minin' gold in the Yukon. Oh, the stories these guys can tell about growin' America.

Well, I'll get back to my original subject. You once wrote and asked about mountain climbin' here in Norway. I saw some beauties between Odda and Hallingdal. In fact if you look on your map for an area called Handanger Vidda (just east of Odda), that whole area is complete wilderness. When I rode up through the pass between Haugligrend and Odda (Haugligrend lies southeast of Odda) I must have seen 10 grouse along the way. I guess the fishin' is pretty good there in Hardanger Vidda too. I got some nice trout in Telemark, mostly in the lakes. Someday man we gotta hit this country again. I figure I am spendin' around $1 a day, sleepin' out, catchin' fish, all I need is a few apples, some bread and cheese, and oatmeal.

Well buddy, I'll write and tell you about how everythin' goes in Aberdeen and the Hebrides. Keep those soles a twistin'.

Headin' west, Steve

1

Afoot and light-hearted I take to the open road,
Healthy, free, the world before me,
The long brown path before me leading wherever I choose.

Henceforth I ask not good-fortune, I myself am good-fortune,
Henceforth I whimper no more, postpone no more, need nothing,
Done with indoor complaints, libraries, querulous criticisms,
Strong and content I travel the open road.

The earth, that is sufficient,
I do not want the constellations any nearer,
I know they are very well where they are,
I know they suffice for those who belong to them.

(Still here I carry my old delicious burdens,
I carry them, men and women, I carry them with me wherever I go,
I swear it is impossible for me to get rid of them,
I am fill'd with them, and I will fill them in return.)

*[from Steve's favorite poem,* The Song of the Open Road *by Walt Whitman.]*

# TRAVELING

*Postcard- postmark EDINBURGH- 19 JUN 1966*
*[reverse is reproduction of McTaggart's The Young Fishers]*

Hobo Dan, I've been in Scotland since June 6th. Man the mountain climbin' here! There are some really fine mountains in the Scottish highlands. I went up Ben Nevis, highest mountain in Great Britain. In reality it's just a long walk. But there are a lot of good rock climbs, and some good schools for climbin' too. I'm in Edinburgh, Scotland today. It's a university town, very quiet and filled with history. It was the home of men like Walter Scott and John Knox, social reformer. As of now I can't get to the Hebrides Islands because of the English shippin' strike. I figure on headin' up the Northeast coast to Aberdeen, Peterhead and Fraserburg to learn as much as I can about fishing. And as soon as the strike is over I'm headin' home. Your comrade, Steve

*Letter- postmark ABERDEEN- 5 JLY 1966*

Dear Hobo Dan, Well, I'm in Aberdeen and for the moment sittin' on the breakwater that protects the harbor here. It's a peaceful sorta place. The small coastal and North Sea freighters have been movin' in and out pretty regularly all day. The large white lighthouse tower catches in itself a feelin' of dominance. It just sort of blends in with the surroundin' grass and rocks and yet at the same time controls and attracts all, in a single scene. The birds seem attracted to it, the wind and rays of sun lend to it. Standin' underneath it, it seems to touch the sky, but here, far back from its base it attaches itself to the earth, belongs and lends all its stormy days and drivin' wind in one solid, never yieldin' structure. That's the way it strikes me today. Solid and yet movin'.

I like Scotland and someday Dan we both have gotta make it here. It's a rugged place, and mighty green, with high grass, for it gets its full share of rain. It's a healthy place. The people are an active lot. Aberdeen itself is Scotland's largest fishin' town. There's at least 300 boats from here alone. I went to the fish auctions today. You see, here in Scotland the fish are all bought by private companies from all over England and Scotland. Every day, except Sunday, the fish are delivered to the fish markets, about four o'clock in the mornin' and by eight the biddin' begins and the fish after being bought are loaded on trucks and sent down south into the populated areas of England and Scotland and there sold fresh. Haddock and Cod are the fish most often eaten and this mornin' there must have been over 5000 cases of them alone. It was an interestin' place, the fish market; we never sold the fish in auctions in Norway. We always delivered to the freezer that took everything we had. I saw a couple of Danish boats today too, but none from Norway.

With the shippin' strike over there's lots of action in the loadin' docks and I did see two small freighters from Flekkefjord and Bergen.

I've been out from Aberdeen, crawlin' around Girdle Ness Lighthouse and even managed to talk with the keeper for about an hour. He was tellin' all about the Scottish lighthouse system and said that he'd been born and raised on the island of Yell (one of the Shetland Islands). If the lighthouse stairs hadn't been wet with paint he said he would have let me go up, but tomorrow he said I'd have a good chance to climb on up.

I figure on leavin' here in about 2 days and goin' north to Peterhead and Fraserburg and Banff and maybe John O'Groats and then down the west coast and into the Hebrides for a short time and then on to Glasgow and see about catchin' a boat to Canada (most of the boats there are English commonwealth boats). If I run into trouble there I'll probably go down and try in Liverpool. But one of the Scottish fishermen who I met in Norway is planning to leave for a trip to Iceland around the 25th of July and said he would have room for me when I talked with him today. At any rate if I make it to Iceland it's only about $95 from there to Montreal, with the Icelandic Airplane Co.

I was in London last week and visited the British Museum, Tate Gallery (art gallery) and the House of Commons, 10 Downing Street, and then Sunday went down to Marble Arch in Hyde Park to hear the some 15 or 20 odd speakers. On Sundays Communists, Jews, Fascists, anybody is allowed to stand up and say anything they want. Most of the fellows spoke against Britain and the US. Some were civil rights workers, some communists from South America and Africa, several Jehovah's Witnesses, along with a few who didn't have much to say. But for the most part the speakers were very serious and the crowd was everything but helping. They threw anything that came to mind, coins and words. The place was pretty heavily policed and they had some additional trouble with some seamen passin' out newspapers and sheet literature. And then all around the place in the subway tunnels and sidewalks the long-haired fellows were poundin' their guitars and harmonicas and people were throwin' pennies, except with a little better aim on to the small cloth in front of the singers. And then all the crowd broke up and filtered down into the bar, pub, &c. for a few pints and then later in the evenin' wandered on home and by the next mornin' were ready for the comin' week. But London was a place of study too. There were those profound faces every so often. There was the grubby student down from Oxford for the weekend. The art boys, who go mighty emotional over a few splatters of bright paint on a canvas, and yet were bored with Rembrandt. London was full of history with all its kings and queens and Westminster Abbey. In Westminster Abbey they even buried a few of the <u>brave</u>, <u>courageous</u>, <u>never failin</u>', British generals who for the cause of the crown died in action during the war of 1776, fought in America. They even had monuments of marble for most of 'em. And England itself seemed plum full of tradition, which holds them back and yet pushes them forward at the same time. And although England looks prosperous on the outside there's unrest in places too, for the country is built on such a complex economic system that unless the buyer keeps buyin' the economy will fall in. If the shippin' strike, for example, had continued for another month England would have been hurtin' perhaps too much. And that's why the settlement was finally made so quickly for what it finally amounted to was not Mr. Wilson against the seamen, but both Wilson and the seamen against the economy. Well, enough about that for today, but I thought since you're studyin' such things you might like a few observations.

(Next Mornin'—) Well, as for now I should be on my way to

Peterhead. I'm thumbin' now, because my bike frame broke in two places (it was an old one to begin with). When I get back across the Atlantic I'm figurin' on thumbing to Beloit and then St. Paul and probably ride home compliments of the NP to Seattle. I just hope they don't ask about my pocket book at customs for it's not goin' to be bulging by any means.

Well, live as simply as you can. Don't work too hard. And I'll hope to see you before this month is over.

Your best buddy, Steve

*Postcard- postmark INVERNESS- 7 JLY 1966*
*[reverse is color photo of the Stacks of Duncansby from the south,*
*John O'Groats, Caithness]*

---

July 6, 1966 Dear Dan—I left  Aberdeen and I'm passin' through Inverness on my way to John O'Groats. I'm getting' to feel like a real bum, hitch-hikin' day after day. I may see if I can't get out to the outer Hebrides by Saturday, but my time really isn't ample for them. It was a fine day yesterday and I spent about 5 hours in Buckie at the boat buildin' shop there and may go back there if I can't find a boat in Glasgow and go with the fisherman from Aberdeen to Iceland. The apprenticeship for boat-buildin' is 5 years here. If it wasn't for Uncle Sam I'd stay here and work as an apprentice. Oh, well, so long for now, your best buddy Steve

CORRESPONDENCE

Hobo Dan, I'm back in Aberdeen today after 4 days of wanderin' around Glasgow docks. It was slim pickin' for boats bound west and I got turned down anyway, so I figured that I'd at least have a chance here in Aberdeen. The only thing is that the boat won't be leavin' here until Friday Aug. 5. It takes 3 ½ days from here to Iceland and then I'll probably fly from there to Halifax ($160). I'll probably leave Iceland about Aug. 12.

It's been hard travelin' for the last 3 weeks, been everywhere, but the Outer Hebrides; Edinburgh, Dundee, Aberdeen, Inverness, John O'Groats, Durness, Mallig, Oban, Glasgow, Fort William, Ayr. Drop a letter or card to the Youth Hostel in Reykjavik so I'll know where you'll be. Address is: Steve Hoyt c/o Reykjavik Youth Hostel, Laufasweg 41, Reykajavik, Iceland. Good travelin' to ya. Your comrade, Steve

*Letter fragment sent to Steve's family, no date-*

It wasn't long before I heard that there were fishing boats leaving Aberdeen almost every week during the summer for trips along the southern coast of Iceland, so I inquired with some of the men who worked on the big trawlers and signed on a boat several days later and around the middle of August was on my way across the North Atlantic to Reykjavik, Iceland. On board the boat I worked on the wheel house during the day, steering, &c. and then helped in the galley during the evenings. Our fuel supply was getting low, so we sailed into a small fishing village on the south coast of Iceland, (about 60 miles from Reykjavik) and the crew all waved good-bye to me (for I had told them that I would work for nothing if they would give me passage to Iceland.) They were a fine group of mates, but really went too far with their brandy and whisky. Some days I didn't know whether they were "coming or going." Anyway, I hitch-hiked into Reykjavik and from there, a week later, flew to New York. I flew Icelandic Airways and it cost me only $160. I got to New York early one morning late in August and by that evening had hitch-hiked to Harrisburg Pa.

---

During the summer of 1966 I took an Anthro course titled Origins of Western Civilization, more German, an advanced Spanish class, and the last of the underclass common course, which involved one longish term paper and I think more weekly themes as well. The teacher for the latter was not that good, but I put in my time, just like he was putting in his, me to get the credit, and he to get his paycheck. My term paper was on Dietrich Bonhoffer, a Lutheran pastor who stood up to the Nazis and was killed for it. One rather thought provoking book that I read while doing the research was Honest to God. I also took my final German class, and passed the proficiency exam at the end of the term. If I had realized that going to Europe promptly might have enabled me to achieve real fluency in German I might have tried for foreign study there instead of going to Japan the following year, but I wasn't as interested in Germany as I was in Japan, no doubt due to reading The Dharma Bums and Snyder's poetry. My Spanish class featured another time server, and time served, although it can't have hurt my rusty high school Spanish as I can still speak very basic Spanish to this day. One additional course I took was sailing, which was a lot of fun; I discovered that I had a knack for it, probably the only A I ever got in PE. The Western Civ class was taught by an elderly professor, an alcoholic according to my fellow Anthro majors. His lectures seemed canned as he thumbed through a stack of yellowed 3x5 cards which a classmate said were the same cards he had used since the '30s. It was interesting to learn of the origin of civilization, farming, armies, writing, money, wars, trading networks, patterns of diffusion, and many related things, but Beloit College did not then have air conditioning in the old Logan Museum, and I seemed to have had some trouble keeping my eyes open at times, perhaps due to the heat, and perhaps due to the worn grooves in the old prof's memory. I chose Anthropology as a major at that time, thinking that whatever the future might hold for me, I could never face the tedium of a desk job that a major in Economics or Government was likely to bring me. As it turned out, I went for years without a "real" job, and it was only when I discovered that I could get paid to dig square holes that I began to develop a career in archaeology (I use the term career loosely here). My memories of the summer also included discovering the music of Johann Sebastian Bach, especially his St. John's Passion, which had a very compelling sense of drama to it, at least to my untutored ear, and I listened to it in the music room of the library as often as I could. By this time I was taking evening walks with my girlfriend, and we invariably ended up lying on the grass in a nearby cemetery in the heat of the early evening, necking passionately, but never going further than that (the dormitories and fraternity houses were strictly segregated by sex at that time, thus making serious hanky- panky problematical for those so inclined). At that time neither of us were ready for commitment; perhaps it was my yearning for the road that kept me from getting too serious.

It was during this summer that I first smoked marijuana, and although it was not something I did often, it had a profound effect on my view of reality, making me question just about everything I had previously accepted about the world I inhabited. Those of us who were interested in the subject similarly saw the more powerful hallucinogens as potential tools in our quest for mystical self-knowledge. I occasionally discussed my (admittedly limited) drug induced experiences with one or two professors, who counseled caution and moderation to say the least. Because of previous, flagrant distortion of the facts on the part of some government officials, I was (at that time) smugly confident that smoking pot had no serious side effects, and perhaps if I had continued to smoke it in the limited quantities that I was then consuming, this might have proved true, leaving my brain less addled in later years. I suppose my attitude was that of Blake's: "the road of excess leads to the palace of wisdom". From an upperclassman, we heard stories such as the students at Beloit who had ordered peyote buttons (then still a legal substance) from a firm in Texas a year or two earlier. They had apparently hallucinated "getting eaten by a Coke machine", and had had other strange reactions to the drug. Along with the more academic texts I read regarding the Native American Church, such stories only served to pique my own curiosity about the effect of the cactus' strychnine like alkaloids on our neurons. We read about and discussed peyote and LSD, but at this time we had no knowledge of how to obtain either of them, so we drank beer and smoked what little pot we had. Toward the end of the *summer term I learned that feral cannabis grew along the sides of cornfields just a few miles outside of Beloit. This was too much of a temptation, and being of the enterprising sort, I biked out northwest of town one day in late August to harvest some. I reported my findings to Doug, and promptly received the following letter from another Railroad Club member from high school:*

---

Danny—I just finished reading your letter to Doug about those plants, well they grow around here too—to be more specific about 400 of them owned jointly by Doug and me here in Doug's room in Everett—green thumbs we!—There they sit in a sweet little window box in the window overlooking beautiful Everett harbor. Is it petunias? Is it daisies? No! It is Pot able to leap... Faster than a speeding... More powerful than a locomotive—(except those endorsed by RR club, of course.)—I am leaving for the East by way of Frisco Denver &c. I'm not certain whether or not I'll be in Beloit but expect me anyhow. Also I may join you and Doug in the Mexico jaunt—Jesus Saves (cigarette Papers, coins, matchbooks, False Idols)—Kim

This is Doug Now

I'm sitting here watching our precious pot plants sprout from the ground while listening to Kim blare out spontaneous jazz tunes on the harmonica.—Now, concerning the trip to Mexico—when I get out of summer school I'll be hitchhiking south into Mexico. It's B___ I'm concerned about, he's such a bigot now. You should understand my feelings about traveling through Mexico digging the natives and smoking grass with him along. But I'm not too sure he is going, it's a bit deviant for him. But as a tentative plan, Kim just declared that he is now a soldier of fortune....... If I don't go to Mexico, I'll hike up into the Olympics for a month alone. Phone me for complete plans, I'll pay the dollar later. I'm home between Friday afternoon and Sunday night. I don't know the complete long distance dial number. [direct dialing was still fairly new technology at that time] Doug——

*About two weeks later I received the following postcard:*

Dan, I am writing you to tell you I won't be getting out of school until Aug. 25th so that leaves little room for a trip to Mexico. My cousin Toni Jean wants to hitchhike with me wherever I decide to go. But if she and I go it'll be in September. Perhaps we can take a trip but it doesn't sound good. I've been doing some hitching- went to Pete Lake & higher & up Mt. Si yesterday. Anthro and Phil. are my interests now but some of my grades have been bad and the draft may take me. The only solution for that fucking system is to get kicked out. Doug—PS the Railroad Club is gaining members.

*A bit later a letter from Kim:*

Danny Boy, My humblest apologies for not writing to you for months. I have been a true derelict as far as that is concerned. Latest neighborhood news: #1 Doug and I are growing pot- lots of it. #2 B___ is more of a right-wing fascist warmongering tool of the capitalist-imperialist conspiracy than ever. #3 I may be thumbing back east soon and I'll stop by Beloit and I'll expect three squares and a bed #4 I hear you have a WOMAN now- way to go Danny!! #5 and, of course, Railroad Club forever. Rodge S. and I are taking a freight to Bellingham soon. #6 I have no job and no money so I expect to be in the Navy in the fall- such is life. #7 I'm going with a 24 year old girl who just graduated from Western. I have no idea why she fell for me, but I'm not complaining, she's tough and I was shacked up with her the last 2 weeks of school getting it nearly every night. #8 Bye for now, check the closing of your choice [ ] RR Club forever [ ] Jesus saves (string, jock straps, AA cups, tinfoil) [ ] Hitler Lives [ ] Love and Kisses
　—Kim

*When he got to the bay area, Doug wrote me another letter:*

I'm sending these books for you to keep & use, if you wish, until I get back. The posters you can also use, I got all but the Zen posters for

working in a bookstore for an hour. I am afraid to send them home.—I
don't know if I told you but I got busted by my parents out in my room
[a small horse barn in the back yard] in early Jan. Kim, his brother &
I were sitting on the floor preparing the pipe for smoking when my
father walked in. It was very serious on their part & they were going
to send me to a psychiatrist but it turned out to be too expensive!—
After that I moved up to Everett with Braden & a South African
Chinese boy. His father is a Chinese diplomat in Johannesburg. He
lived in China for many years & the boy knows a lot about Chinese
culture. He really turned me on to China for two months. After I quit
school I spent three weeks trying to find cheap passage to Formosa.
The cheapest I found was about fifty dollars more than I had room
to pay.—This month or next month I have to take my S.S. [selective
service, i.e. the draft] physical of which I'm not looking forward to (to
state the obvious). I got three very good assurances of working for the
forest service, one a lookout out of Darrington. It's a shame they're
a month or two late, so I'm not accepting their offers.—I'm leaving
for Mexico tomorrow & if I like the country & people I'll go down to
southern Mexico & explore some Mayan ruins & live with the natives.
I could very easily disappear in the southern Mexico jungles for quite
some time & if I get down there & really like it I may do that. It all
depends on if I like Mexico. If it's too hot and uncomfortable or the
draft board calls me right away I will come back to the states. Most of
all I think it will be the people in the states that bring me back. I've
learned so much on this trip. Its like I've gone through a great rebirth
and I came out with a big broad grin on my face. My thoughts are
clear and crystalline, I'm understanding people, ideas, the psyche so
beautifully that I catch myself laughing & screaming "Oh, the joys of
living." People make it. They can destroy themselves in the awareness
of nihilism' existentialism, ego-games, social farces, intellectual koan,
& a hundred other intellectual understandings then like a great rebirth
they can create love & swirl in a fantastic heaven of living, creating
orgasms of thought & beauty, & Buddhas & Christs, & awarenesses
like a fantastic symphony of reality & newborn discoveries. It's like
when I heard Gary Snyder read his Mountains & Rivers without End,

sitting cross legged with a candle lit in front of him & incense burning throughout the room with oranges, & apples & fir boughs all around. Reading about Marblemount, & the Cascade mountains & hitchhiking down 99 & talking with mountain hermits; stopping his poetry words to look up at the audience with a big Buddha grin. I ask myself what do you do with so much love? You spread it around like peanut butter, it's catching you know! Doug

---

*As the summer wore on, all of us stuck in Beloit felt a bit antsy, and one day my friend Hank announced that he was going to catch a freight and get the hell out of town, he just couldn't stand it any longer. We thought that this would involve a short "40 miler" over to Savanna, but he ended up on a fast freight heading west and couldn't get off until Aberdeen, South Dakota if I remember correctly. He had shoplifted some lunchmeat at a Safeway due to hunger pangs, but made it back, penniless, after four or five days, none the worse for wear. At least he had gotten it out of his system.*

*During my first year of college some very great rock and roll music was first heard; Bob Dylan, the Beatles and the Rolling Stones were all still on their upward trajectories, the world was young, and anything was possible. Related to such anthems of the era, it was at this time that I first became aware of the richness and variety of American folk music whence rock and roll had originated. While every generation no doubt feels the same about their music, the 1960s folk music revival enabled us to reconnect with an older, rural side of American culture. Although I had listened to old Tex Ritter recordings on the "78" as a child, I had never before encountered original recordings of Woody Guthrie, the Carter Family, the Stanley Brothers, or the Delmore Brothers and instinctively recognized the authenticity of these artists. Even more exotic to my untutored ear was the blues. At first I had trouble comprehending what I was hearing, but the powerfully compelling music by the likes of Robert Johnson, Son House, Leadbelly, Sonny Terry and Lightning Hopkins opened a new world of aesthetic enjoyment for me. As I became increasingly familiar with this music, I came to realize that it was a small part of a greater truth, hinting at many other contributions to American culture made by individuals who had been ignored in the* textbook versions of history I had grown up with. With my friend Ed, who was quite gifted with the guitar, I eventually became somewhat adept at playing blues accompaniment on the harmonica, a pastime which no doubt helped both of us to endure the less stimulating tasks inherent in our "four walls education" at Beloit.

As I researched hallucinogens by reading everything I could find on the subject my political attitudes were also undergoing a shift from conservative to more liberal. I do not doubt that the growing war in Viet Nam and the accompanying draft had the effect of drawing my attention to the Johnson administration's change from a war on poverty to "Let's you and him fight!", with me (and well over two million other young Americans) being asked to go over to Viet Nam and shoot some guy that I didn't particularly have a quarrel with. Although my political attitudes did not change overnight, I began to question the war, and the more I learned about it the more disaffected I became. An amusing response to such widespread concerns by draft age college boys was a mock notice posted on a bulletin board in one of the dorms, promoting a "foreign study" opportunity called the "Saigon Semester—all expenses paid!" One would be given clothes (a uniform), personal security (a gun) and poor grades were "no obstacle to participating in this great opportunity to get to know people of a different culture, and then shoot them". When it was time to head back to the northwest at the end of the summer term I was ready to let my hair grow long, grow a beard, and thus identify myself with the counterculture of the day. I can only say now in my defense that I didn't drop out of school, and I never wore bellbottoms. I can still remember the intense heat and humidity of the upper Midwest, fireflies swooping through the cemetery as I lay on the grass, my arms around a healthy and attractive young woman, the music of Bach and the Beatles, Dylan and the Rolling Stones running through my mind, all combining to make this a memorable summer, but one characterized more by yearning than fulfillment. Steve's postcards describing his travels in the UK stoked my own wanderlust. Now that he was back on the road again, I too was itching to do some traveling.

*From Steve's journal-[Steve later told me he had awakened in a moving boxcar as he rolled through Terre Haute, Indiana and thinking to himself "This is Theodore Dreiser's home town".]*

Notes:

Regular trains west from Harrisburg, a large division point. Between 6:00-8:00 Wednesday, perhaps daily. Evening trains west between 8:00-10:00. A chance of one after midnight.

I just talked to the engineer; said the 6:00-8:00 was a regular daily run. He gave me two sandwiches too. Altoona seems to be a division point with most lines heading west, but with difficult access. An hour stop. Luckily I wasn't switched off in Pittsburgh, but at Ambridge-Beaver Falls. I found myself in the re-classification yard and walked up to the end of the main yard, caught a westbound train. We made good time between Ambridge-Beaver Falls and Columbus, stopped only once in a small yard. When I got to Columbus I found myself again in the classification yard, so I walked up to the westbound end and I'm on a train bound for Indianapolis.

| WEST | STOPS* |
|---|---|
| Left Harrisburg | 8:00 Wed. morning August 24 |
| *Lewistown, PA | loading stop |
| *Altoona, PA | A major division point |
| *Pittsburgh | Division point—time 12:00 midnight |
| *Ambridge | Major yard—5:30 Beaver Falls |
| Crossed the Ohio State line—7:00 | |
| *Columbus, Ohio | Major division point—11:30-almost noon |

*Letter fragment to Steve's family, no date-*

From Harrisburg I caught a series of freight trains to St. Louis and from St. Louis crossed the Mississippi River and hitch-hiked on to Kansas City, through Nebraska, where I caught a ride with two boys who dropped me off two days later in Idaho Falls, Idaho. From there it was on to Billings, Montana and then through the mountains to

Spokane. In Spokane I waited until the next morning and rolled out on a fast freight to South Seattle. I got switched off in Pasco, so I went into town, had something to eat and got cleaned up and that evening I was on another train bound for Seattle. The next morning I woke up in the middle of a familiar looking yards and hitch-hiked home to Kirkland. I arrived home on September 1st.

---

*Once the summer term was finished I hit the road immediately. The trip home from Beloit was my longest trip by freight train to date. I hitch-hiked up to the Twin Cities and once there soon located a small switching yards. A worker there told me I would find westbound freights being made up over at Union Yards on the west side of St. Paul, and even offered to put me on a transfer freight if I wanted to wait for it. Being young, dumb, and full of beans, I instead decided to walk over, following the main line across town. Once at Union Yards I learned that I wouldn't catch out until after midnight. I killed time by reading a paperback I had picked up at a bookstore, ate some of my travel rations, and finally spotted my ride and climbed aboard a car carrier loaded with US Army jeeps, no doubt headed for Viet Nam. I got a lot of smiles waving to folks at the crossings as I "drove" my jeep across half the country on the "high line" (in those days there were no jerks with cell phones to drop the dime on you) and two days later I was in Seattle, hitching around the north end of the lake toward home. The entire trip had taken me three days and cost me less than $4, all for road food.*

*A few days after getting home I had shared some of the "Wisco Weed" I had harvested at Beloit with Doug, and the following day drove down to Renton to apply for work at "Boeings", as it was locally referred to. As I was waiting between job interviews, I wandered into a big box drugstore, still feeling the aftereffects of my marijuana high of the night before, and had a sort of epiphany; as I gazed around me, I realized that I really didn't need almost all of the stuff festooning the shelves of this giant emporium. This was perhaps the major turning point for my worldview, although I did not realize it at the time. I had changed from basically accepting the fundamental rightness of the American way of life to a much more critical and questioning attitude, which I have only gradually modified as the passing years have given me added perspective. Steve's views on America's materialistic march toward self destruction now made increasing sense to me.*

2

You road I enter upon and look around, I believe you are not all that
   is here,
I believe that much unseen is also here.
Here the profound lesson of reception, nor preference nor denial,
The black with his woolly head, the felon, the diseas'd, the illiterate
   person, are not denied;
The birth, the hasting after the physician, the beggar's tramp, the
   drunkard's stagger, the laughing party of mechanics,
The escaped youth, the rich person's carriage, the fop, the eloping
   couple,
The early market-man, the hearse, the moving of furniture into the
   town, the return back from the town,
They pass, I also pass, any thing passes, none can be interdicted,
None but are accepted, none but shall be dear to me.

*[from Steve's favorite poem,* The Song of the Open Road *by Walt
Whitman.]*

# BREMERTON

*Back in the Pacific Northwest, Steve enrolled in the community college in Bremerton, Washington, having arranged to live rent free in a small cabin on the east side of Bremerton as a caretaker. I was about to begin working the swing shift at Boeings—they were cranking out 707s as fast as they could at that time and gladly hired any high school graduate who had once taken a shop class.*

*But before classes began for Steve we squeezed in a trip up to Saxon to visit the Nesset farm, riding the freight to nearby Sumas of course for our transportation. The farm, on the far side of the south fork of the Nooksack was backed up against the foothills of The Sisters, a double peak just south of Mt. Baker, and was a true Norwegian bachelor farm, run by Steve's cousins, two brothers and their sister. The buildings dated from the turn of the last century, with the hand hewn timbers of the original log cabin covered with clapboard siding to give the house a much more recent appearance. The old sagging barn had the dates of the first salmon sighted for a number of years chalked on the structural timbers in charcoal. It also featured a small sawmill and various farm equipment, and the old grey car with the Technocracy symbol painted on the doors with the latitude and longitude of their farm beneath it. The Techocracy symbol, a red and white yin-and-yang monad reminded us of the Northern Pacific's logo on the sides of their rolling stock. Spending time at the farm was truly like walking back in time, maybe to the '30s or '40s at least, and was a nice break from the more stressful life across the river. On the morning we left we watched elk graze in the south pasture, ambling leisurely aside as we hiked down the long gravel drive on our way to Sumas to catch a freight back home.*

*On weekends, Doug (still enrolled at Everett JC) and I were able to do things together as we were both living at home. On one weekend we took our bikes up to Sumas (by boxcar) in an attempt to locate the rather obscure Sumas Mountain Cave, and in early October we climbed Mt Stuart on my 19th birthday. With Steve, the three of us climbed Mt. Shuksan that fall, bivouacking (and cooking) in a single two-man tent in the snow. This climb in some ways exemplified Steve's lackadaisical attitude toward serious and potentially dangerous endeavors; he showed up without adequate gear—*

Steve and myself waiting to catch out at Sumas in the fall of 1966. Steve was laughing because of my idea for combining two photos to get one like this.

*pitiful looking boots, an old sweater, no sun goggles, no flashlight—and I had to lecture him about the "ten essentials". I had taken a climbing course in high school but it was already in my character to make the lists and check off the items one by one. Doug was somewhat less detail oriented, but didn't skimp when safety was at issue. While Steve always saw the big picture he never seemed to achieve the kind of safety consciousness that Doug and I had drummed into our heads during our Search & Rescue training. On our hike up past Lake Ann to our bivouac I remember Steve giving me*

Norwegian lessons, repeating the Norwegian weather reports that he had heard every morning when fishing in the North Sea. His lilting Norwegian sounded very poetic as he rang off the place names of the Norwegian coast, making me wish I had gone to St. Olaf College so I could have studied Norwegian instead of the (to me) more stolid sounding German. The next morning we summited Shuksan with a group of young climbers from UBC, and after signing the climbing register, we sat in the swirling mist and were treated to brief glimpses of nearby Mt. Baker. We naturally talked about the Pacific Northwest from the respective viewpoints reflected by our two nationalities, and the subject of logging and clearcuts eventually came up. We Americans bemoaned the ongoing damage to the environment and accelerating loss of the old growth timber on our side of the border, which prompted one Canadian to smugly opine that "they'll never be able to cut all the trees in BC!" But another Canuck quickly countered that "that's what folks had been saying on their [the American] side not too many years ago". We ended the discussion by agreeing that we were all in favor of less logging and more wilderness.

After my epiphany in the drugstore, I had gone over to the U District to locate some books on Zen Buddhism, and also procured a copy of Thoreau's Walden, which I promptly read, along with his Essay on Civil Disobedience. After I had been back home for about a month, my erstwhile girlfriend wrote me to say that we were probably not meant for one another. Although disappointed, I soon got over it as my combined interests in Buddhism, Thoreau and the poetic landscape of the northwest continued to grow. While working at Boeings, I happened to meet an old black guy who regaled me with tales of growing up on the south side of Chicago and riding the blinds when a young man. I had never heard railroad workers or hobos use this term and asked the old guy what a "blind" was. He explained that on passenger trains between the first passenger car and the coal car (located immediately behind the engine) there was an accordion type connection between cars which would be open to a stowaway when the train was stopped or moving slowly, but once underway the blind would close again, thus enabling the rider to ride without being seen. Passenger trains of course had priority over virtually all freight trains so this was considered the fastest way to "beat one's way over the road" as it was termed. The *flip side of this mode of hoboing was that in contrast to the relative lack of scrutiny in the freight yards, the passenger stations were crawling with railroad personnel, making the illicit boarding of a fast passenger train a difficult feat for even the most agile and cunning of hobos. I had by this time read a few books recounting personal tales of the hobo life, but meeting an old hobo with similar stories to tell first hand only increased my own yearning for the road. After reading The Dharma Bums, I had also applied for the job of fire lookout on Desolation Peak and since very few wanted to work as fire lookouts in those days, the fire control officer at Marblemount Ranger Station had practically promised me the job the following summer. Thus, when I returned to Beloit for the winter-spring term I would have something to look forward to while immersing myself in "four walls education" once again.*

*Postcard- postmark BREMERTON- NOV 17 66*
*[reverse is Daumier's The Beer Drinkers]*

---

Hobo Dan, Thank you so much for your card. School is coming along fine. I woke up this morning and rode down over the hill towards school and oh!! The Cascades stood out so vividly and Mt. Rainier towered so high in the south that it seemed just like a wilderness of rolling green, fenced off by a ragged white fence, with Mt. Rainier as the entering archway. It was so cold and clear that I could almost see Sumas. I've got a real yearning to see that fair little town, right soon!! And buy a few helpings of good old Sumas Café chili. In fact I dreamed a few nights back that you, Doug and I jumped aboard at the Woodinville clubhouse and saw all the old sights; Wickersham, the Nooksack, Acme, Sumas Mountain. Well I'll be coming home this weekend and I'll give you a call on Saturday. Take it easy!! Steve

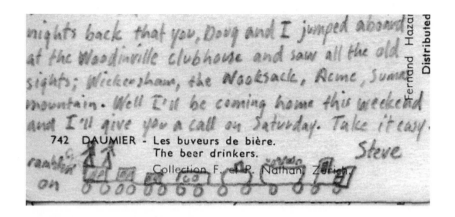

nights back that you, Doug and I jumped abound at the Woodinville clubhouse and saw all the old sights; Wickersham, the Nooksack, Acme, Sumas mountain. Well I'll be coming home this weekend and I'll give you a call on Saturday. Take it easy.

742 DAUMIER - Les buveurs de bière.
The beer drinkers.

Steve

ramblin' on Collection F. et R. Nathan, Zürich

*Letter- postmark BREMERTON- DEC 66*

Bremerton, Washington, Dec 4, 1966

Hobo Dan, I thought I'd drop you a couple of lines to let you know that the trains are still running over here, across the sound, and their long, low whistles drift in occasionally through my open window playing a sweet tune, ROAD MUSIC!! That's what it is, OPEN ROAD MUSIC!! Apparently there's a daily run from Tacoma to either Poulsbo or Port Orchard. But the train itself consists only of about 15 cars, sorta like the Redmond to Issaquah run.

Well, since I saw you last I made the trip down to Chehalis and spent three days down there, mostly working with my cousin. We managed to pot about a 1000 small shrubs and bushes that he hopes to sell next spring. We also spent some time gathering in a couple cords of firewood. Anyway there weren't many idle minutes. My cousin's wife raises pigs, sort of as a side line, and Thanksgiving evening one of her sows produced a total of 17 piglets, which caused great moments of elation through the whole place. Even the cats and dogs gathered around to get in on the goin's on. Oh, yes, my cousin's children really go in for mushrooms, so when we were out choppin' wood they managed to find over 2 gallons of "fairy cups" and two big "shaggy-manes". They had so many projects goin' on around the place; 4-H, square-dancing, football games, county fair, it's quite a community "old Chehalis". Well, I left Sunday morning from Chehalis and got back to Bremerton that evening.

The quarter is coming to a close over here, Dec. 14 is my last day. I signed up for 16 hours next quarter; English Comp., Botany, Russian, a class entitled "The Novel" and basketball. What I'm ultimately studying toward is an English degree plus a foreign language minor. Russian is by far my most interesting class; my teacher is an old Russian herself and really shakes things up. She's even spending class periods telling about some of the geography and natural resource distribution, &c. The class itself is geared toward conversation more than a study of grammar, verb endings, language cases. Learning to write Russian helps to pass the long weekends.

I imagine you're still spending time with "Walden" and "Zen". I'm a little further back down the road and reading *The Soviet Family* by David and Vera Mace. It's an interesting book for the most part, telling about the various aspects of city and country families in Russia today. David and Vera Mace traveled around in Russia themselves for several months, living with Russian families in their sod and log homes, in the regions just north of Moscow and also with families in Kiev, Leningrad, and Moscow. The areas of the Balkans, Ukraine, Poland and Hungary are places where a fellow could do some "good traveling". At one time last year I was contemplating on whether or not I should see if I couldn't get to Poland and Leningrad, but the 10 kroner a day wage didn't seem to allow for the extra cash I was in need of.

During the evenings or when I'm on my way home from school, I really get to missing "good old Norway" and wish that I could be back out on the North Sea. I got another letter last week from a lady I knew in Egersund who I used to bring cod to on a Saturday evening and who would cook up a good Sunday meal and invite me over on a Sunday afternoon. The things I remember the most are the folk in Egersund and all the action around the harbor, big herring trawlers from Hammerfest and Tromso, freighters from Amsterdam, Copenhagen, Liverpool, Le Havre, Hamburg, Aberdeen, Scotland, and the junky German and Polish boats loaded with fish boxes and radio aerials. When you get to Norway you'll have to stop in Egersund, for my sake and see the little place for yourself.

Listen, I'm planning on being in Kirkland on this coming Friday evening and plan to go up to Sumas, Saturday, if you can go. I want to see Tom and George Nesset before Christmas and show them some of my slides of Norway, &c. It's hard to believe that three months have gone by so quickly and I guess it's going to be a good long while before you'll be back in this neck of the woods again. I'm saving all I can now for travelin' this summer, and I'm plannin' on using my passport while it's still valid. It's too early to make anything definite right now, but if the trawlers run in the right directions I may get back to Norway sooner than expected.

For extra money I've been making Christmas wreaths with some of the fir and cedar around the place. [Steve's cabin was located at the Mountaineers' outdoor "Forest Theater", surrounded by woods.] I'm going to sell some more this week and next. If sales keep up I may clear enough money to keep me going for the month of January. The woods are so full of animals that every time I take off through the trails there's a raccoon or a squirrel, a flicker or a pheasant, making it's way through the undergrowth or up atop the fir branches. If you don't have anything planned for the weekend after this next one, why not plan on coming over here and maybe we could go up along the peninsula, around Poulsbo and Port Orchard. Anyway you're welcome to come over and sit around the fireplace or split wood for the Mountaineers, besides getting a few "good olde Mountain type" meals. The roof leaks a little when it rains real hard, and the mice are always around to clean up the leftovers, but the place is still standin', which counts the most. The Mountaineers built this place around 1910 and have remodeled it some since then. I've got a couple of old photographs that show how this area looked around 1920, including some of the old Mountaineer members, which are sort of interestin'. The Mountaineers have been quite an active group through the years.

Well, I hope all is runnin' smoothly there in Kirkland. And I'll see you this weekend. Keep the old file movin' with vigor [a reference to my work at Boeings, making 707s that fall.] and skillful-handedness!!

Your comrade, Steve

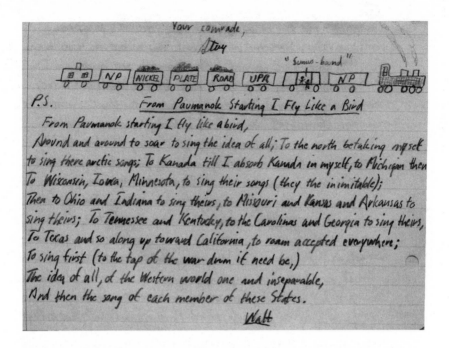

Your comrade,

Stuy

"Sunus-bound"

P.S.    From Paumanok Starting I Fly Like a Bird

From Paumanok starting I fly like a bird,
Around and around to soar to sing the idea of all; To the north betaking myself
to sing there arctic songs; To Kanada till I absorb Kanada in myself, to Michigan then
To Wisconsin, Iowa, Minnesota, to sing their songs (they the inimitable);
Then to Ohio and Indiana to sing theirs, to Missouri and Kansas and Arkansas to
sing theirs; To Tennessee and Kentucky, to the Carolinas and Georgia to sing theirs,
To Texas and so along up toward California, to roam accepted everywhere;
To sing first (to the tap of the war-drum if need be,)
The idea of all, of the Western world one and inseparable,
And then the song of each member of these States.

Walt

*In late December I quit my job at Boeings before heading back to college.
On the 28th Steve and I had gone to Woodinville to catch out on the old
NP, heading south towards Portland, but having arrived just as it pulled
to a stop, Steve was knocked off of the boxcar ladder as we were hastily
boarding the train. I had climbed up to the top of the car and didn't see him
fall off, but what was worse, I was unable to get off the train by the time I
realized he was not on it. When the train finally stopped in Auburn, I was
able to get to a pay phone. From his sister I learned that Milo, the friend
who had dropped us off, had already left to find Steve. Unable to do more at
that point, I returned to my freight train and continued south to Portland,
Oregon. The following morning I called from there to learn that Steve had
been hurt but was by then patched up. Disconsolate at Steve's situation, I
nevertheless had to get back to college, and in Portland I switched to hitch-
hiking, intermittently following Highway 99 and Interstate 5 south to a
rendezvous with Doug in the Bay Area.*

*I found Doug staying at his cousin's place in Berkeley. He had just scored
some acid, so we agreed to drop acid together a day or two later. We spent*

the next day touring San Francisco, the high point being a visit to City Lights Bookstore where we talked with an old beatnik running the store. He told us that *The Dharma Bums* was still out of print, and that Jack Kerouac now lived in a house in Florida "with a big wall around it", essentially a recluse. We found this very hard to accept, but the guy claimed to know all the beat writers, and seemed to be in a position to know what he was talking about. To me this was disheartening if true, and, unaware of his addiction to alcohol, I still cherished the idea that Kerouac had not abandoned the lifestyle he had made synonymous with his name. The next day, Doug and I were back in Berkeley. We walked up the hill above Derby Street to a grove of eucalyptus and split a cap of acid Doug said was from Czechoslovakia. We then waited for some indication of a change in our perception of the world. The sun was mild and warm, there were a few people out enjoying the view overlooking the University of California and San Francisco Bay, and although I felt strangely aware of it all, I was waiting for some kind of obvious hallucination that would confirm that I was not just imagining an acid trip. A boy with a small motorbike tried repeatedly to get it to go up a steep section of trail, and then came over to us, requesting help pushing it up the hill. We were in fact tripping on the acid, although we did not realize it at the time, unable to take any kind of quick or decisive action. We put him off with vague suggestions, all the while observing him and ourselves as if we were watching a drama in an open air theater in the round. Seemingly out of nowhere another guy walked up the hill and took charge of the gutless motorbike, gunning the engine and powering it up the steep stretch with what seemed to me to be an endless reservoir of skill and determination. I still didn't realize that my reactions to what I was experiencing were being influenced by the LSD, but as Doug and I wandered around the hillside I remember looking at the leafy end of a small branch, recently emerged from its bud. I commented that it almost seemed as if it was trying to tell me something. Doug asked me what that might be, but I could not put my feelings into words. Eventually we wandered down the hill to his cousin's apartment, and at some point I picked up a copy of *Zen Flesh, Zen Bones*. After reading a few lines of a zen koan, I suddenly understood the afternoon's events in a new way. As I began to explain my insight to Doug he immediately got it and we began laughing, exchanging what must have seemed to the other people there as somewhat cryptic comments to each other. My first acid trip had been minimalistic, interesting and tantalizing, making me want to try it again, preferably in a slightly larger dose, but at present duty called and I prepared my pack for the road again.

From a dealer acquaintance of Doug's in the Bay Area, I had scored some marijuana and some peyote buttons. These I sent via the "dirty dog" (Greyhound Express freight) to my address in Beloit, and then headed there myself, thinking to avoid the worst of winter weather by continuing south and then east from Southern California. After taking a city bus down to San Jose, I caught an SP freight south to San Luis Obispo. In Watsonville some old hobos in a gondola evidently thought I was worried about riding with them and told me, "Don't worry kid, we won't give ya any trouble." I was impressed with how much warmer the weather was once we had cleared the tunnel and dropped down into the valley where SLO was situated, but after a few hours of waiting there for another train to be built, my patience grew thin and I headed over to the freeway, continuing south by thumb. Interestingly, on this train I had met another couple of young hobos who were going to one of the Claremont Schools and knew a couple of the smarter kids from my high school physics class. Hitch-hiking at this time was much like the old days of hoboing; one would meet people who knew people you knew; it was all connected together.

I managed to catch a series of shorter rides as far as Barstow, and then Needles, where I finally got a longer ride with a Texan who looked about as scruffy as I did. He stopped to buy a large bag of hotdogs and another of potato chips, and we ate these, the hot dogs uncooked, as we drove east on Route 66. I did my best to be entertaining as it was growing increasingly colder with every mile closer to the continental divide and I certainly didn't want him to tire of my company. At Holbrook we cut south through the back country, as he was heading toward Socorro. Around midnight he asked me if I would drive for awhile, to which request I readily acceded. As he dozed in the back seat I did a rough calculation of how many miles it was to our destination and realized that at our present rate of travel I would be standing by the side of the road at about three in the morning. I accordingly slowed down a bit, enjoying the clear sky above and the hints of true desert landscape illuminated by the headlights, thus managing to delay our arrival until about 6 AM. It was still well below freezing in Socorro, but at least the sun was coming up, and I had hopes of catching a ride north to Albuquerque.

In Albuquerque I visited Milo, who was able to fill me in on the details of Steve's recent mishap and recovery. Milo was attending the University of New Mexico, so I was able to cop a few free meals and a place to crash. The following day he dropped me off at the local yards where I caught a nice empty down to Belen and then nearly got busted by a "suit" when I inquired a bit too freely about trains heading to Kansas City. I quickly ditched that guy and located a car knocker who was more accommodating. He told me when the next hotshot was due out, and suggested that I ride the units, as otherwise it would be pretty cold riding, even in an empty. I managed to get into one and, with the connivance of the train crews, to ride all the way to KC, where I arrived at night, snow falling, with the temperature at about 10 degrees.

While inquiring about any transfer freights going across town to the Milwaukee Road yards I met a conductor working a (local) transfer freight who put me into his caboose and promised to drive me over the next morning as it was on his way home. I settled into the "way car", as he termed it, and was writing in my journal when a couple of switchmen came in to warm up. They immediately concluded that I was writing a book, and one of them quipped that I should be sure to put "old Red" (an engineer that they seemed to hold in low repute) in it. This comment produced an inordinate amount of hilarity, my host laughing as much as they did but I now can say that I have fulfilled their request. I was able to get some sleep that night as the conductor's transfer freight shuttled back and forth across town, and true to his word, we drove over to Knoche yards in the morning. I was given a guided tour of his neighborhood as we crossed Kansas City, and at one point we approached a crossing with the lights flashing and the bells ringing. He continued on through as if there were no approaching train, calmly explaining which train it was, assuring me that it wouldn't beat us to the crossing, but before he was able to finish his explanation we were in fact crossing the tracks. I looked in panic at the approaching nose of a big diesel directly to my right, not having had time to digest all this, but he did indeed know his stuff; the train was only moving at about five mph. I hardly had time to heave a sigh of relief before he was pointing out the apartment of his favorite whore, whom he described in some detail. He seemed to appreciate her all the more as she was not paying off the local mafia that ran the town. Like an Arab transferring his guest safely into the custody of a neighboring tribe, at Knoche Yards he introduced me to the dispatchers in the Milwaukee Road yard office and bid me adieu.

The dispatcher there asked a yard worker to fix me up with an empty shanty, and I was soon soaking up the heat from a coal fired cast iron stove, writing in my journal. I had missed the morning train to Milwaukee and thus would have to wait another day for the next one, but as the day progressed, a number of workers stopped in to chat when they had free time and before long someone had set me up with a ride as far as Savanna, Illinois in the caboose of the Chicago train. I passed the time reading a paperback and finally was able to cook the last of the hot dogs I had inherited in Soccoro, frying them directly on the top of the shanty's cast iron stove. Around dark I was once more on a freight headed east, taking all night to cross Missouri and Iowa. I tried to sleep when I could, but did talk with the conductors and brakemen as each crew passed me off to the next one. The dispatcher had given me a forged pass at Knoche Yards telling the conductor to "Please haul this man to Savanna", but the guys in the caboose working their divisions didn't much mind having me ride and never asked to see my "ticket". We were in our own world between midnight and dawn, frozen, snow covered farms inching by as the train inched its way eastward toward the Mississippi River. Since I had gotten on the engine unit in New Mexico, I had been treated kindly by all the railroad men I had encountered, and felt that working for the railroad would be a lot more enjoyable than most desk jobs I might aspire to once I had a college degree. In Savanna I encountered the same situation as I had in Kansas City; I now had to wait about twelve more hours for the Milwaukee train. I inquired at the dispatch office, and was told that I could stay in a caboose that was not going anywhere for the next while, so I promptly rolled out my sleeping bag and "copped some Zs" until that evening when I began waiting to board the train that would take me the last eighty miles to Beloit. Due to my earlier inquiries at the dispatch office, I was again offered a ride in the caboose, and stepped off the train in Beloit just before dawn the next morning, walking up the hill to the campus in the dark. As I crossed the campus I wondered if the sound *of my vibram soled hiking boots hitting the bricks of Red Square in front of Middle College was anything like the sound of one hand clapping. I was back for another term of "four walls education".*

Letter- postmark BREMERTON- JAN 16 67

---

Bremerton, Washington January 15 1967

Hobo Dan, It's a beautiful day Sunday mornin' out here and I'm sittin' on my porch, takin' in the movement of the wind as it drifts through the branches of some of the surrounding firs. The sun is filtering in from the east and as the wind continues to blow, the trees and sun combine to form an ever changing pattern of light and solid green motion. The patterns change from a very restless, chaotic action to a gentle, drifting motion and then back again without any conceivable warning, like a hobo on the drift, striking out with untold capacity and force, and then gently drifting down the tracks, movin' on, allowed to stop, only as long as the wind would care to.

I'll try to tell you as concisely as possible what happened Tuesday, December 28 in Woodinville although so much of the action that night is unexplainable. Well, because my sack and sleeping bag were thrown carelessly around my shoulder after I got on the car ladder and as the train began to gather speed I lost consciousness and slipped off the ladder onto the [Sammamish] Slough bridge. As far as I could tell afterward I must have been out cold for about 30 minutes. When I finally did come to I discovered I had a good size hole in the back of my head, so I went down to the Woodinville gas station, washed up and phoned Milo. After he looked at the cut we decided to go down to the hospital in Kirkland and after arriving there and being told they would have to bring out the thread and needle and do a little sewing I figured I'd save $50 and have Milo drive me into Group Health hospital, since I'm a member there. Well, about 12:30 in the morning I was lying face down on the old doctor's table and he was leaning over me with clamps in one hand and needle and thread in the other, joyfully sewing away as if he were patching up a sock. My cut went right down to my skull, so he kept beating his little hammer against the bone, so I could have the pleasure of listening to a low, indescribable, hollow-like sound, each time he hit my drum (head). They let me sleep over night at the hospital and then said that I'd be OK to leave the next morning. Since Milo had planned to buy some climbing gear at the [REI] Co-op, he stopped by and picked me up along with Sunny Jim and I was almost tempted to have them drive me over to Woodinville again for another try. My neck was so stiff though, that I could hardly move it one way or the other, so they dropped me off at my place and I spent the rest of the week reading *Tom Jones* and yearning to be in Chehalis. Man, Dan, I was glad when I felt better and could come back here to Bremerton. My cousins in Chehalis were sorry I couldn't make it and sent me a nice get-well card (the whole bit).

Well, the sun has moved up farther into the sky now, and looks more like a big expanding star lighting up the tops of all the trees. My next break from school comes about March 27, so I'm planning to go down to Chehalis then to make up for a little lost time and help my cousin with some of his spring planting. I can sense the days becoming a little longer now, for as I ride down the hills to school each morning the sunrise is a little brighter, and indeed, full of renewed strength. It will be good to see the approach of spring here with all the poplars down along the road throwing on their green coat and rushing out to meet the summer sun. It's nice to stay in a place for one complete year, you begin to see it in its entirety and it begins to take on a completely different pattern, a picture of completion and fulfillment.

I'm sending my application for federal employment up to Marblemount tomorrow as it's all filled out and ready to go. I'm still planning to go to Iceland, but thought if I sent my application into the Forest Service now and then discovered in March that my friend in Trondheim (he's moved now from Reykjavik to Trondheim, Norway) can use my help this summer, I'll be able to write to the Forest Service then and tell them not to consider me for a summer job. However, if I decide not to go to Norway I'll have a good chance to find work on the trail crew if I get my application in now.

I hope you'll write and tell me about your trip across the states. Say, did you find there were good connections in Kent for trains going south to Chehalis? Milo said you had called from Kent to tell him that I'd fallen off the train. What's it like to be back in the flat country again and how are classes this semester? I've been reading on the weekends, several different Russian authors, namely a biography about Boris Pasternak and a story by Maxim Gorky entitled "Mother". The book was written during the time surrounding the 1917 revolution and is very descriptive and conveys the mood in Russia during 1917. My novel class is interesting and worthwhile, but for being only a two credit course, it takes up over half of my time, at least during these last two weeks it has. As soon as I'm finished with the seven assigned books for the class and write a critical analysis, comparing two of the books, I'll be able to allow more time for Russian and Russian literature, and also some Norwegian and Swedish books by Sigrid Undset and Selma Lagerlof. I found an old Norwegian book (written in Norsk) over at the Seattle Public Library last week telling all about coastal travel through the North Sea from Oslo around and up the coast to Trondheim. The book is written in a relatively easy style so it's easy to understand.

I haven't been back in Kirkland since the 2nd of January so haven't heard anything from Doug and how his trip went, down to S.F. On my way to school in the morning I always recall those old hobo songs from the south and while drifting along with the approach of morning light, let go with some of those movin' tunes.

The sky is so blue now and the sun has cleared the trees in its journey to the top of the sky. The wrens and sparrows are coming down out of the trees to look for some food in the front yard here. I suppose I should go in and make up some stew for this afternoon and maybe go down to see what's wrong with my water pump. I've been short on water these past few days.

Well Dan, write when you find time and may the good God of the Hobos watch over ya!!

Your pal, Steve

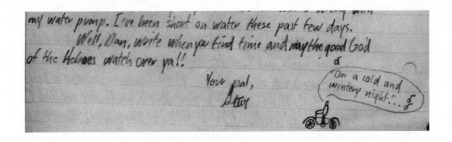

my water pump. I've been short on water these past few days. Well, Dan, write when you find time and may the good God of the Holmes watch over ya!!

Your pal,
Dan

"On a cold and wintery night..."

Dear Dan, I want to thank you so much for your letter, and that the journey back to Beloit went so well. For $9, all in all, it sounds like you got a worthwhile bargain. Did you get any long rides from LA to Kansas City? I guess it must have been beautiful in the SW this time of year, especially in Oklahoma.

My head is healing up now, but I've been pretty busy with school and all, so haven't had a chance to make a trip up to Sumas. It's been such a mild winter this year that the trees are already starting to bud and the crocuses are a bloomin'. It's good travelin' weather, and in about two weeks I'm hoping to make another attempt to make it down to Chehalis (during the quarter break). I'm home in Kirkland today and as I'm sitting here the long pervading tone of the local can be heard between Black River and Woodinville. I talked to Doug's father last night on the telephone and he said that Doug is planning to go down to Mexico when the winter quarter concludes next week. Doug was up in Everett yesterday so I didn't get a chance to see him. I'm going down in the afternoon to see if he's home and to see what his plans are. I guess he has probably written to you already tellin' about his forthcoming journey to the south. If everything works out I'm hoping we can ride down together as far as Chehalis, but I'm not sure yet what day he plans to leave.

School has been fine this quarter. As of late, Russian has been so interesting that it's difficult to set the book down and go to bed in the evenings. Some nights I feel like just reading right on through until morning. I was able to find some Russian readers and short children's books. It's helpful just to sit down and start reading a simple story. The grammar becomes a reality when it's written out in the form of a story. Next quarter I've got a course in British literature and one in American contemporary prose. There will be only 8 short weeks in the spring quarter and by the 5th of June I should be on the road. A letter came this last week from the Forest Service in Marblemount saying that by the 1st of April they would know if they could use me on the trail crew. But as of now my chances look pretty good for going to Iceland in June. But I think if you do get accepted and I find that they will still need me too, I'll stay here this summer. Just think how great it would be up there and oh!! Milo is hoping to work up there too. If you are home in the first week in June we could take the train up to Acme and then walk from there to the Twin Sisters [a nearby mountain] and then down into the Marblemount district, stopping along the way to climb on a few of the ridges.

The skiing has been wonderful this winter, but most of the weekends now are difficult to find enough time in, but I've been up to Hurricane Ridge and another time to White Pass. I may go up on George Washington's birthday. White Pass is a wide-open type of place with a lot of long runs and not packed to the edges with folks.

I've been reading books for a course on the novel this quarter and haven't had a chance to locate any books by Mr. [Alan] Watts. Right now I'm reading *The Stranger* by Camus and a couple of short Japanese novels, one, *The Sound of Waves* by Yukio Mishima (a story about a Japanese fisherman) and also some stories by Turgenev, a Russian short story writer.

It is so peaceful out at my place in Bremerton, the birds come down every morning to sing and feed on the oatmeal crumbs scattered around the front yard. And just lately I've had a few foxes running by the place in the early mornings. I met a Swedish lady who lives only a mile or two from me who does a lot of weaving and who let me copy the dimensions of her loom. As I mentioned to you before when you were here at home, there is enough room in my place for a loom of about 5 feet by 6ft., so when I'm down in Chehalis I plan to see if I can't get started on fitting some of the pieces together so that by next fall I'll be ready to turn out a few fabrics, &c. At least it will be a start. This

Swedish lady was telling me (when I was over at her place again last week) about life in northern Sweden (where she grew up as a child), the logging, the sheep herding, the winter weaving and skiing, the means of travel. Have you ever thought of looking around up in that part of the world. I imagine that there is a lot of work there in the logging industry. Anyway I've got my eye on the eastern coast of Sweden as a place to settle down. As the days go by I'm becoming more and more convinced that the States is definitely not the place I want to settle down in for any length of time. It seems like many times the one thing a fellow has an opportunity to do here is to build freeways. I heard that the next plan under way in Seattle is to build another floating bridge and then put another deck on the Seattle Freeway. We're starting it now even in our road construction (destruction). I was reading in the East Side Journal last night that a big four-laner is going in between Juanita and Woodinville by 1968. I begin to wonder now what the old home land will look like in another 20 years. And, oh, what a beautiful land we do have, or would have if there wasn't this need on our part to develop at such a rate.

Well how is everything there in Beloit (school and otherwise)? I've been hearing on the radio that the weather in Wisconsin and Minnesota has been pretty cold and snowy. How cold has it been in Beloit? Almost every day I see that it's -30 in Minn. And that the schools are all closed down, &c. I don't think we've had a day below 32 since the 1st of February. Well, I imagine it will be good to see that first day of spring in Beloit.

I just wanted to send along some of the latest happenings on this side of the mountains, so I'll close for now, and let me know how things are in regards to your summer plans for work, &c.

Your Itinerant cohort, Steve

*Letter- postmark BREMERTON- MAR 6 67*

---

Bremerton, Washington, March 4, 1967

Hobo Dan, Things are rollin' along smooth (like a freight running down off Clearview hill) out here today. The spring sun is the only visible thing in the sky now, except for an occasional 707. You know how beautiful a blue summer day is out here, well that's what we've got today. It's the afternoon and the sun that has been movin' slowly westward has finally set itself between the top of two pine trees and looks as if it could suddenly drop straight down between their trunks and burn a shaft of gold in among the branches. The wrens and sparrows have been feeding on the pine seeds in the front yard while a squirrel has been busy (some 70 ft. above where I'm sitting) shelling pine cones and dropping down the husks all around the base of his home and coming mighty close on several occasions in his attempts to see if he can land one on one of the birds. Now and then he'll become so happy inside that he'll rise up on his back legs and laugh at the sun. Just like a hobo would laugh as he's racin' across the prairies of Nebraska or North Dakota and a watchin' the sun rollin' west, <u>his direction</u>, goin' west to find work. It's been a fine day for growing, both for the plants and man, <u>growing closer to things</u>; the roots hugging in closer to the earth and the souls of men rooting themselves in closer to the appearance of the sun, as its force absorbs into the soil, leaving the earth <u>changed</u>, <u>altered</u>, never again appearing in the same manner. Although I'd like to be on the road today it's good to stay here all day and watch the sun. And to save travelin' time for a day that will identify itself as one made for <u>boot poundin'</u> and <u>steady rollin'</u>. That day will come and present itself in due time, but today is a good one for <u>growin'</u>.

Well I haven't been in Kirkland now for over two weeks, but the last I heard, Doug is still here. This Friday I'm planning to go home and will stop in at his place in the afternoon to see how his plans are comin'. I think he said he plans to leave sometime next week, but I haven't seen him for a while and I'm almost positive that his winter quarter at EJC [now Everett Community College] will conclude next week as does ours. I'm going to leave for Chehalis in the afternoon or evening after my finals and plan to be down there for a short week. Spring quarter starts the 28th of March. So you'll be here on or around the first of May!! I'll be in school until June 5th, so I wouldn't be able to go on any long trips until then. My plans for going to Iceland this summer still look pretty good, but if things don't work out I'm a hopin' the ranger at Marblemount will be in need of me. I had a fellow offer me a job on a fishing boat this summer fishing for salmon, out along the coast, so one way or the other I'll be able to earn a few dollars for next year besides seeing a little bit of the country.

So you're planning to homestead up in BC. Well, I still prefer the Scandinavian countries myself. I think when you get to Norway you'll think the same thing yourself. But wherever a fellow stakes out a claim it's a good feeling living with the land; it's a worthwhile experiment, and now is the time to begin to prepare the <u>raw materials</u>.

School is coming along fine. I've been reading some books by Albert Camus and Jean Paul Sartre these last few weeks. Camus' use of imagery (the sun and sea) in his novel *The Stranger* carries with it tremendous depth on his part in attempts to capture the sea and sun and relate them to his main characters. It starts you thinking about the blending in nature, of objects that when they combine together there is formed a meaningful medium. You can relate some of your own experience into the text and the blending of his words, with the representation you associate them with, made solid, bold print into words that <u>roll</u>, <u>pound</u>, words that <u>move</u>, <u>west</u>. *The Stranger* is in many ways parallel in style to Hemingway's *The Old Man and the Sea*. It is this type of literary expression that I feel draws closer to things. It leaves room for wandering out along the sides of the page. If you have some time in your next letter, reflect a little on the thoughts that you have on <u>existentialism</u>. The modern novel and its various forms that are with us today come as close as any form of expression in the <u>interpretation</u> of nature.

The Mountaineers have been around here the last couple of weekends and are planning to hold a climbing school here during April. They are a fine group of people and have some mighty good times out here in the early summer. They invited me to a get-together party next month too. I thought I'd at least show up to meet some of the fellows in the group. They are planning, I've heard, to climb some of the Olympic peaks in May. And then the last weekend in May the Mountaineer plays will be starting at the theater here, so I'm hoping

Steve learning to dive, Bremerton, 1967. Photos courtesy Daryl Hoyt.

to see one production before hitting the road. This little place has been mighty quiet these last 5 months but as the snows are starting to melt off the folks are a finding their way back to the old grounds. It's nice to have folks stop by and sit out on the porch here. You get to feelin' like old Henry, do you remember his chapter in *Walden* entitled "Visitors"?

Well, I've got some reading to do for class on Monday, so I'll sign off and hope all is well for you as you prepare to move westward again. Keep up the studies, too!!

Hobos forever, Steve

PS I get to thinkin' some days that after I've completed two years here at Olympic, I'll leave the country and finish years three and four in either Oslo or Stockholm. Right now most everything is in the planning stages, but by next year about this time, I'm a thinkin' the yearning to be on a long road trip will be with me <u>strong</u> and <u>poundin'</u>.

At about this time, Doug had been attending EJC for more than a year but had not found academia much to his liking. The college had an FM radio station, replete with student disc jockeys who did their best to parrot the prevailing hip and groovy sound of the local AM and FM commercial stations. Influenced by the different approach at KRAB, Doug had wanted to get an hour slot to provide not only a different kind of music, but without the hype. It seems however that the powers controlling the college station did not feel such programming would serve the educational goals of EJC. Near the end of the term, he encountered yet another discouragement in his pursuit of knowledge at this institution; he was called in on the carpet on the explicit charge of "slovenly attire". The dean of students calmly told Doug that if he didn't clean up his appearance she would not let him return the next term. Although it is difficult to imagine such institutional bullying today, this sort of generational skirmishing was common as the '50s mentality slowly yielded to that of the '60s. Thoroughly disgusted, Doug finished his classes and headed south, stopping in California to visit friends there, but eventually he continued hitch-hiking south, crossing the border at Nogales to spend a couple of months in Mexico. He did not speak Spanish, and at 6'5" was physically imposing, but being a gentle soul he had no difficulties communicating with the people he met, riding cheap busses and sleeping on the beach once he hit the coast at Guymas. When he finally returned to the US from his wanderings he had achieved a new perspective regarding his studies. When he moved in with Steve at the cabin in Bremerton and enrolled at Olympic Junior College he only took classes that interested him, finding that achieving passing grades was suddenly easy.

*Comment from Doug in 2011:*

Looking at my EJC & Olympic Community College records I find: "reinstated Jan.67" (if I cut my hair, and did not show radical [i.e. counter culture] tendencies; as specified by the Dean of Students). I quit school soon after this and went to Mexico. When I returned I attended Olympic [Community College] in the fall quarter of '67.

The Dean of Students' comments and conditions regarding me became very outdated within a few years due to the social changes happening on campus. At the time, there was another person, on EJC campus, whom I would describe at that time as a brilliant, very original thinking, radical Beatnik. I still remember to this day the originality of his thinking and his scruffy appearance.

*Letter- postmark BREMERTON- APR 17 1967*

---

Bremerton, Washington, April 15, 1967

Hobo Dan, It's Saturday afternoon, and I'm sitting out in the front yard, reading some books concerned with realism and naturalism in American Literature at the turn of this last century.

I've been thinking about you and half-way expect to see you coming up along the tracks with some of your cohorts from school before the close of the month. And before I relate some of the latest from around here, I want to remind you to be sure and drop me a postcard as to when you'll be <u>rolling in</u>.

Well I went down to Chehalis as planned (a few weeks back now) and spent a week (in total) digging fence post holes and chopping wood. I was down there over the Easter holiday and so managed to get to the <u>First Methodist</u> on Sunday morning with my cousins. I got to thinkin' at the time that I'd fancy travelling around the States for a year or so and every Sunday drift into a church, be it in the heart of Boston or in the backwoods of Mississippi. You know, just to see if a fella couldn't do a little comparing between denominations and such. Sitting and listening to lectures every day (and particularly English professors speaking on some aspect of literature) it's interesting to go to one of the local halls of redemption and study the sermon structure and presentation of one of the "men of God" as he appeals to or reassures his "good people". At any rate, I really enjoyed the good old Chehalis First Methodist. Instead of going down by the train I thumbed from Tacoma after getting a ride with a schoolmate that far.

When I was in Seattle (almost a month ago now) I noticed along the streets a number of young fellows (San Francisco Bay boys) passing through. And met two boys from Canada, each with bedrolls, who were making an extended tour through the States, riding the trains for the most part and hitchhiking now and then. They were two pretty swell fellows; fine comrades.

School is going to continue here until the 5th of June, and as it looks now I'll be leaving for Norway on the 7th; I'll let you know for sure by the time you get home. Subjects this quarter include British Literature, American Literature, and Composition. I managed a 3.3 last quarter. I'm thinking that next year I'll take fewer hours so I can concentrate on Russian and outside reading. By the end of this quarter I'll have almost 50 credits for this year, so I'll have 5 credits to begin with this coming September and subsequently will only need 40 more to graduate from here.

It's been so beautiful here, now that the sun and rain have agreed on more or less equal time each day. The weather has been cold for April, but for the most part clear. I hope it continues so, for your trip west!! I wouldn't fancy riding on a rainy car-carrier if you are planning to come the northern route!! At least not in the sort of rain we've been blessed with on several occasions this month.

I've been reading a group of foreign and American novels since I last wrote; Lord Jim, Madame Bovary, Red Badge of Courage, Herzog (by Saul Bellow) and Huckleberry Finn and Innocents Abroad by Mark Twain. Joseph Conrad seemed to me to be a man who had good insight into the nature of things, particularly human relationships and comrades vs. nature. I want to read all his books, and if you're going to be working on a lookout in Lolo, be sure to include one of his books. I haven't read much from good old Walt lately, but the greatest poem that ever found its way onto the printed page is "Song of the Open Road. The whole piece moves; it includes aspects of traveling that live, move, pound. It expresses freedom, a soaring moment of freedom.

> Well, have a good trip across, keep free and write.
> Man, it will be good to see you again,
> Your comrade, Steve

*Postcard- postmark  BREMERTON- MAY 5 67*
*[reverse is Le Dejeuner Des Canotiers by Renoir]*

---

Hobo Dan, I thought I'd be hearing from you this week. I'm hoping you'll be able to stop by before the 1st of June, if not sooner. There's nothing better than having fellows stop in for a couple of days. The forest is so beautiful over here now, with the blendings of the evening sun through the cedars and there's plenty of room to go on some good hikes. The meals aren't the best, hamburger meat and corn, but there's plenty of it. And maybe you could come a day to school and have a look around Bremerton. You should bring your sleeping bag or a few blankets because I'm short on 'em. Otherwise I've got most everything else. Hope to hear from you soon. Bring your harmonica. Your comrade, Steve

---

*At about the time this postcard was mailed I had ridden a freight to Seattle with friends from college and then spent most of May hitching and riding freight trains up and down the west coast, finally free for a while to indulge in my lust for travel. My brother drove Ed, Hank and me out to Woodinville where we caught a Portland bound train, but once there we had the misfortune to meet with the long arm of the law. Standing in an empty boxcar as the Coast Starlight rolled by, we waved and gloated at the suckers who were paying to ride, but shortly thereafter a yard bull walked up to our car and conducted us to a waiting paddy wagon. Although this delayed our arrival in sunny California for a week much to our chagrin, the experience was one I would not now trade for another week added to my life span; we were free to mingle with a motly collection of winos, mentally retarded individuals, a homosexual (as they were then referred to), some very bad drivers, and a guy who made the mistake of hitting the cop who had slugged him for no good reason. We were the three hippies in the group and were accepted as no better and no worse than anyone else. The cop told the judge as we were about to be sentenced, "I figgered that these college boys could do with a little education here in Portland".*

*Once free of our captors we hitched the rest of the way to the Bay area, and soon found our way to the hills above Berkeley where we dropped*

acid together as previously related. The next day we of course headed for Haight-Ashbury in San Francisco, the acknowledged center of the much touted summer of love, but almost immediately we were sorely disillusioned by the profusion of gaudy superficiality and sketchy characters. From there Ed headed back to Beloit for the summer term, while Hank and I headed south for a brief taste of Mexico, catching a ride with a couple of guys who happened to be on the run, scooting out of their San Francisco apartment and psychedelic drug emporium just ahead of the cops, heading for the LA airport. They had been dealing (pot and LSD they told us), and had been tipped off on the impending bust, but hadn't wanted to chance getting nabbed at the San Francisco airport. They were planning to fly to New York City, figuring that the east coast might not be quite so unhealthy for them just then. We hopped out before the airport, declining their offer of a free car, realizing that it might soon be hot, if it wasn't already, and besides, we didn't want to squander our dwindling cash on gas; hitchhiking was free. Sometime after midnight we found a place to sleep beneath some palm trees by the side of the road. The next morning we packed up and began hitching along the road, not really knowing where we were, but heading south, when a long, slow freight crawled into view. It didn't take much discussion for us to catch it on the fly, and we were then treated to a leisurely tour of the back yards of East LA, finally ending up in the vast rail yards of San Bernardino. There we caught another freight heading for Yuma, where a couple of state bulls gave us a less than friendly reception, but eventually let us go. Due to having little cash, we couldn't go beyond the border town of Mexicali, and we soon headed back north, catching a series of freights back to LA and then another heading north from there. We woke up in a boxcar the following morning near Monterrey and, wanting to head down to Big Sur, we jumped off the freight as it slowly rounded a curve. We began walking down a country road, resilient enough to just enjoy the peaceful rural surroundings. After catching a couple of rides we figured out about where we were and were considering how best to get to Big Sur when a gaudily painted bus full of hippies stopped to pick us up. They were scouring the area for the likes of us as part of a "Be-In" that they were holding the following day. Hank and I of course went along for the ride, and this time felt that we were experiencing something more like the idealized version of California's "summer of love" we had heard about. The Be-In turned out to be a bunch of people making music and dancing in a big circle, with the rest of us sitting around watching, and I soon became bored with the whole thing. Hank and I again decided to head for Big Sur, and not too much later were picked up by a couple of girls who had cut classes to go camping at the state park there. They asked our help in getting their Coleman stove to work, and we gallantly agreed to camp with them that night. In the morning Hank and I asked the girls to drop us off at a vast grassy hillside above the Big Sur highway. As they headed back to their classes we climbed up the hillside and dropped acid, spending most of the day gazing out over the blue Pacific Ocean. Once more I experienced a mental state impossible to explain in words; the chemistry seemed to be rewiring the circuits in my brain that worked at a level of awareness deeper than language. But I was beginning to realize that aside from the questions generated with each new acid trip, in all this wandering I was still not finding what I was searching for. I had to admit to myself that I really didn't know exactly what that might be, and that rather than doing more acid, it might be a good time to ruminate on my vision quest experiences thus far. I decided to head back to the northwest, knowing that Steve would be getting out of classes soon and we could take a trip together. Hank and I hitched back to Berkeley and from there I caught a freight back north, ending up back home in early June.

Once home, I got in touch with Steve and Doug and we soon rendezvoused for a bike trip around Hood Canal. We started from Steve's cabin in Bremerton, stopped along the way to hike up to Lake Lena, where we attempted to climb The Brothers, but rainy weather made a climb pointless; we would have only become soaking wet and gotten no view. Still, the trip was the perfect way for me to mull over my vision quest experiences in California as we pedaled along the scenic back roads, sweating up the hills and coasting back down, slowly moving through a landscape we had grown up in. Soon thereafter Steve left for Norway, spending his summer working on a marine biology research vessel, cruising along the coast of Norway and Scotland, diving for corallines.

Back in Juanita, Doug agreed to host me and another friend as we took LSD. As it was the first trip for our friend we both were able to act as guides, me experiencing the same trip as he would and Doug as the straight caretaker. This time I chose to take two of the capsules, hoping to reach a deeper understanding of what we jokingly called the eternal verities and put an end to my confusion which would occur as I came down from the experience and reentered a more normal level of consciousness. I got more than I had bargained for, and did experience a merging of my own self awareness with the larger world that we normally conceive of as external to our bodies. For a brief moment all was a pulsing pattern of glowing, flowing light. I remember talking with the acolyte, but I suspect that anything said was hardly unique, let alone profound. For me however, the experience was indeed profound. Still, after this very intense trip, I had no more desire to drop acid for quite a while and soon began to pack for my summer work as a fire lookout.

In late June I reported for work at the Marblemount Ranger Station, where I was immediately told to shave off my beard. The political climate at the ranger station was one of circling the wagons; all the guys on the trail crews and fire crews, even the lookouts, were, along with being clean shaven, required to wear a uniform of green shirts and pants. Crew cuts were the style in the Skagit Valley. We were a long way from San Francisco's summer of love. I was unaware of the cause of this quasi-militaristic atmosphere until we were shown a slide show about the wilderness area to the west of Ross Lake, the same patch of mountains that Doug and I had traversed four years earlier. This Primitive Area, as it was then termed, was soon to become a national park, which meant that the size of the Marblemount Ranger District would be reduced by more than half. The head ranger was thus not a happy camper, his Texas sized district was soon to become a Rhode Island. As the slides had been forbidden to be shown to the general public, we forest service grunts were the only audience left, so we watched image after image of snowy peaks and verdant valleys, voiced over by a grandfatherly forest ranger with smarmy promises that the trees would never be logged while in the bailiwick of the Forest Service. Having seen logging trucks roll out of the foothills all my life, I had my doubts. Everybody openly joked about the lip service paid to the official slogans of "sustained use" and "multiple use" and understood that the timber desk was the tail that wagged the dog in the northwest; the real deal was called "get the cut out and worry about the rest afterwards".

The "void" of Mt. Hozomeen as seen from Desolation Peak Lookout in 1967

*I spent a week at fire school, and then a couple of weeks mowing and remowing the vast lawns at the station until it was time to man the lookout atop Desolation Peak. Although it had been about a dozen years since Snyder and Kerouac had reported for duty in Marblemount, there were a few stories still being repeated about these two writers. I suspect that like many urban legends, these stories had been transformed as they were repeated, but as the practice of Buddhism was unheard of in rural America, Snyder's sitting zazen in the bunkhouse at 5 AM was bound to raise eyebrows in the early '50s and was still talked about, along with Kerouac's jonesing for tobacco while up on Desolation. I was able to explore a bit of the valley before the fire danger was high enough to send me up to the lookout, and made a point of hiking up to Sourdough Mountain lookout for an overnight stay, getting a foretaste of what was in store for me once up on Desolation.*

*The trip up the valley was first by truck which was driven onto a barge at the end of the road and back off at the base of Ross Dam. Once above the dam* we loaded everything onto a pack team of about 8 horses and were hauled up Ross Lake on another barge to the trailhead. I set off in front with my loaded back pack, but fortunately did not have to carry my summer's worth of canned goods and books in it up the six steep miles of trail to the lookout. Once there, it took another day to get the station operational; the radio and aerial, a weather station, the fire finder, wood stove, and the cistern all had to be dealt with and tested before the fire control officer gave me his parting words of advice and the pack train headed back down the mountain. For the next two days I was socked in with a visibility of about 20 feet, but on the third day I awoke to a bright ring of peaks and ridges surrounding me, with a sea of clouds covering the valleys, making Desolation an island in the middle of it all. I spent the next week identifying all the ridges and drainages visible from the lookout, using the 7x50 power binoculars and cross checking with the map on the fire finder. In this very necessary task I was aided by an ancient photograph from the '20s, old mules on a picket line in the foreground. It was pasted together in a 360 degree panorama with all the principal peaks marked; they had not moved in 40 years.

As Kerouac has already described the view when he manned the lookout in 1956, I will only add that I was not disappointed. I could see as far west as Mt. Baker, well up into Canada, and had a nice view looking down Ross Lake towards Sourdough Mountain Lookout. To the east the landscape was dryer, with fewer trees. There was no sign of humans visible in any direction, which suited me fine. I could see the trail for nearly a mile as it snaked its way down the ridge to the south, and consequently felt free to do a bit of sunbathing without worrying that I would upset the ranger down in Marblemount with conduct unbecoming to a forest service employee. The entire peak was in an area closed to all motorized vehicles and devices, which also should have kept me safe from prying eyes, but helicopter pilots make their own rules and I was caught shoveling snow into the cistern when a helicopter popped over the top of the ridge one sunny day. I grinned, held the shovel tastefully over the family jewels and waved, and the pilot waved back. That evening during lookout hour (from 8 to 9 PM the lookouts and trail crews were given free use of the airwaves, largely to keep the lookouts from going stir crazy) I was asked obliquely if I had finished filling the cistern with snow, and were there any lady sasquatches around. Interestingly, this minor contretemps found its way into Kresek's encyclopediacal *Fire Lookouts of the Northwest:* "Yet another disoriented soul from the big city wandered around the peak naked all one summer." I don't feel particularly embarrassed at the remove of nearly 50 years, especially considering the sweeping changes in attitudes about such things since then. Kresek's brief comment however exemplifies the creation of myth out of fact; disoriented I may have been, but I was far from being from "the big city", in fact having grown up in a rural area having the quaint name of Farmer Brown's Corner.

After learning all the ridges and drainages and mastering the alidade (Osborne fire finder), I settled into a routine of sending in the weather reports. When my pancakes were overdone, I left them as burnt offerings for the local deer. An inquisitive hoary marmot came up to the cabin door once, and I occasionally stumbled over ptarmigan and their chicks which frequented the peak. I even tried my hand at writing poetry in a vain attempt to emulate Kerouac and Snyder, but soon realized that I was cut from different cloth and settled for just enjoying the snow clad peaks surrounding the lookout. One duty that I had no difficulty with was scanning the ridges and valleys with a pair of high powered binoculars. I would spend hours looking down into all the crenellations, admiring the ridge lines and marveling at the peaks high enough to form glaciers. I soon realized that the shadow cast by my cabin was a natural sundial, the color and texture of the tree covered slopes changing with the angle of sunlight that illuminated them. At the very point of the shadow, the trees seemed to glow, a luminous, rich, dark green halo, but slopes with the sun behind them were a deep mauve, purple, blue, especially later in the day as I looked toward the setting sun. As the sun set I would often find myself looking to the west, Mount Baker peaking up from behind the Picket Range, less than 50 miles away but seemingly half way across the world with nothing but rugged, uninhabited mountains in between. I yearned to share all this beauty with someone, but had to content myself with solitude. In the evenings, the lookouts and trail crews were allowed to chat on the radio, but I was usually at a loss for words. When not scanning the horizon for smoke or sending in the weather report, I spent time whittling knick-knacks, reading, practicing on the recorder and harmonica, cooking and chopping firewood, shoveling more snow into the concrete cistern as it melted, but mostly I just soaked in

Steve diving with Dr. Adey in Norway, summer 1967.
Photos courtesy Daryl Hoyt.

*the feel of being there; Hozomeen and Jack Mountain were almost like old friends by the time the fire season ended.*

*Letter fragment from Steve to his family: Monday, August 14, 1967*

We are on our way now toward Egersund and at the moment are just south of Larvik on the east coast. Since we left Oslo we have managed to complete another two stations, one in Oslofjord and another near Larvik. Dr. Adey has decided now to continue right to Egersund where we will fuel up for the Shetlands. Since we won't be putting into land until we arrive in Egersund I'll mail this letter from there...

Now we are scheduled to run for the next four days and plan to do several stations in the Shetland Islands by the end of this week. On Saturday we anchored near an island just off the coast from Larvik. The island is about three times the size of Eigeroy and was connected to the mainland by a bridge. At any rate, Torve (the Norwegian boy who I work with mostly) and I took the evening off and went to a big country dance in a small community on the island. There were over 250 people there and we had a great time. The music was mostly Norwegian and they had all sorts of different dances. It was a lot like the night we spent at the mountaineers dance near Bremerton. We both had such a great time that we hated to leave when the dance was over. There were a lot of nice Norwegian girls, &c.!!!

Friday Aug 18. I've had little chance to continue this letter for the last couple of days and today we have arrived in Egersund. We had very poor weather between Arendal and here and were forced in by some gales, one blew outside Kristiansand and another near Flekkefjord. However, things are fine now, although it took us two days longer than expected to reach Egersund...

At the moment I'm not sure as to how and when I'll be returning to the States, for Mr. Jorjusen is not here to verify whether or not I'll be able to obtain passage on a Norwegian freighter...

I would like so much to go up to Nesset and work for a week or two, but that would mean that I'd have to leave Dr. Adey now, and all summer I've been looking forward to the next few days; our journey to Scotland. We will probably stay in the Shetlands for about a week and by that time I'll be leaving the Bjorneng [the research vessel] and start for home. If I'm able to save the $200 difference between plane and boat fare it will certainly be a great help.

It sounds like you had a nice vacation in B.C., despite the usual mishaps. I'm hoping some day soon to take a trip along the coast of B.C. and up to Alaska myself, maybe next summer!! Dan and I have been talking about it for several years now, and perhaps we may sail up there next summer.

Although times have been pretty busy since we left Oslo, I've been finding some time lately to get caught up on some reading, studying, &c. I managed to find several helpful books for studying and reading Russian while I was in Oslo, so I've been brushing up some and also reading a novel by Theodore Dreiser entitled *An American Tragedy*. Dreiser, I think, is my favorite American novelist. He writes mostly about the period right at the turn of the century when America was growing and expanding. He is very good at developing very realistic characters, action, &c. and he has in his style a manner by which he links together the individual and the community he was part of. His central theme is the effect that industry and economic growth plays on the spiritual growth of an individual and a nation...

*Another writing fragment, probably part of a letter: summer 1967-*

The work under the sea as we continue to explore the coast is more interesting, particularly by comparing one area with another. In essence this is one of the things that allows Dr. Adey to get a complete picture of the North Atlantic. By relating one area with another not only a better understanding of corallines is gained, but also a knowledge of all other aspects of the sea; animal life, algae groups, rock formations, substrates for plant life, and the relationship that temperature, light, and salinity play on algae. The combination and relationship of one plant to another in the vast sum of the whole tend to make Dr. Adey an artist as well as a scientist. I've often thought of him as more of an artist than anything else. The relationships that the artist attempts to reveal, the symbolism involved in the sum total of the parts of the sea, life, all crop up in the work.

Dr Adey has lived most of his life in Newfoundland and he has told me a great deal about both contemporary and historical eastern Canada. He has travelled around almost all of eastern Canada, working here and there while he was in high school and college. His wife Pat is a real nice person, with a real love for the sea and sailing. They make a fine couple.

Conversation around the galley table ranges from politics to art. Usually we find ourselves discussing contemporary conditions and modes in the U.S. and Europe. Many times we end up by laughing and joking around... The work builds up so much that at times it's great to spend an hour in the evening discussing various thoughts that have little if anything to do with our work. Pat is interested in literature so we often find ourselves discussing various authors, particularly French, Russian and American. The nature of the work tends to make us search for the relationships between anything we happen to discuss. Many times we'll be relating and associating several different topics at one time and as the discussion enlarges we'll attempt to link opposites with each other.

*The day after coming down from Desolation I was on a plane to Tokyo, where I spent the next ten months at Waseda University, studying the Japanese language and culture and living with a Japanese family. After my experiences with LSD the previous spring and a summer of virtual isolation on a mountain top, Tokyo was daunting. I was intimidated by its intensity but simultaneously impressed by how ten million people were able to live and work there with much less friction than Americans would have exhibited. Because of my initial inability to speak Japanese I experienced the first few weeks in direct impressions, perhaps analogous to someone with a kind of autism, and even with my fellow (American) students at the International Division I was initially extremely shy and reserved.*

*My first cultural lesson was practically a zen koan. At the first dinner with my Japanese family I was served various foods, most of which I had neither seen nor heard of. I gamely tried each one in turn, and found many to be quite tasty, but one item bothered me a little, a white glob with convolutions much like a brain. I asked what it was, but my hosts' English was not adequate to translate. For the rest of the meal, I had the intriguing experience of one part of my brain telling me how good it tasted, a rich nutty flavor that kept begging me to take another bite, while another voice in my head continued to repeat, "It's brains! It's brains!" After dinner the family got out a Japanese-English dictionary and looked the word up. I had been enjoying a kind of fish liver.*

*Aerogram- postmark EGERSUND- 9-9-67*

---

Dear Doug, My mother wrote me several weeks ago and mentioned something about you living with me at the Mountaineers' cabin this fall, as you planned to attend OJC [Olympic Junior College] this year. I hope everything works out and you will be able to move in with me. In fact, when I think about it now I don't know why I didn't try to persuade you to change schools and live out at the Mountaineers'. From what my mom writes the president of the Mountaineers seemed to think that there would be a place for us this year. When I left Bremerton in June they told me then that they were planning to tear down the cabin I was living in and they would build a new one, but apparently they have decided against that. If they do let us live there I plan to fix up that little cabin, (the one we ate dinner at when you were there last May) and use that instead of the big place. We would have to hook up electrical wires and so forth, but that can be easily done, since most of that is already installed. These are all things I was planning to do before school started this fall, but time has passed so quickly over here that I'll be lucky if I get home in time for school. I may be at least a week late. If everything is going as you have planned go ahead and move in, if you haven't already. Of course the Mountaineers have the final say about everything but I found last year that they really didn't seem to care one way or the other as long as the place was kept clean and neat. I sure hope things will work out, it's a good place to live, as you well know. I plan to ride my bike again this year to school to save some money and get a little exercise to boot.

We'll have a lot to talk about when I get home. I've been working at several jobs in Norway this summer (managed to earn enough to pay for passage over and back), which was what I had originally planned. Last year when I was in Iceland I met a man who was studying algal growth in the North Atlantic and I spent about 2 and a half months working with him along the Norwegian coast between Trondheim and Oslo and several weeks in Northern Scotland, the Shetland and Orkney Islands. These past two weeks I have been in Egersund helping a fisherman and working some days at the herring meal factory here. The money is good at the herring meal factory, $125 a week, but the work is pretty wearying. I work with about 8 other men loading 100 lbs. sacks of herring meal onto freighters. Although it's the kind of work that makes you sleep for a good 12 hours every night, it satisfies just the same. Most of the fellows I work with are drifters, mostly from Norway and Sweden, and a few from England. Each with his own philosophy, each very much of an individual, but at the same time all good comrades. Some of the fellows were working here last year too when I worked at the factory for about three weeks during the winter. Some of them have been all over the world, rode freights around the States in the '30s, been to the Far East, Russia, South America, <u>Seattle</u>.

Of course the English are the most interesting to talk to because we both have the experience of knowing the same language in a way that we can more than just understand the words passed between us, but can give to them some type of meaning, interpretation, explanation, symbolization.

I had originally planned to work in a freighter that was scheduled to be here in Egersund last week. The boat was to be loaded here with herring meal and then sail to Baltimore. But as luck would have it the boat was held up in Holland for two weeks and now won't be here in Egersund until next Wednesday, the 13th. The boat will leave here in Saturday the 16th and probably arrive in Baltimore the 30th of September. I'm still thinking about working on this boat and if I do, of course won't be home until October 1st which wouldn't give me a very good start in school this year. The only other possibility I have is to work here in Egersund all this next week and then fly home, arriving in Seattle, Sunday night, the 17th. I'll have to wait and see this next week.

I imagine Dan is already in Japan if his plans worked out. Say hello to him for me if he is still in Kirkland. It will be good to see you again, we may end up doing a little travellin' ourselves this coming fall; Sumas, Chehalis, &c. I'll see you in the near future, Your itinerant comrade, Steve

---

*Doug moved to Bremerton that fall and began attending Olympic Community College, sharing the cabin in the woods with Steve. While telling me about those days, Doug was reminded of an example of the difference between Steve and ourselves. When going to Seattle, Doug had a trick of getting free ferry rides. When hitch-hiking to the ferry he would ask the driver if he could hide in the trunk of the car, and often got permission. Doug had also (I must now confess) told me of a way to scam the "dirty dog" when riding the bus on longer hauls. He would buy a ticket to a closer destination such as Tacoma, and then merely stay on the bus until it arrived in Portland. But such tricks were apparently not for the likes of me, as the one time I tried it, I ended up standing on the side of the road in Drain, Oregon in a heavy downpour, the roads flooding. I had the only ticket going there, and had to get off when the driver stopped. Maybe it is experiences such as these as much as what we learn at our mothers' knees that encourage us not to cheat in life, but maybe there is also a thing called karma. As much as Steve was into living cheaply, he would not have felt comfortable with such chicanery and I doubt that he ever stooped to such tricks. On the opposite side of the ledger, Doug also told me that while he was living in Bremerton, Steve tried to get home to Kirkland every weekend he could, as his youngest brother needed a father figure, having been quite young when their father had died. Steve would play ball in the sandlot with John, and also try to give him the kind of advice and guidance that he otherwise would have only had from their mother. Steve felt such responsibilities deeply.*

*Letter- postmark BREMERTON- OCT 10 1967*

---

Bremerton, Washington, September 25, 1967

Dear Dan, Thank you so much for your letter which I received this morning. It was so good to hear from you (I guess it's almost 4 months ago now that I last saw you in Bremerton.) I'll never forget the trip Doug, you and I took around Hood Canal. We'll have to do it again someday. I'm glad that your plans worked out for your trip to Japan too!! I saw an article in the September issue of the Nat. Geographic about 10 boys from Dartmouth who travelled by kayak along the southern coast of Japan (from the southern tip to Tokyo). The Japanese must be very gentle people, the pictures in the Geographic seemed to expose the people more than anything; the young children, the old farmer, the gentle girl, the family. How do you find the people yourself? I imagine many of them to be rather poetic. When I think about Japan I can't help thinking about the novel *The Sound of Waves*. For me it was so well written and such a gentle story of love. If you haven't read it already may I suggest it. Certainly the Japanese, especially in Tokyo, must be a very active people; sports, dances, plays, music, industry, shipping, travelling, and very much on the grow (so to speak). How do you find student life there? Quiet? Busy? Basically are there any fundamental differences in the life of a student; the student community between

Japan and the US? I think the most interesting course besides the Japanese language there at Waseda would be your study of Far Eastern religions. I'm starting to read some of the books Doug has here by Lin Yu Tang, and A.W. Watts. Certainly it is the type of study that provides growth for the soul. I find the poetry to be the most vivid expression of Japan and for that matter all of the Far East.

I'll tell you a little about my trip across the US. I arrived in New York about the 12th of September after finally having to fly from Stavanger to New York. Unfortunately the freighter that I had planned to take from Egersund to Baltimore was held up because of shipping difficulties for about 2 ½ weeks, so after working in Egersund for about 2 weeks I decided to fly so that I'd have some time to hitch-hike across the States before school. I arrived at JFK Airport early in the morning and by 10 o'clock that same night was sleeping in an old car about 10 miles over the Canadian border, 40 miles from Montreal. I really fell in love with Vermont, especially northern Vermont, the Burlington area. The trees in red and orange, the cold nights, the sun racing through the trees, the oak, the elm, the birch, the maple. R. Frost had a nice place to live!! Good farmland too. I may go to school there next year. Well, to get back to the road, I continued up to Montreal the next morning and spent the whole day in Montreal at Expo 67. Saw mostly the Russian exhibit, listened to three marching bands from the US, Russia, and Greece. I think all the music there was what impressed me the most; hundreds of new books; lots of action; internationalism 100%. I met a girl from London at the fair who I enjoyed talking to most of the day. From time to time on the road I find myself drawn toward someone, sometimes an older man; a young girl or boy. Someone who silently waits for a meaning, an expression, someone with an untold meaning who waits for a moment, an hour, a day of revelation. Walt Whitman expresses it in his poem:

TO A STRANGER

Passing stranger! You do not know how longingly I look upon you, You
    must be he I was seeking, or she I was seeking (it comes to me as of
    a dream,) I have somewhere surely lived a life of joy with you,
All is recalled as we flit by each other, fluid, affectionate, chaste,

matured, You grew up with me, were a boy with me or a girl with
me. I ate with you and slept with you, your body has become not
yours only nor left my body mine only,
You give me the pleasure of your eyes, face, flesh, as we pass, you
take of my beard, breast, hands, in return.
I am not to speak to you, I am to think of you when I sit alone or
wake at night alone. I am to wait, I do not doubt I am to meet
you again, I am to see to it that I do not lose you.

When I start considering the hidden meanings between these lines
my meeting with this girl becomes as meaningful now as the hours we
spent together in Montreal. Of course as I continued across eastern
Canada after leaving Montreal I met others; several young fellows on
the road; hockey players; miners; made strong from the soil.

(days later) October 5. Well almost 10 days have past when I first
started this letter, but I have some time this afternoon to write so I'll
try to progress on in some direction. Doug is at school and should be
home in about an hour or two. Last week we went over to Interbay
[Balmer RR yards, between Queen Anne Hill and Magnolia in Seattle]
on Friday evening, but had to wait until Saturday morning to get a
train over to Wenatchee. Because the train was so slow on its way
up the pass we got off the train in Skykomish and hitch-hiked down
to Edmonds in the evening. The next morning we went out fishing
around Indian [Scatchet] Head, but the weather was so poor; rain and
wind (reminded me of the North Atlantic). We didn't catch anything
and came back here to Bremerton Sunday afternoon. The rains have
continued all this week; every day we get another inch or two. Most of
this week has been spent reading Kerouac, Dostoyevsky, Camus and
Wordsworth. I've been reading portions of *Desolation Angels* today,
much better than On the Road, Kerouac's style, the tremendous
moments of feeling, highs, lows. A lot still to think about.

Doug and I are planning to ride down to Belfair tomorrow (Belfair
is that little place at the end of the canal) to see if we can buy some
maple and alder wood. I'm hoping to make some tables and chairs this
winter, perhaps to sell, most likely just to use around here. If things

go all right I'm going to start work on a small Norwegian work boat. I want however, to start with furniture first, for the sake of spending some of these rainy afternoons working with wood. I remember the chess set you made last year; there's something about wood, just the feel of it, you know…

Your bicycle is getting a lot of use now, sometimes 20 miles a day. I fixed it up last week and everything but high gear is in good condition; middle and low gear are all we really need.

I guess I should continue on where I left off in Montreal. Well, in the evening I rode out of Montreal on a bus and hitch-hiked through the night on to Pembroke, Ont. The man who I got a ride with to Pembroke invited me into his house to sleep for a couple of hours before hitting the road again. In the morning I left Pembroke and got a series of rides through to Pt. Arthur, Ont. via the Trans-Canadian Highway. From Pt. Arthur I went south into Minnesota, came into St. Paul about 10 o'clock at night and by 3 in the morning was on my way out of the GN Yards in Minneapolis on No. 97. I stayed on the hot-shot until Havre, Montana, but because I didn't have a sleeping bag and the evening frost was beginning to form on the ground I got off and waited for a train with some empty cars going to Spokane. The trip was beautiful along the southern end of Glacier Nat. Park and on into Whitefish, Mont. The train waited in Whitefish until the late evening and I finally rolled into Spokane yards just as the first pinks of the morning were beginning to erase some of the stars. About 8 o'clock a train left for Seattle and I rode in a gondola to Wenatchee and then got in an empty from there. I met an old migrant in Wenatchee and we rode together to Everett where he got off. He was very interested in Dostoyevsky and we spent most of the afternoon talking about literature and trains, the States, the 30s, the future. Well, when we got to Everett the old man drifted away into the night, along the beach to cook some coffee and 45 minutes later I jumped off the train myself just as it entered the yards in Seattle. You must know, too, how good it feels to catch the smell of the Pacific and race along the beach after being away for a while.

(Saturday morning the 6th) Last night Doug and I spent the entire evening reading aloud the poems of Robert Service. The range of feeling that Service had in his work made us want to keep reading and reading until we both almost fell asleep on the floor. We have both been studying Robert Burns this quarter in British Literature and Service seemed to be influenced by him particularly in his rhymes and Scottish words. Of course Service was born in Scotland himself.

The weather is looking a little better today so we'll probably go down to Belfair as planned. We are both becoming more interested as the days pass in Dostoyevsky, Theodore Dreiser, and James T. Farrell, the fellow who wrote *Studs Lonigan*. Kerouac too, ties in with these three writers; the schools of realism and naturalism. They break away from the Romantic writing of earlier American and English novelists. However there seems to be a break between Kerouac with either Dreiser or Farrell. Mainly that Dreiser and Farrell devise a plot and tell the story by standing apart from the characters, studying them, making studies of them. Whereas Kerouac is moving along the road with highs and lows, telling his first impressions, hoping that in the end that the story will be a true representation of the <u>Beats</u>. Both methods of writing are fascinating to read, sometimes I begin to think that Kerouac is perhaps one up on both Dreiser and Farrell. If you get a chance to read either *Studs Lonigan*, *Sister Carrie*, or *The American Tragedy* you'll see the difference almost immediately between these three books with any of Kerouac's, although they are basically all about the same subjects.

Maybe you are in the mood for a poem now...

AS, THE RAIN
The gentle rain; October
Rivers running down the darken surfaces of
Wood and glass.
The flowing together; drops
Small collections of love coursing together.
The realization of swelling puddles.
The gentle receiver.
The long stems of reaching grass; drops and grass.
The slow, flowing movements of October rain.
Alone.

...the symbols in <u>As, the Rain</u> can be translated in a variety of different ways, it's probably best placed as a love poem, a blending of nature and love.

Well we will hope to hear from you again soon and may "The Great God of the Hobos" lead you in the paths of Zen.

Your comrade, Steve

---

*Even before I was able to utter more than a few phrases of Japanese I was initiated into the fraternity of drinking. It took about a week for my fellow students to discover that being less than 21 years of age was not going to be a deterrent to visiting bars and the more gregarious of us would, when classes ended on Friday, catch the Yamanote sen to Shinjiku where we repaired to the Kirin Beer Hall for an attitude adjustment. A "nama dai" (1 liter draft) cost 260 yen, a little less than six bits in American dollars and one could procure a plate of passable spaghetti at a reasonable price as well. We often cajoled a couple of the more adventurous members of the office staff into coming along and attempted to get them drunk enough to let down their hair, as they made a point of remaining absolutely proper while at work and we felt that they deserved a little fun in their otherwise regimented lives. I am embarrassed to say that I accumulated a collection of beer hall mugs from this establishment which I drank from for years afterwards, but perhaps the karma of such irresponsibility led to the development of what the Irish call "the weakness". It took me about 20 years of serious drinking to get to the point where I realized I had to quit, before I graduated to what the Irish call "the failing". There was one older student among us who was already well down this road however. Having reached the august age of 40 he had been given a small apartment of his own whereas the rest of us boarded with host families, supposedly to keep us from the more egregious forms of unsupervised behavior. Roberts, with a room of his own, was thus free to indulge in nightly forays in Tokyo's bar scene, which (as opposed to his supposed major of architecture) was his true calling. He described his "Roberts' Method" of drinking on the other guy's tab: walk into a small bar, buy a bottle of beer and then pour a glass each for the customers sitting to*

*your right and to your left, and then spend the rest of the evening letting*
*them fill and refill your glass. He would often say, "Tokyo has over 30,000*
*bars and I'm going to visit every one of them!" The rest of us were a bit more*
*responsible, as we had to return home to our families every night, and also*
*we were young enough to be lacking his worldly weariness.*

Aerogram- postmark  BREMERTON- NOV 2 1967

---

Dear Dan, At the moment I'm sitting in Woodinville yards listening to
the several local trains as they move up and down the tracks between
Kirkland and Woodinville. It's a beautiful morning, the sun, the leaves,
the long double line of tracks, the whistles, the wind. The Sumas
train came early today so I'm waiting now for a local up to Arlington
or Snohomish. A good day to be on the road. I've been finding out
more and more about trains around the US and Canada. Apparently
the Black River-Sumas run now is hauling a lot of extra Canadian
freight because most of the train is made up of either CN or CP cars
and trailers. One of these days, I'm going to go up to Sumas and then
across the border and see just where the major division point is for
cars going east through Canada. I'm almost sure that some of the cars
they are hauling on this line are going to places out along the main CN
tracks. There must be trains going almost every day to Alberta. Doug
and I will probably go up to Sumas next weekend. We want to do a
little mountain climbing before it starts to snow here.

School is going fine, but even better than school, Doug and I took
a job on Seabeck Road. We are cutting firewood for a man who lives
down the road from us. Instead of working for money we've decided
to have him pay us with maple and fir trees. All in all he owns about 70
acres of forested area and he wants us to thin the alder and maple trees
out of the rest of his forest. There's enough work there to keep us busy
until next spring and if we do a good job we'll get enough wood from
him to make some furniture and a work boat, like the kind they have
in Norway. This is the basic design:

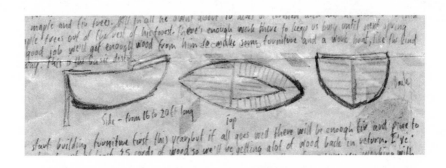

We are going to start building furniture first this year, but if all goes well there will be enough fir and pine to build a boat. We plan to cut at least 25 cords of wood so we'll be getting a lot of wood back in return. I've still been thinking a lot lately about the coast of BC and about living up there for a summer, working with the salmon run and exploring around the coast. The total cost of the boat wouldn't be more than a couple hundred dollars, because there's a sawmill near Seabeck that cuts wood for a reasonable price, and they dry it too.

I've been reading mostly novels lately, *Studs Lonigan* by James Farrell, Dreiser's *Jennie Gerhardt* and just lately some Plato and philosophy in general, English Victorian writers Huxley, Carlyle, Emersonian philosophy, expressions of Thoreau, essays by Whitman. Doug has become interested in the French writers, naturalists and realists and also Franz Kafka. *The Family of Man* is one book that we think about much of the time. The impressions of the road are right there in that book, the country people of Kansas, the logger, the young children.

Doug and I are trying to get by on as little as we can and try to make things instead of buying them. We have a lot of buckwheat, oatmeal, bread, and potatoes, lamb and beef stew. I bought some meat from my cousin in Chehalis for about 2/3rds off. So as close as we can figure we can do real well on $4.00 a week for the two of us. Some weeks it's less than that. Kitsap Way and the Olympics are so beautiful now, the weather has been mostly sunny and nice here since the last of October, and although it's been cloudy most of the time we've had few days with rain.

I've been studying Russian too quite a bit lately. I want to continue on with it next year, but I'm not real sure as to which school I'll go to next year. Maybe U. of W., UBC, U of Minnesota. I'll have to decide pretty much by Christmas, it all depends on what I decide to do this next summer. I've been sending in applications to the Forest Service districts around the state but I'd rather be able to get on the road again this next summer and find some work along the way. If you get Desolation Peak lookout again next summer I may decide to work up the Skagit for a while and spend the summer in the northern Cascades. I've got a chance to work in Norway again, maybe in Ontario with the Forest Service.

How is school going now in Tokyo? Have you been learning a lot of Japanese? What about traveling around Japan? Is it a good place to go by bicycle? Is there a lot of work there? Farm work? What have you been reading lately? Doug and I were thinking that since you are so close to Russia that maybe you might decide to go from Tokyo to Vladivostok on your way home and then come across Russia on the railroad. You could fly from Luxembourg to New York for $170 if you were there before June 20th and then ride the trains across the States. It may cost you a little more but I don't think any more than $100 at most. I believe the fare from Vladivostok to Europe is about $150. I talked to several fellows in Germany who had been across that way. When do you get out of school in the spring?

Doug is still in fear of being drafted soon, but we are hoping now that since he is in school that when he appeals that they will let him continue with school this year. He's doing real well this quarter. We have the one British Literature course together. We have been studying as of the last two weeks the romantic poets, Byron, Shelley, Keats, Wordsworth and now we have begun on the Victorian era and its novelists and philosophers. Lately the draft board hasn't been so tight and as long as Doug stays in school there is a chance he may get his 2-S [a student draft deferment] again. He has been thinking about joining Vista and maybe working in the Ozarks or Pennsylvania instead of going into the army. I wish he could stay at Olympic the whole year, but after this quarter he'll have over 90 credit hours. I think he likes Western Washington [State College (now University)] and if things work out with the draft board he may go up there next quarter.

You know they took down our old clubhouse [an abandoned house near our catch-out spot] here in Woodinville, but it is still so beautiful around here, especially when I look up toward Snohomish with all the blendings of the leaves and the flowing motion of the wind against the poplars along side the tracks here. I imagine autumn is nice in Japan too. As Doug and I have been working this last month we've been thinking about the gradual growth of nature, the steady force behind the growth of moss on the maple trees, the song of the rolling earth, the change that takes place in the forest every day, the big trees and what they represent, the feeling that the forests, even if they are destroyed, have a force to grow back again and in time grow over the marks that men have left, the peace between the individual trees, the peace they bring to the workers, the way the sun shines through the branches and sinks in the west, the walk home, the stacking of alder and maple into rows, the reliance upon nature to feed and clothe, the implication and the underlying meanings of it all, the small bodies of birds against the sky, the miracle of a freight train, the way it stays on the tracks, the needlessness of cars, freeways, airplanes, the growth that comes through hikes in the mountains, along the roads and paths, the tracks to Woodinville.

I remember when we used to sit here waiting for the train. The Song of the Open Road. Write when you get a chance and let us know how things are going. Your Comrade, Steve

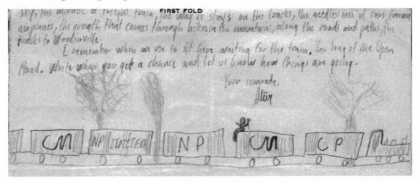

One of the things that had drawn me toward a year in Japan was my

interest in rock gardening, and the many parallels between the rugged and misty mountains of Washington State and those of Japan—moss and rocks, steeply plunging rivers, twisted and gnarled pines, all framed by swirls of mist and fog as in the sumi paintings I had admired in books. By the time our first academic break occurred I was ready to see the famed rock gardens and temples of Kyoto, and caught a train heading there with a few fellow students. First we of course headed for the most famous garden of them all, Ryoanji, a spare rectangle of raked gravel punctuated with seemingly randomly situated groups of large rocks, islands in the sea of white gravel defying the viewer to make sense of them. Not too distant, the north side of Kyoto had much more, a complex of Zen Buddhist temples and sub-temples founded in the 14th century, each with its own rock garden (although to refer to these works of art with the mere words "rock garden" is like saying that Van Gogh "painted landscapes"). The specific shape and texture of each rock had been painstakingly sought out and carefully arranged into a larger pattern, reminding me of French Impressionism; each garden's designer had created his own vision of perfection in a formal and limited space, raked gravel swirling around the rocks as waves swirl around rocky promontories. In one garden the gravel remaining after raking the flat area was neatly deposited as perfect cones in one corner. Another garden had been planned to reach maturity over a hundred years after it was first created, its moss slowly growing into crevices originally visualized in the mind of a zen monk hundreds of years earlier. Although I had been a bit disappointed by the few gardens I encountered in Tokyo, the ones in Kyoto lived up to my expectations, making me vow to someday create similar landscape art out of the abundant raw materials to be found in the Pacific Northwest.

Aerogram- postmark BREMERTON- DEC 15 1967

---

Dear Hobo Dan, Thank you so much for your last letter. The days roll on for both Doug and me now and I've been meaning to write to you, forgive me for being so slow. I know how much it means to you to get a letter from the States. When I was in Norway I would run down to the post office every Saturday, after being out at sea all week, and be so happy when I received a letter from either you or someone else here in the States. We both wish that you could be here, especially when we're on the road together.

About three weeks ago Doug and I hitch-hiked down to Chehalis and worked for 3 days at my cousin's place, wood chopping, pickin' apples, feeding the pigs, and had a fine time just running around the farm kicking the football after work, &c. Apart from the visit itself and the work we both got to thinking how nice it would be to travel around the States and stop and find work in small towns like Chehalis. The small, isolated places appeal more in the first place and secondly, community life in a small town lends itself to being written about, like Steinbeck's theme of Cannery Row, California fruit pickers. American life in a small town seems to me to be one of contrasts. The people themselves are half-way between complete isolation and the big city. Some in the town are materialists, some idealists, some bankers, some farmers. Places like Spooner Wis. In some towns the people gossip and deal with social position in the church, club, in others like Middlebury, Vt. the New England tradition patterns its inhabitants toward transcendentalism and the workings of the soul of a man, the community, the manner of life. We were thinking that the best way to travel would be to spend several weeks to a month or two in one particular place working at whatever seemed most to our liking, farm work mostly, the only thing we'd be qualified to do at present. Of course if a fellow had a teaching degree he might find a year's stay in a place as rewarding as just only a month. Right now, years seem like a long time to be in one place. At any rate we got "filled" with the spirit of the road as we were travellin' down 99; if it weren't for this cabin we probably wouldn't have come back, but it's nice living here and we've gotten to know a lot of people in the community so I guess right now we're on what you might say is an extended stay on Seabeck Road.

We're still cutting wood, but lately I've been working at a holly farm in Silverdale. The fellow who we cut wood for has a holly farm and at present his holly trees are in full swing being transformed into Christmas wreathes. I'm mostly cutting holly from the trees to be made into wreaths. Also working there are about 5 Japanese fellows who have just come over within the last few years from Japan. They know a little English but they speak Japanese among themselves. I like working with them, so gentle and they love the earth and cold December days. I'll be able to make enough to help pay for over half the up-coming fees for winter quarter. There's a nice Norwegian girl who is from Poulsbo, who works there making the wreaths.

Well I've been reading Nikos Kazantzakis lately, *The Last Temptation of Christ*. It contains so much that I have a great deal of thinking to do about the underlying themes of the book itself. Basically Kazantzakis explores the soul of Jesus, the hermit, who travels the roads of his country in search of his identity with God. Jesus, in Kazantzakis's mind was not the sinless man, the lamb of God, but rather he was a young man filled with the roots of good and evil, two words that were difficult for him to define and difficult to live with, the interweaving of the joy and pain of the soul comes out as one of the many themes of the book. Nature, in Kazantzakis' book is so vividly portrayed. What can I say Dan? The book just flows through your body, the movements of the trees, the rolling of the earth, the movements of Jesus down the road, the dust filtering the sun, the rain planting its seeds in the earth, the light playing with the walls of buildings in the morning; they are all part of the book. The book continues to flow, to overwhelm and confound. It's the closest book that, for me, has ever come near to explaining the interwoven qualities of nature and the blendings of a man with the trees, grass, sea, and with his comrades. It makes me want to be with you even more, travelling down the road, "on the long brown path wherever we choose", "the earth is sufficient and ample, it may be full of contradictions, but it satisfies, the earth may seem difficult at first but it will provide for the soul." The best cannot be told anyhow.

Doug took last week off school and went up to Indian Point [Scatchet Head] to be with the sea and beach, it rained most of the week, but he had some strange experiences he says, just watching the waves lap up along the beach during the last windy days of November. I'm going to go up to Sumas this weekend and spend a couple of days at the Nessets' place fishing for steelhead. Finals aren't for another two weeks so I don't mind missing a couple of days, in exchange for being up on the "good old Nooksack." I plan to take my bike and hope the train stops in either Wickersham or Acme. I guess Doug plans to work around here this weekend, but by the end of this week I'm sure I'll be able to convince him to come with me. We are both planning to go on a road trip during Christmas vacation, but just where we're not sure. Maybe up along the Nooksack to do some hitching around and a little train ridin' to boot. My cousins Tom and George Nesset are still logging at their place so maybe they will need some help. Every time I go up there I start thinking about the roots of the old family, the Nessets, my great-grandfather, and Norway, but so much of that is gone now. I remember when I was younger, about 5, my great grandfather, and the impression he made, the old man, 95, working and walking along the river; he thinking about his younger years, probably through me, and I exchanging with him his oldness, his gradual growth into the elements of the river, trees and fields, the land that had been his expression through so many years. What can I say Dan?

Well the weather has been exceptionally bad this last week. We've had so much rain and wind that some of the coastal towns have been labeled as disaster areas. It sure is nice to be inside reading during these wet nights. The mountains are full of snow; the Cascades at the passes have about 4 feet already, just in this past week. Maybe Tom and George Nesset will take us skiing up at Mount Baker.

My brother Daryl is going to Germany at the end of this month as an exchange student so if Doug and I decide to go up to the Nooksack during Christmas we'll probably go up to Vancouver where he plans to leave by train, to Montreal. He will be in Germany until next September studying the German language. He wants to travel around some too during the summer, the Slavic countries and Danmark, Sweden and Norway. I'll let Doug finish the page. Take care of yourself. Your comrade, Steve

> ...s month as an exchange student
> we'll probably go up to Vancouver
> ...y until next September studying the
> ...o, the Slavic countries and Denmark
> ... Your comrade, Steve [drawing]
>
> sittin here with my feet
> ...es I'm still smokin - its
> ... growing up. Last week
> to the old house on Whidbey
> " + people but the little
> ...er's Franny & Zooey & his Nine

Hi Dan- (the real meaning of the word high) yes it's me your friend Doug-I'm just sittin here with my feet to the fire & smoking my pipe- yes I'm still smoking- it's just part of the crap you pick up growing up. Last week upon reaching my maximum I went to the old house on Whidbey. The house is gradually being destroyed by the "elements" & people but the little shack behind it is really quite nice. You ought to read Salinger's *Franny & Zooey* & his *Nine Short Stories*, they've affected me tremendously, but if you're not interested that's fine. I could even send them to you- He presents partially the Zen thing in a western approach- I consider the Western Way considerably more maddening. Mickey the Monk [Doug's dog] was hit by a car again (he can't seem to comprehend these things) breaking his front leg- you should have seen him with his cast on running around the neighborhood on three legs. Steve won't let me tell you what I want to say- he's deceitful. Here's the most poetic poem I've written in years: [followed by empty space]

*Aerogram- postmark BREMERTON- JAN 9 1968*

---

Dear Hobo Dan, I'm in Kirkland today and now that Christmas has passed I plan to be on the road during this next week before going back to school on Jan. 4th. Doug and I plan to go up to Vancouver and stop at the Nessets for a couple of days to do a little steelhead fishing. Last week another friend (Tim from O.J.C.) and I went up to

Sumas and stayed with the Nessets for about 3 days and all in all, the trip went real well. Tim and I caught the train in Woodinville about 11 o'clock in the morning and the train stopped in Wickersham so we hitch-hiked from there to the Nessets. We've been having some cold weather as of late, and the day after we arrived at Saxon it snowed about 8 inches. George and Tom are still trapping. Do you remember the beaver George had when we were up there last year? This year he has had pretty good luck, especially with weasel, muskrat and beaver. Tim and I went out with him, checking all his traps, but while we were there he didn't manage to get anything, only one small water owl. We tried to catch some steelhead too, but the river was too cold and ice was floating all over the place. The guides on our poles finally froze up so we decided to go into the house and sit around the wood stove. We left the Nessets' place the day before Christmas and hitched up to Sumas, but had to wait almost 7 hours for the southbound train. The train finally left Sumas about 9 o'clock in the evening and we got home about 3 in the morning after walking home [about 8 miles] from Woodinville. The NP and GN have merged now, but as yet there has been no change in the NP run here. There has been an increase in the size of the trains of late; a lot of Canadian cars are making up the trains now. B.C. is really starting to develop particularly up in the northern section along with Vancouver itself.

I'm sorry that I've been slow at times in writing. I'm beginning now to formulate in my mind just what the possibilities are for this summer in terms of work. Most of my applications are in for the Forest Service, although I want to send several more to Montana and Idaho. I also have a chance to go fishing in Alaska, but I've been thinking now seriously of trying to get into either Swedish or Danish school for this coming fall so that I can study there instead of going to the U. of W. The university here has a good Russian department; I'd be able to live in the Russian house close to the campus and everything, but I really want to get on the road this summer, leave here for the first week in June and ride the freights across Canada, try to find work in Ontario or New Brunswick, Nova Scotia, and then take a ship from the east coast to either Iceland or England in July and then work in the herring-meal factory in Egersund until school begins in September (about the 25th). If I'm not accepted for study abroad then I'll stay here during the summer and go to the U. of W. next fall.

How are your plans shaping up for the coming months? How is the language study and the courses on history and philosophy in Japan and China? What was Christmas like in Japan? A lot of my old friends here in Kirkland along with my three brothers and I have been playing football together these last few days. It is good just being outside on those cold, overcast days, running and passing with the football; a welcome change from school. With all the good Christmas food the pounds are starting to mount up; I almost wish I was good enough to play pro-football (just a whim I guess, but it seems like a real challenge; at least it is on the sand lot here in Kirkland).

I've been reading Emerson a little this week and plan to start another book by Nikos Kazantzakis, *St. Francis*, and then *Freedom or Death*.

Doug and I plan to continue to cut wood through the winter, our furniture projects are still in the beginning stages, but these next few months we're hoping to earn enough for school in the spring quarter by selling more cordwood. Doug, I think, will probably take some composition and literature courses, while I plan to take sociology and philosophy.

(Almost a week later) Well I'm back again at the old cabin, the fire is slowly dying out into the evening, Doug is across the room reading and I've just about completed *St. Francis*, and in the meantime I've been thinking about getting this letter off, even though it doesn't have much to relate. Thanks so very much for your letter, which I received several days ago. Sounds like you've been doin' a lot of travellin' lately! All Doug and I talk about nowadays is Canada, and come this summer how we plan to ride the freights all over Canada. I guess you'd call it the pre-spring blues. School looks pretty shabby by comparison. Yeah, you'll be proud of us however; we both got 3.00 pts this quarter, although I never have as yet figured out just what good it all is!! If you know what I mean. Right now I'd be satisfied with a 2.00 pt in Freight-hopping 101 or Winter Mountain Trips 212 (courses not included unfortunately).

I've got Geology this quarter along with Sociology and Psychology and Doug is taking Genetics, Composition and Social Psychology. We made $20 this weekend selling cordwood. You'd almost call us capitalists at present; all this wood and all these dollars!! I really can hardly express to you Dan how much we're both looking forward to this summer now, and the train trip around Canada. I'm really starting to yearn for some of those travelin' impressions, passing through towns, going over the mountains, the Rockies and Cascades, across the flat plains of Alberta, Manitoba, drifting down into the States, Minn., Wis., Ill., Vt., N.H., Mass., Maine, eastern Canada, Montreal, Quebec, St. Johns, Halifax, New Brunswick, meeting people along the way, travelers, working people, attempting to get a feeling stirred up inside about Canada and the U.S., the industry, the farms, the small town, the big city, the mills and seaports, New England traditions, to be receptive to nature, the earth, the fields, the hills, trees, rivers, lakes, to camp and not be in any place, to watch the shifts of the road, the images and the intensity of meaning and symbol, the image of the road as Whitman described them in "Song of the Open Road" and the meanings, the symbols , the implication between the images, the link between the body and the soul, as he would say. Doug and I got a book from a friend at school which has maps and freight schedules of all the trains in the U.S. and maps of all the Canadian routes too. A true bible!! Let me know how things are going, Your buddy, Steve

And Now the voice of Doug interjects-Hello Dan- soon I will write you a long letter but now there are too many words and too many ideas- wanting to get out of that realm. I'd like to stop & just tell you about local news & friends- Milo went down to Yucatan for Christmas and Jim will be working in a mental hospital for his work period, Mike Davis has gone Hip & Mickey is being Mickey & I am & the freights still run but now they go to hobo heaven.

*Aerogram- postmark BREMERTON- JAN 30 1968*

---

Hobo Dan, I'm in Kirkland today. The morning sun is shining across at an angle into the dogwoods. It has been cold. Northern winds have set in since last Wednesday (four days ago now) the sun has been out bright. There is already a noticeable change in the duration of the day to night. Darkness came last night about 5:30. I'm counting the days for the coming of spring and eventually the freedom of the road. Yesterday afternoon some of the fellows I've known around here since childhood had a big football game. As the game progressed the sun and the wind combined. We played right on into the night as the big red glow of sun rolled on over towards you. There was a layer of darkening clouds in the sky and as the sun moved between those clouds and settled in the mountains I was thinking how great it is going to be to have you back here and hoppin' freights together and climbin' all over the mountains. Doug and I were thinking abut the same thing earlier this week when we first started noticing the longer days and the new sun.

This last week we received application forms for the Univ. of Stockholm. As yet I haven't decided for sure that attending there next year is what I'll do. In terms of being accepted there chances look very good. Of course, the biggest criterion is grade point average. I've got about a 3.2 at Olympic and hopefully by the end of the year it will be a little higher. The school also seems like it has an interesting group of courses, but Swedish is what I want to learn while over there and in the summer travel around Russia if it is still possible by that time.

Doug has started to ride his bike to school with me. We're trying to get in shape for this summer. There's nothing greater than ridin' bikes all over the country, just watching the wheels roll. Dan, you'd never believe the changes that are taking place around Kirkland all because of this crazy economic game. The latest word is that within another year the state plans to build what they call a super interchange which will pave all the area between our house here in Kirkland all the way to the Kirkland-Redmond highway. You know the Overlake interchange there in Bellevue? Well, the state has promised all the beautiful people here that Kirkland's interchange will be even bigger and prettier than Bellevue's. It's not the interchange itself but the implications behind Dylan's words: "It is easy to see that not much is really sacred." Ford Mustangs seem to have taken over here and the rucksack revolution has a long hill to climb. Our generation seems to be moving in the same materialistic direction and it appears the only thing that will alter that direction is an economic change and not a philosophical change. Protest is followed by direction and that direction needs to be established with our generation. A return back to the land, an awareness of nature and development of transportation that supports an appreciation for what we believe to be sacred in life, the sun, wind, leaves, grass, the love between comrades, the love between a man and a woman, all designed after the movement and patterns of nature's growth in each of our lives. But at present it's the twisted sorrow of the business game and economics.

Nikos Kazantzakis has taken the place of Walt Whitman as of late and I've been reading and re-reading his books. I know you would like *The Rock Garden* by him if you haven't already read it. There lies at the core of that book the best selection of Kazantzakis' thought and expression. The setting for the story is in Japan and China. The man himself is certainly one of the closest to a sense of nature that is important and necessary for people here in the States to become aware of to its fullest extent, to the point of blooming growth. The hippies here have moved underground; those who are still here. Most of the action is still protest, but new directions are beginning to be discussed in the underground papers. Dylan just came out with some new songs that are really good in terms of images, and images are certainly one of the best forms of expressing direction. Most of the songs are about travelling around the States and working in the big cities, or just greeting the sun. I've been writing more myself of late...

Your Hobo buddy, Steve

---

*Waseda Universtiy was located inside the Yamanote line, a ring of train tracks which circle most of the significant locations of greater Tokyo, and the campus had no significant open space or park-like atmosphere associated with large universities in American cities. It did have a rather long walkway extending through the campus from one end to the other, broken up with a series of steps and terraces at the upper end, leading down* to the Kokusaibu, or International Division where our classes were held. During my year at Waseda there were numerous student demonstrations held here, with this main thoroughfare often filled with banners and large black and white kanji posters voicing opposition to the Vietnam war and the concomitant presence of US troops in Japan. Interestingly, although anywhere we went we were instantly identifiable as Americans, at Waseda we were treated as if we weren't there; we were not seen as being responsible for the war or all the GIs in Japan. A lot of the Japanese students' political groups were similar to the student clubs at Waseda. We learned that joining a club at a Japanese university was more akin to joining a fraternity; once you committed to one it received your complete allegiance and all others were off limits. The protesters engaged in a great deal of choreographed marching and chanting, columns of students four abreast, helmets and armbands idendifying which branch of the ideological tree their group hung from, arms linked and being led by what can be best described as a cheerleader guiding the snaking column around other groups of protesters and temporary information booths, often with a flag or baton waving or a bullhorn bellowing, showing the rest of the world what they stood for. We understood that at the end of their time at Waseda they would all enter a company however, and become a "salaryman ", a white collar worker cog in the big machine called Japan, Inc. At the end of January of 1968 the Tet offensive began in Vietnam, with the city of Hue being fought over for another month before the Vietcong were finally repulsed. All this intensified the demonstrations on campus, but aside from an occasional copy of Time or Newsweek in English we received a very filtered and garbled version of the war; television images needed no translation, but resulted in a more emotional than factual impression. But we knew then, as we hadn't before, that the troops wouldn't be home by Christmas, not even the one after next, and it is just as well that we were spared the doctored body count that General Westmoreland fed the civilians back home in order to bolster support for the war. As for the daily pageant of demonstrators, we understood that they were experiencing one of the few periods of relative freedom in the life of the individual in Japan, and were for the most part only putting on the style, but as we Kokusaibu students were generally appalled by the growing fiasco in Vietnam we sympathized with the protesters.

Hobo Dan, It was good to get your last letter with the picture of Desolation Peak. You must have had some beautiful days on top of the mountain last summer; the combination of night with day, the flowers, the dust in the late summer and the trail from the lake to the peak, the sun against the mountains in the late evening; the gradual progression of hot summer days into the resting of September growth of frost and cold. Living in and around the cabin these growths and stems of direction begin forming, not only those growths of buds and roots of moss along the side walls, but the link of one with the movements and patterns of these growths. Pictures do tell a thousand words!!

At this very moment Doug and I are sitting out front of the school and in another half hour we'll be leaving for La Push with the geology class I'm taking this quarter. It's a one day field trip, but the weather is clear and sunny as we are sitting here waiting for the bus. I'll be writing this letter while we are on our way out to La Push and Doug said he would write some of his impressions too, so we'll combine efforts. In the meantime I'll mention a few things we've been doing as of late. The weather has been so nice that Doug and I have been playing handball and football with some of the boys who live down the road from us. I've been reading Dostoyevsky's *Brothers Karamazov* this week. Dostoyevsky was moved by spiritual feeling in his book and he goes into the life of a Russian monk and the basic separation of spiritual vs. scientific interpretation of the life forces. At present the question as to the validity of what Kazantzakis writes about and the revealing of the earth through the science of geology seem more or less basic in terms of the direction in the coming years. Even though geology is fascinating and certainly provides a method to view the natural formations of the earth, a blending or filtering of science with spiritual awareness and interpretation may be another one of the fusings of Whitman's opposites. These thoughts have been stirring now for several years but with the gradual growths and symbols in nature it is difficult to accept, <u>point blank</u>, science (the molds begin to form). Oh, I was up at Mt. Pilchuck last week and began thinking that if I do remain in the States this summer I'll work the first half of the summer and then wander around the Cascades in August. If you are going to be working at the lookout again I'll probably use that area as base camp and work mostly south and east of there. Doug and I are planning to smoke several lambs down in Chehalis this spring so we'll have plenty to eat through the summer. I got a lot of ideas in reading *The Dharma Bums* and how Kerouac ate while in the mountains and on the road.

(Well, it's already the next day now Friday the 16th) the trip was beautiful, the sun and sea, the birds and land receiving the sea along the shoreline, the foam along the edges, the bits of wood and straw up against the hillside, the distant ships, with the offshore islands, the rocks rolling with the currents beneath the foam, the gradual progression of the day and the long drifting into night, the filtering of sun against the clouds and into the mixed movement of the sea, a piece of quartz held up against the sun at noon and again as the sun fell at 6, the unity of gray stones and black sand, the ebb and flow of the rocks against the sea walls, but the unity of all into one and the natural progression, the working of this natural progression to form growth and direction, to form symbols, and be aware of the image and the symbol and their interaction, the feeling is hard to explain but I think you understand and have felt the same concepts in your own way. We are now planning, if the days allow, another trip out to La Push and a hike from there to Cape Flattery. When the urge begins to grow as it did yesterday, I'm going to drop things down to a slower pace and build that small boat that I was writing to you about last fall. I sometimes regret not staying on in Norway in '66 for I had a chance then to work in a boat building company in Egersund. A couple of years experience in building is worth a great deal. But the machine age needs machine people so hand work is not given much importance anymore. It comes down to the serious question as to whether one feels the present way of life is best, and if so, then a complete involvement in our culture, and if not, a partial if not a complete rejection of all these machines that profess to have magical powers to make an individual really know the experience of being alive. I believe in the linkage between man and his environment to the extent the men feel the depth of nature and the land and are influenced by its movements and patterns in a spiritual sense. This theme Dostoyevsky uses in *The Brothers Karamazof.*

I'm anxious to know just how your plans are coming for this summer, for I'm hoping that we can be together for at least part of the summer. When will you be leaving Japan? And how is the language coming now? I'm starting to realize just how great knowing some Russian (as a base for Slavic languages) may be in the coming years, and I'm thinking that traveling over into Eastern Europe is definitely included in a long range plan, if one can at all be made. In the years ahead the Russian language will be taught in the States too, so there is always that possibility. The romance languages like French and Italian would be worthwhile while on the road too, but there's hardly enough time to study them in school now.

Next week is Washington's birthday here, so I'm planning to go down to Chehalis to work a couple of days, and get some lamb so we'll have enough to get through April. Living has been so inexpensive this year and we're discovering new ways all the time to eat well on about a $1.50 a week. [A gallon of milk in the mid '60s cost about $1.00.] Doug has managed to get a lot of surplus food and usually we buy everything in bulk. Milk is still the biggest item, which runs about 50 cents a week. Being that there is no rent and only about a $3.00 light bill every month the average month runs about $12-$15 including all forms of transportation. Working just on the weekends is enough to pay for school which turns out to be about $25 a month. Driving a car, most students are spending $20 a month for gas [around $.30/gallon at the time] and repairs alone. But it's more than just the money saved, riding around in the morning and in the evening, watching the formation of color against the hills, Rainier with the Cascades, the Brothers and the entire Olympic range have been so bright and clear these last few weeks.

There is a large faction of people in the northwest who are planning a rapid transit system for the greater Seattle area. There was an election last week in which a bill for rapid transit was defeated, but many feel in Sept. when a re-vote is planned on this issue, that the rapid transit measure will win [It did not]. The freeways here are now so congested that unless they build another bridge over the freeway people will be able to ride their bikes to work and get there at a reasonable time. Boeings is bringing in people by the thousands and by 1975 the city planners say there will be the equivalent of another Seattle around Lake Washington. I read in the Eastside Journal that Kirkland is planning to develop its downtown area with a big shopping mall, one way streets, and a multi-level parking area. It is hard to believe it all could really be this way. The town itself has become a version of the Bellevue area. [Bellevue got the first bridge across Lake Washington in 1940 and subsequently grew at a much faster rate than Kirkland, much to the chagrin of Kirkland's business elite.] The site where the original town of Kirkland is so beautiful, with the lakefront facing hills which seem to form a huge Greek amphitheater. Doug and I were thinking this week just how beautiful Kirkland is and that if it were to be developed with a great deal of consideration to the surrounding landscape it would be a fine community, but direction for the town at present is in the hands of the highway commission and economic junk dealers in town.

Well I guess I'll have to finish this letter myself and send it along so that you receive it before you start on the trip around Japan. The weather has been beautiful here; the new growth is becoming more evident each day. I just found out a few days ago that Doug and I will have ten days in March between winter and spring quarter and we are planning to ride back to St. Paul on the hotshot if it warms up in the Midwest in the next couple of weeks. We plan to visit your brother at Beloit and go to the Univ. of Wis. to have a look around the campus. It might be that I'll go there next year if the town of Madison itself holds some possibilities for cheap living like we have here in Bremerton. Doug is thinking that he may go "Army" in the fall, but I'm hoping things will work out this summer and he will be in school next year. The draft situation is changing day in and day out so that both of us could possibly be drafted by next year, or the end of the war could be within the next six months. Either way I think that before this election year is out some big change in the present situation will take place, and at present we'll just have to look for indications. If it looks like I will be drafted I intend to go in as a two year Navy medical assistant, if I choose to go in at all. I've made out four or five applications for admission into Canadian schools in Ontario and Nova Scotia in case of that possibility for next year, or I may end up back in the North Atlantic fishing on a trawler or working along the coast of Norway. Comrade, Steve

---

*That I was able to hitch-hike in Japan came as a great surprise and delight. It turned out that the license plates of the long haul trucks had kanji (Japanese characters) indicating where they were based, and thus one could quickly identify a truck from Osaka. I soon learned to ask the driver if he were returning there (usually a "yes") and would he give me a ride, also usually a "yes" after a bit of surprise that the gaijin (foreigner) could in fact speak Japanese. During our academic breaks, I hit the usual cultural icons with the other, mostly American students, but I did most of my hitch-hiking solo after my friend Ralph broke his leg just before our planned trip together. In a last minute change of plans, I hitched south to visit another student who had been studying shakuhatchi in southern Shikoku, and from there I began walking north, following the main railroad tracks. I was going to say through the rural parts of Shikoku, but the smallest of the four main islands of Japan was then pretty much entirely rural. I hiked above terraced rice paddies reaching up the sides of steep valleys, as the tracks left one populated valley and cut through a series of tunnels to reach the next one. Towards the end of the first day I met a young Japanese guy who was going the same way and walked with him that day and the next. Whenever the trains caught us in a tunnel, I would drop to the ground, making like a bead of putty where the outer edge of the tunnel wall met the floor. My companion merely flattened his body, spread-eagled against the wall of the tunnel, perhaps concerned that someone might be using the "benjo" (toilet) on the train as it went by—no holding tanks on the trains in those days. The following morning we reached a major road crossing the railroad line* and I began hitch hiking again. I soon got a ride, and as we drove along the deep valleys of central Shikoku I did my best to converse with the driver. While the little Japanese I had command of was fluent, my vocabulary was decidedly limited. In Japan there is a saying for foreigners, "the better the Japanese, the fewer compliments", and as we were all novices we were continually hearing how well we spoke Japanese. The driver of my ride however, after a few minutes of formalities, said, "Your Japanese isn't very good is it?", which was so unexpected as to make me burst out laughing, as I heartily concurred. We stopped at a roadhouse and he bought me breakfast, a bowl of miso soup and a bowl of rice, with an egg on the side. I ate the miso and rice, wrapping each bite in nori (dry seaweed) as he questioned me further about my background, academic goals, and impressions of Japan. I was sort of doing as in Rome as far as the food went, but I had left the egg alone, perhaps thinking it was hard boiled and I could eat it later, but once my interlocutor had finished his rice and miso he summarily broke his egg into his bowl, whipped it up with his chopsticks, and then sucked it down in one noisily smooth vacuuming gulp. As he got up to pay the bill, I slipped my egg into a side pocket and once outside, discreetly flipped it into the bushes when his attention was elsewhere, not wanting to let on that gaijin couldn't handle raw eggs. I told myself that it would be different if it weren't so early in the morning.

When he let me off in the next town I stopped at a Japan Travel Bureau office to get my bearings and noticed a travel poster of some rather primitive vine suspension bridges over a narrow gorge. I asked about this and on the recommendation of the ticket agent I soon found myself on a small bus heading up a winding dirt road in a steep sided remote valley, heading for the village with the old vine bridges. These were originally defensive structures built by the Taira clan when they retreated to the remote back country after losing the Genpei War to the Minamoto clan in the 12th century, but now they were a tourist draw for a small farming community which would otherwise be forgotten. The bus climbed gradually above the valley bottom, and soon I was staring down into near vertical drop-offs as my side of the bus rounded the curves. At one point we stopped for a photo opportunity at a sheer cliff of well over 100 meters. One of the braver students sat with her feet dangling over the edge of the flat rock while her friends took her photo, but I noticed that she quickly removed herself (with a nervous laugh) from the potentially perilous situation when her friend approached her to hand back her camera. Back aboard the bus she attempted to engage me in conversation, but my limited Japanese was alas not adequate for anything beyond fairly straightforward description of my status at Waseda and my interest in Japanese culture. When we arrived at the end of the line, I was met by astonished looks on the faces of children as I stepped off the bus. In Tokyo foreigners were perhaps unusual and would often draw stares and turned heads, but these kids had never encountered a gaijin and when I greeted them in Japanese they were so astounded as to be unable to respond, much to the amusement of the girl who had been talking with me on the bus. We walked over to the vine bridges and took a few photographs and then wandered down to the river bed to admire the water sculpted rocks. I explained that I was camping out to save money and as she left to find a hostel I found my own patch of woods to unroll my sleeping bag, spending the night more peacefully than I would have at the hostel.

Later in the spring Ralph's leg was still in a cast, but we nevertheless decided to spend a one week break in Kyoto, taking the train from Tokyo. I had a tent and we both had sleeping bags, and we managed to economize by pitching the tent in empty lots behind the large temples and rock gardens on the north side of the city. Our biggest coup however was when we snuck into a temple after dark and managed to sleep on the balcony of a large temple overlooking the town. At around 4 AM Ralph shook me awake and whispered that there was a strange sound approaching. Sure enough, a series of rhythmic swishing  sounds, each followed by a sharp crack, gradually became louder and then faded away. I rolled over and went back to sleep, but soon I was woken again, just as a young Buddhist monk came around the corner of our veranda, sweeping the walkway with a kind of dry mop. Although we were both prone and encased in sleeping bags, Ralph having a full length leg cast as well, we both bowed from our horizontal positions and greeted the bonze with an "Ohayo gozaimasu!" He replied in kind and we then asked if it was OK for us to sleep there. He said "Daijobu" (OK) and continued about his duties, exhibiting a savoir faire completely in keeping with a zen monk's training.

A few days later Ralph and I were riding a streetcar in Kyoto when I was approached by another gaijin, who asked me if I would like to go on a hike the following Saturday with Gary Snyder. I was naturally eager to meet the author of Cold Mountain Poetry, the writer who had inspired Kerouac to write The Dharma Bums, and arrived at the rendezvous on the north side of Kyoto at the appointed time, while Ralph spent the day in one of the zen rock gardens nearby. I chatted briefly with Gary and his wife, mentioning how much I had enjoyed reading Snyder's poetry during my summer on Desolation Peak. The hike seemed to reflect my basic experience of the Japanese landscape. At first we walked along inhabited streets, and then into waste ground, climbing towards a ridge line. There were small trees planted about three meters apart, each nearly identical in size, waiting to be cut down before they reached even 20 cm in diameter. At a certain point Gary said we could now safely drink the water, as there were no humans living upstream. After we crested the ridge top we entered a forested area and followed a well maintained trail to an unusual Shinto shrine, the Kami being some kind of white snake. During the hike I did get to talk with Gary a bit about the hippie movement. The previous spring I had read an interesting transcription of a conversation among Gary, Timothy Leary, Alan Watts, and Allen Ginsberg in the San Francisco Oracle. In front of an audience they had been discussing the question of how to drop out, and related issues concerning the future of the hippie movement. I still had some questions on various points that they had touched upon, and here I had the opportunity to learn Snyder's opinions without any complicating dialogue on the part of the more idealistic, ideological, or mystical members of the original discussion. I commented that I saw the world going to hell in a hand basket, and all I could see to do was find a decent place to live in a wild or rural area and find some decent people to hunker down with. Snyder was more optimistic, commenting on rural hippies who were moving back to the cities and saying that big (positive) changes were coming in the larger, established parts of our society. I had my doubts, especially as I knew then that I would never be happy living in a city. (How sure we are about such things when we are young).

Hobo Dan, Thank you so much for your last letter. Since I last wrote I've been doing some travelling too, mostly in Canada. From what you mentioned in your letter you've been free this last month and circling Japan with your thumb. I can't fully express to you how good it was to be on the road myself again this last week, but I'll try as best I can. After working for the first half of last week I hopped the freight to Sumas, hitched across the border and then on to Vancouver. I have a friend attending UBC whom I met while in Europe so I stayed with him while in Van. The weather was beautiful during the first several days and he and I took a one day trip to Nanaimo and up the east coast of Vancouver Is. The coast is very wooded and much like Norway's in that the mountains are all over the place and they come right down to the sea, especially in Howe Sound, a great place for backpacking trips. Incidentally this boy I know in Vancouver knows Alice Purdy, the girl we met from the UBC climbing club [while climbing Mt. Shuksan]. I guess they are still doing a lot of climbing. While we were on Vancouver Island we spent most of our time walking along the beaches and gathering oysters, just north of Nanaimo. In Parksville there were several large oyster beds and we loaded our packs and came back to Vancouver late in the evening with about 50 lbs. in all. We were still eating oysters the day I left there. I noticed a great deal of lumbering in and around Nanaimo; some of the mills there were working in round-the-clock shifts. On the ferry I met several loggers who were on their way up to Campbell River to cut some cedar, all in all it looked like a good way to be living, working in either the mills or the forests, with always the coast range mountains near at hand. The clean smell of fir and cedar around the mills, the salt air along the beach, the wind down off the snow covered mountains and all the blendings and filtering of the day made the road a good place to think about Canada as a future home. I'm planning to apply to Simon Fraser University this next week, and hopefully if the draft board allows it I may go there next year. One thing I like about the school is that it is not too far from Sumas and the Vancouver freight yards, so it would be easy to get around and see some of the country and find out more about Canadian trains in general. I found out a great deal while I was up there last week, mainly that there is good daily service from Vancouver both north and east. While in Vancouver I spent a day around the main CN and CP yards and saw several long trains pull out just during one morning. CN has tracks to Prince George and Prince Rupert with daily runs on both. CN also has tracks to Edmonton and from there to Montreal. My friend's brother in Vancouver has ridden through the Rockies as far as Winnipeg and from what I could gather there is good daily service anywhere between Vancouver and Montreal. It was interesting being around the main yards and shipping area in Vancouver which border one another. There were boats from Japan, Russia, China, Greece, Holland and Norway that I saw and I got a chance to speak with some Russian seamen from eastern Russia. This is another reason why I like Simon Fraser so well, because Vancouver is always filled with ships and there is always a good chance to use Russian. Canada even has exchange programs with the USSR. The Russian boats in Vancouver were being loaded with large cedar logs; I guess that cedar does not grow in Russia for it seemed funny that Russia would be hauling logs from Canada since their own country is covered with forests too. I know cedar didn't grow in either Norway or Sweden so such could be the case in Russia. As I was riding around the harbor I was wondering if it would be possible for you to find passage on a ship from Japan to the west coast here. I know that there are over ten Japanese ships that put into Vancouver during a normal week; I saw at least that many while I was there. You may be able to save several hundred dollars. Well, I was mentioning Vancouver Is. earlier and while in Nanaimo I even saw two ships from Japan. The last few days I spent in Vancouver I rode a bike around town to get a general idea of the city, its parks, beaches, UBC, downtown area, and North Vancouver. Vancouver was so international with new immigrants from Poland, Italy, Germany and Scotland; it seemed like everybody was speaking a different language, even some American fellows. The trip from Vancouver back to Kirkland was beautiful; I hitched out the Trans-Canadian Highway to Sumas and waited until the late afternoon for the train home. It was a clear night and I climbed in a big gondola, on the way home watching the lights of Sedro-Woolley, Arlington, and Snohomish cast their patterns on the inner sides of the car, at times singing away and making up all kinds of poetry about the train and the links between the shadows of the night, the beat of the road, the filtering of the sun, the hardness of the steel, the rolling of the earth, the stars, the vastness of the night, the outline of the darkened hills, and the final jump back down to the earth again in the Woodinville yards. And to speak in more realistic terms, the whole trip was about $3 (always something worth mentioning here in the States), plus a lot of things that money can't buy.

I start back to school in a couple of days again and will be finished by the first week in June. Let me know what you have planned for this summer if you have changed your mind about anything. I'm planning to work for most of the summer, but I will have some time off perhaps a month or more. I want to save up enough money this summer so that I'll be able to invest in some land if I decide to in the next few years. I'm thinking that it would be nice to get some land in Canada and develop it into a place for farming or just a place to be between road trips, and buying land is a sure investment. I'd like to find a place with some trees and fields, like Nesset's on the Nooksack River.

I received another letter from you today. I feel now that what is needed most at present is more experience with the road and farming. I want to know Canada better for one thing, before I decide to do any moving there for good. Also, the situation with the war seems to be changing or at least revolving to the extent that we may find the war in V.N. altered a great deal by this next fall. We are waiting and hoping for the best at present and in the meantime climbing lots of mountains; I plan to go up Mt. Si, The Brothers, and Mt. Adams in the next couple of weeks. The spring is here now, the maple and alders are green, the wind is stirring, the sun is with us most every day, the growths are forming with the land, the approach of summer is on a gentle path. You bet, we'll hike all over the Cascades this summer. Comrade Steve

Steve contemplating "mountains and rivers without end," Kelly Butte, 1968

Shortly before I was to leave Japan my Oka-san (Japanese mother) told me about a "kowareta omiya", a bombed out Shinto shrine, that she had visited with a friend. She gave me directions to find it and I set out the next weekend, taking a couple of trains to a small village on the outskirts of Tokyo where I began walking up a small road between rice paddies. The road eventually left the paddies and began rising as I climbed into bamboo forested hills until I came to the ruins of the shrine. It had apparently been the policy of the US Army Air Force to expend any remaining bombs on such targets of opportunity once they were headed back to base, perhaps with the idea that bombing the equivalent of churches would demoralize the Japanese people. The old wooden building was flattened, but the elaborately carved dragons from what I guessed had been a huge lintel remained intact, the detail of the scales, fangs and eyes unblemished. There were a number of hand painted silk banners adorned with noble looking eagles which seemed to be of a military character. They each had names on them followed by the kanji for "safe return", and I realized that these were essentially prayers for the safety of the young men who had been conscripted to fight the US just one short generation before. Perhaps due to the natural optimism of youth, and certainly due to my lack of experience with war and death, these banners registered in my consciousness only superficially at first, but as time passed I came to understand them as the saddest thing I encountered while in Japan, affecting me far more deeply than the gory and shocking exhibits depicting the indescribable at the Hiroshima Peace Memorial Museum. The terrible and pointless waste of their lives only reinforced my own reluctance to go to Vietnam, in spite of my government's insistance that I should.

14
Allons! through struggles and wars!
The goal that was named cannot be countermanded.

Have the past struggles succeeded?
What has succeeded? yourself? your nation? Nature?
Now understand me well—it is provided in the essence of things
    that from any fruition of success, no matter what, shall come
    forth something to make a greater struggle necessary.

My call is the call of battle, I nourish active rebellion,
He going with me must go well arm'd,
He going with me goes often with spare diet, poverty, angry enemies,
    desertions.

*[from Steve's favorite poem,* The Song of the Open Road *by Walt
Whitman.]*

# ALASKA

*Steve finished his second year at Olympic Community College and with Doug, he flew to Kodiak Island in early June of 1968 to find work fishing for salmon. Steve hoped to make enough of a stake to buy a piece of land, a home base for himself while he continued to explore different options for his future work and travels. Doug stayed in Alaska after the fishing season while Steve returned via Prince Rupert, probably catching a ride there on a Seattle bound boat. He wanted to ride a freight train at least part of the way home, as he jumped ship in Prince Rupert and caught the train to Prince George through the Skeena Canyon. His description of rolling past Indian villages with totem poles along the Skeena River greatly increased my own desire to see that part of northern BC someday.*

*Letter fragment to his family: June 1968*

---

...with the crew we have we'll be able to set at least 5 to 8 more sets a day. The boat I'm on, the "Marcris", is one of the largest in the fleet, with all extras in engine power so we are set to work hard right through the season and stand in a pretty good situation by the middle of August. Kodiak Island is so isolated and far out from any civilization to speak of that the only good reason to be here is to catch a lot of fish. There are about 30 boats that fish in the same general area where we are so it is quite crowded at times. For the most part I prefer fishing in Norway as compared to here. One reason being that the dollar is the main and primary concern here and subsequently there is with many fishermen a constant pushing and lack of concern for anything but the dollar. However I have been able to meet some fishermen from the Seattle area who I'd like to work for and the experience aboard the "Marcris" will enable a chance for working on almost any boat next year. On the weekends there is a lot of work around the cannery with making and repairing nets and boat motors, so I'm hoping to learn all I can about the running and maintaining of the purse-seiner, so that the possibility of building and making of both boat and net would be something to work on while going to school this next year. I'd like to make a small gillnetter at first and fish along the Washington coast.

Here in Alitak there is a large salmon cannery, with Norskies, Swedes, Slavs, Polish, English and American students working in all the different processes of the canning industry. Fish thus far have been slack, so not much is being done here at the cannery except for general maintenance work and supplying and outfitting the various boats that fish out of this cannery. The boat we work on is owned by the cannery, and they supply us with all the equipment, except for food which we buy from them at a small fee. There are a number of old Norwegians working here and I've already had some good opportunities to speak Norsk with them. Some are builders here at the cannery while others work as fishermen. I got to know a boy last night who was born and grew up just north of Egersund. He moved from Norway about 5 years ago and has been fishing here ever since. He seems like a good fisherman, for within the 5 year period he has been here he has earned enough to buy a small boat and become an independent fisherman here at Alitak. I also met a fellow this morning from Yugoslavia. His boat was docked next to ours yesterday and today so I got a chance to speak with him while repairing some of our lines and net... Anyway this fellow from Yugoslavia, Nick, spoke Russian well and has travelled all over the world. He said as a young boy he worked with his father on the coast south of Dobrovnik. He said that he left Yugoslavia to escape Tito's army and went to France.

All of the fellows I work with are from Washington,...all experienced fishermen and their methods are much improved over the old Norwegian ways of fishing around Egersund. There is more machinery on these boats but the hours are much longer I think here in Alaska because of the short season for salmon. We have a large crew so that we can work in shifts and help one another through both the day and night. The food is the best ever, with the best of everything. There is a big meal hall here at the cannery that serves big, delicious meals day in and day out, meat, vegetables, pie, ice cream, the works...

Although I've only been here for several days it seems like almost a month. It seems like every time I fly my sense of time and place is altered so greatly that it takes several weeks to really become established. The coast is so beautiful here and since I last wrote we have seen over 50 miles of Kodiak coastline, which is so much like Norway, except for the lack of trees here. Two days ago Gordon (one of the fellows on our crew) and I saw a big Kodiak brown bear just above another cannery that we stop at to pick up our net. The bear had a cub with it and just sat and looked at us for about 10 minutes before wandering further up the hill. This is certainly the country of "mountains and rivers without end". It seems like everywhere we go there is another mountain range equal to the Cascades. For miles and miles there is an endless wilderness, and the towns are so small that the whole of Kodiak Island takes on the aura of being a very isolated place.

---

*Back from Japan, Farmer Browns Corner, the landscape of my youth, was being radically transformed. The first thing I perceived as I got out of the car after being driven home from the airport was the bulldozer cuts had finally reached the edge of our property, leaving a four foot drop-off to the dozer blade marks on bare earth, punctuated by the brightly colored plastic flagging tape tied neatly on the lines of grading stakes. I was reminded of the texture and pattern of an Indian basket as I looked at the parallel scars on the tan colored mineral soil, disturbed for the first time since the glaciers deposited it. With Doug I walked across the now wide open swathes of what had been our woods, my mind endlessly recalculating where I thought we were, attempting to conjure up a mental map which was now forever out of date.*

*Although the eradication of the woods was upsetting to me, I was immediately occupied with getting together the wherewithal I would need to keep body and soul together on a fire lookout down by Mt. Rainier, my job for the summer, and this kept me from obsessing too much over what to me bordered on an environmental crime. These thoughts were mostly on an unconscious level, but it seemed a rather clear message that I would have to light out for the territories once I was out of college; my home place had been damaged beyond repair. Two days after I returned from Japan I was on Kelly Butte Lookout, located approximately 25 miles north of Mount*

*Rainier in the Washington Cascades, my duty to spot any visible smoke and immediately radio its location to the fire control office of the nearest US Forest Service ranger station.*

*No postmark-* Alitak, Alaska, July 10, 1968

---

Hobo Dan, Well, buddy, although it has been some time since I last wrote, the road has been good as I trust it has been for you. As you can see by the postmark I'm on Kodiak Island, at present fishing on the southern end of the island. I left Kirkland about the middle of June and plan to be here in Alaska until the middle of August and then return to Washington for several weeks before hitting the road again. Doug is up here too, I saw him a couple of weeks ago, but not since. He's got his copy of *Leaves of Grass* and *Zen Flesh Zen Bones* and I've been reading John Updike and Leo Tolstoy and a collection of transcendentalist writings when time permits.

At present, the fishermen on Kodiak Is. are striking against the canneries for more money, and subsequently we haven't been out on the wide blue sea for over a week. The settlement is in view now and we should be back fishing by the first of next week.

Alaska is the land of mountains and rivers with no end. Wilderness for miles, the mountains, the rivers, fields of flowers, cliffs of sea birds, the northern sun along the shoreline, the Eskimos and Indians, the old fishermen and seamen. Kodiak Is. is equal to one word: fish. Everything is fishing here, salmon, halibut, crab and shrimp. There are very few trees; the land is rocky, with high snow capped mountains, bays, inlets, fjords. The murres, puffins, cormorants and seagulls inhabit most of the island, with a few Indian villages and Kodiak City as harbors for the fishermen. Weather is windy, with cool rains now and then. So much for Kodiak Island.

I hope this letter gets to you before you head off into the mountains. When I get back to Washington I'll come up and see you if you're still in the lookout before I hit the road for the east coast. I plan to meet my brother Daryl (who is in Germany now) in New York near the end of August and we'll bum across the northern part of Canada on the CN, getting back around the middle of September. I think I'll be going to Western Washington this next year, maybe live down around Bellingham Bay and sail around Puget Sound, climb in the northern Cascades &c. this next year. Vancouver is a nice town with lots of Russian seamen and places to ride to with the bike so Bellingham will probably be home for a while anyway.

Of course I'm still thinking about leaving the States and the themes of Canada keep ringing loud and clear, especially since being on the road this past month. Russia is still under consideration, Greece, Yugoslavia, and Norway, but I'd like to be able to come back to the States [If Steve had been willing to apply for political asylum in a country such as Sweden he could have dropped out of school, but until the amnesty of the late '70s he would of course not been able to return to the US without being arrested for draft dodging.], so at present I figure going to school is the best thing, reading and writing in the winter months and getting to know the waters of Puget Sound and Vancouver Island.

Just before Doug and I came up here we sailed around Puget Sound with his sailboat. We started in Seabeck on Hood Canal and four days later landed in Edmonds the day after RFK was shot. Sailing provided a lot of new room for growth with the natural elements along the beach, the drift of straw and wood, the evening sun, the trees with blowing leaves in the afternoon, the lights from the lighthouses, the sandstone cliffs and grass fields forming with the interior of the land, the projections of the sea, the currents and shifts of tide, the glare of sun on open water, the drifts of the sail and the gentle force of the wind on it. By the time we reached Edmonds it was good just to sit on the beach and let the breeze filter through our senses; it was a good trip.

Most of the fishermen are up here to make money and there is a constant rush, rush, rush to make the dollar. I think if I make it through this season I'll bag this type of fishing, for all in all it's a bum trip when the only value in life is the dollar and friendship comes second. The more they make up here the more is wanted, the same old story. All talk centers around the dollar, new investments, new car, &c. A couple of times I've almost wanted to just bag the whole thing, but inside the ring of materialism there is a great deal to learn about the moods and patterns of the sea. When I talked to Doug about this several weeks along he felt the same way. One can really see the directionlessness of values in the States here, to the extent that character is a very loose and contradictory matter. At any rate, if I stick things out, I'll see you in August, about a month from now, if not sooner. Forgive me for being so slow in writing.

Your itinerant comrade, Steve

*Letter from me to Steve- July 1968*

---

*Steve-Well I have just finished listening to a composition w/ John Cage telling some very interesting stories. Meanwhile I watched the valleys for smoke & built a fire in the stove. Just as Cage said: "My grandmother said sharply, 'John, are you prepared for the second coming of the Lord?'", I was standing on the porch taking a leak. There apparently is a lot to Cage & his new music. But I don't feel able to write much now, especially since I am writing this on the top of the stove. I am on Kelly Butte Lookout in the White River District near Mt. Rainier. From Enumclaw get a U.S.F.S. map & they'll tell you how to get here. Bring FRESH food if you want, but I have enough food already. There is no refrigeration tho. I will be here until the end of August. I hope that you can come up. It is very peaceful, esp. after a year in a city of 10 million. I hope to hop a freight back to Beloit with Roger S. in early Sept. School starts for me on 6 Sept. I may have to fly back in which case Roger still may want to take the trip. –Your not so mobile comrade, Dan*

*PS- I would add something about the draft, Canada, &c. but I expect to see you. If you plan on not going into the army tho, you better get professional advice.*

*letter- postmark ALITAK RUR- AUG 10 1968*

---

Hobo Dan, Everything is going fine up here on Kodiak Is. I received your letter the other day, and was glad to hear that you managed to get back from Japan and find a lookout for the summer.

I plan to head south again in another two weeks and should be back in Washington about the 20th. I'll hike up and see you when I get back so you can expect me between the 21st-26th.

The salmon run has been relatively good this year so I've been able to make a few dollars besides seeing most of Kodiak Is. We have fished everywhere on the island except the northernmost point. Doug is on a boat that fishes on the west side of the island so I've only seen him a few times this last month. We plan to ride the freights from Prince Rupert to Vancouver and then hitch-hike to Sumas and ride the Sumas-Woodinville freight the rest of the way home. At least this is my plan; Doug may decide to stay up here until he is called for the draft.

As far as I know I'm still II-S [the draft deferment for college students], and my plans are to attend Western Washington this fall quarter, although I'm beginning to feel even more strongly opposed to staying in the States so I don't know quite what I'll do this next year or the one following; I'd like to go back to Norway, or perhaps Canada.

I really enjoy the fishing here and although the hours are long between 18-20 a day it is good to be at sea for a week at a time fishing along the coast of Kodiak Is. Alaska is truly the land of mountains and rivers without end and the natural beauty is both very gentle and harsh, full of northern moods. We fish only 5 days a week so I do have weekends to read and do some writing. Right now it is about midnight and we are waiting for a tender to come and pick up our catch for today. The average wage for our boat this week has been about $150 a day, enough to save and buy a few acres of land and do some farming. I may buy a few acres just south of Bellingham and live there while going to school and then hopefully sell it for a better price in a couple of years. Right now I'd like to find some land close to Bellingham Bay and spend this winter working on some weaving and boat building, perhaps complete plans on the small boat which I drew up this last year and maybe build a small sailboat like the one Doug has out of marine plywood. Working here this summer I've found plans for several small fishing boats that would make good winter projects. My cousins who live on the Nooksack are still logging and I hope to buy some lumber from them and get it cut and kiln-dried in Deming or Bellingham.

I imagine you're able to get a good deal of reading time in this summer too. I want to read Nikos Kazantzakis again when I get back home along with the various American naturalists and realists of the early 1900s, such as Theo Dreiser, James Farrell, Frank Norris, Steinbeck, Dos Passos, and Jack London. Right now I'm reading *Anna Karenina* by Tolstoy, a book full of the movements of the earth, the simple change and balance of human elements linked with the drifts and implications of natural growth. There are sections in the book where Tolstoy goes into a description of the flux and flow of freight and passenger trains between St. Petersburg and Moscow, his writing flows with distinct images, the human expression, the light and reflective qualities of the sun in the afternoon, the silence of the night, the vastness of Russia itself.

Well, thanks again for your letter and I'll see you in another few weeks; it hardly seems like over a year since we parted in Bremerton. Your comrade, Steve

---

*Having spent a season as a fire lookout I knew what to bring with me to fend off boredom on the lookout: around 80 books, my new guitar, carving tools, a kite, sumi painting materials, an empty notebook, and a small radio among other items. I remember hearing reports of street demonstrations in Seattle as broadcast on KRAB, the reporter interviewing several angry young black people (as they preferred to be called at that time) and other unusual programming not to be heard on the commercial stations, but I felt isolated, above it all on my mountain top. I read books, carved small figures in wood, painted, and flew my kite, but what I really craved was human companionship as the days passed, each one much the same at the one before. Time slid by slowly as I contemplated the hazy lump of the Seattle skyline about 80 miles to the northwest; all those people down there and me up here with no smokes to report. It turned out to be a damp and unexciting fire season.*

*Towards the end of the season Steve finally showed up. He and two of his brothers came up the steep Kelly Butte trail one afternoon in late August.*

Later that day we picked a quantity of blue huckleberries and made a grand pie in a tin wash basin, the largest container that would fit in the oven of the wood stove, using up the lookout's last vestiges of Crisco augmented with bacon grease to make the crust. Although not remembered as great gourmet cooking, it looked like the Mt. St. Helens crater (after 1980) by the time we finished eating. As the pie slowly baked, I remember Steve picking out a plaintive tune on my guitar: "a woman, song and a good guitar, the only things that I understand...." A wave of moisture blew in from the Pacific the next day and I got the call to close up the cabin and hike out to the trail head, where we caught a ride back to civilization.

With the fire season over I rode freights and hitch-hiked back to Beloit, taking the central route across Nevada, Utah, Wyoming and Nebraska to get back to the Midwest. My memories of that trip included the impressive red rock mesas coming into Utah from northern Nevada, but the weather was hot enough to make me concerned about running out of water. Getting off my freight in Ogden, I took a short side trip to visit the center of Mormonism in Salt Lake City before continuing east. In the middle of Nebraska I hiked about five miles in hot and humid 100 degree weather to avoid the yard bull at Grand Island, and less than a day later walked across the Missouri River on a railroad bridge at dawn to make a connection for a freight across Iowa. About the time I was thus crossing the heart of the country the police in Chicago were having their own riot/demonstration as Humphrey was nominated to run for president. By the time I got back to Beloit the convention was over and there was an air of impending doom as far as the idea of our generation somehow waking America up and turning things around. I voted in my first election that November, and was disappointed but not surprised at the outcome. I was starting to realize that youth and idealism were not going to be enough. On campus, the attitude towards the war that fall had become quite negative and one day as I walked out of the dining hall I saw a giant board game chalked onto the pavement, forming a square of boxes which were based on Monopoly. A giant pair of dice were rolled as each volunteer entered the game, walking around the board, acting as their own playing piece. But the game was rigged, and everyone seemed to be getting sent to jail or going broke, and perhaps one or two being sent to Vietnam while another would escape to Canada or Sweden. A small band

Cutting firewood on Kelly Butte Lookout, August 1968

Picking blue huckleberries on Kelly Butte, August 1968

*The Letters of Steve Hoyt*     185

Steve on Kelly Butte

*played a current anti-war song of Country Joe and the Fish, "Put down your books and pick up a gun,… we're gonna have some fun!"*

*I taught Japanese at the newly formed free university at Beloit that fall, thereby meeting Diana, a young woman who had lived in Japan when her dad had been stationed there in the Air Force. My dreams of living in a rural or wilderness environment were shared by her, and as we got to know each other we began talking about the possibility of making a go of it somewhere out on the west coast.*

---

15

Allons! the road is before us!

It is safe—I have tried it—my own feet have tried it well—be not
  detain'd!

Let the paper remain on the desk unwritten, and the book on the
  shelf unopen'd!

Let the tools remain in the workshop! let the money remain
  unearn'd!

Let the school stand! mind not the cry of the teacher!

Let the preacher preach in his pulpit! let the lawyer plead in the
  court, and the judge expound the law.

Camerado, I give you my hand!

I give you my love more precious than money,

I give you myself before preaching or law;

Will you give me yourself. will you come travel with me?

Shall we stick by each other as long as we live?

*[from Steve's favorite poem,* The Song of the Open Road *by Walt Whitman.]*

# BELLINGHAM

*After making a modest stake fishing out of Kodiak, Steve moved to Belling-*
*ham and made a down payment on a two acre plot of land on the east side*
*of town, where he hoped to become involved in growing food and eventu-*
*ally building a small place on it to live in. Some notes he made indicate his*
*thoughts and plans at this time:*

THE PROPOSAL

Living off campus-Finding a place for less than $10,000, perhaps
    $5,000.

Method of Buying

To buy some land and later build a small place on it.

Or to buy a place with less land and then have a small house.

Transportation Necessary. Car or bike.

Distribution of property

Close-in property would be more.

Advantages:

Building experience

Gardening experience

Land property experience

The cost (?) after investment

Meat- working to earn

*Vegetables- growing*

*With a few other guys in a driveaway car (being reimbursed for gas money*
*to deliver a new car from one city to another), I came back out to Seattle*
*during the Christmas break. On a day when the temperature was close to*
*zero, Steve, his brother Daryl and I hopped the freight up to Bellingham*
*from Seattle, loaded ourselves and our gear in his old pickup truck, and then*
*drove out to Lake Ozette on the west side of the Olympic Peninsula. From*
*there we hiked out to the Pacific Ocean and the old Ozette Indian village*
*which was then in the beginning stages of an archaeological excavation. Out*
*on the windswept coast I encountered prehistoric petroglyphs for the first*
*time, not realizing that ten years later I would not only work at the Ozette*

Steve in boxcar, December 1968

*Above*: On our way to
Ozette, December 1968

*Left*: Hiking at Ozette,
January 1969. Photo
courtesy Daryl Hoyt.

*dig, but then spend years documenting rock art as a field archaeologist. Shortly after these diversions, I returned to Beloit for my final term.*

*By late 1968 Steve was camping in a shack with no amenities next to the two acres he had bought on the east side of Bellingham and he was keeping his expenses down, in one letter telling me he was surviving on about $15 per month. Then as now, America seemed to me unconscionably wasteful, making it easy to live on the discards of less frugal individuals, and in our avoidance of rampant consumerism many of us found dumpster diving a very productive activity. Steve's gleaning activities extended beyond mere dumpstering however. I remember him once arranging to scavenge potatoes and beets in October after the mechanical harvesters had been through the fields in nearby Ferndale. Thoreau would have approved. Steve's next letter reached me soon after I got back to Beloit.*

*Letter- no postmark - Bellingham, Washington, Jan 16, 1969*

---

Dear Dan, Hope you got back OK to Wis. Since you left we have had quite a bit of snow and continued cold weather, but things seem to be breaking up some now.

I rode the GN to Bellingham a wet rainy morning on the Monday after you took off and last weekend went down again to Seattle to get some used books and art supplies. I walked around the U district for several hours with Yuki and we stopped at the House of Rice to eat some sushi. Yuki works at the U of W hospital so in the afternoon I said goodbye to her, as she had to go to work and hitched home to Kirkland and took the Sunday morning train back up here. While I was in the U district I got a hold of Snyder's *Rip Rap and Cold Mountain Poems*, as I have a poetry teacher here who will be including him in the course work.

I'll probably go up to Vancouver next week to see if there are any Russian boats in again to keep in practice with the language. The national Russian hockey team is playing in Vancouver then too, and I hope to see them.

I think Doug may have gone to California for I haven't seen him since the 5th and he told me he expected to come up to Bellingham that week. I've got several art courses this quarter along with a drama course and one in poetry. I have classes three days a week and I'm working down at the fish harbor a couple days a week. I'll probably go fishing between quarter breaks to earn some extra money; most of the trawlers here are short men. There are about 20 out of Bellingham fishing up along the western coast of Vancouver Island. Pay is about $400 a week.

After coming back from Ozette and realizing again how great it would be to be back on the road, school is kind of <u>HEAVY</u>. As soon as the weather gets better I want to start sailing around the Bellingham area and probably keep the boat down at Kim C.'s place on Chuckanut Drive.

In art class I've been working on some abstract painting ideas with freight images; doors against doors, steel rings and ladders, night lights and shadows from the sun. I remember our trip north on that cold Sunday and how we were looking through the empty doors and watching as our shadows flashed closer and farther away against the

Sketch by Steve, no date. Courtesy Daryl Hoyt.

trees and over the fields as we rolled along. My goal is to take natural abstract things that are apparent in the yards and out on the main line and combine them together or in a series of images. There is a great deal of writing to be worked out this quarter too. Right now I feel like writing on the confining qualities of education in the institution and link that into poems of the open road and the drifts of the natural world and basically show the advantages of the open road over the institution as a method of experience and expression.

Well, I'll close for now and hope to hear from you again.

Steve

---

*After working a while building log cabins in Alaska's Matanuska Valley Doug returned to Kirkland early in the winter of 1968, summoned for his draft physical. He told me that over a hundred other guys were there to get passed and then shipped out directly to boot camp. Just before he left Alaska he had been working on a fishing boat and had had a wet bunk while on board. "There was a section of the form we all filled out which asked about psychological stuff: Did you ever feel depressed? Were you a homosexual? &c., &c". Doug told me he checked the one about being depressed, as he was very depressed about his situation at that moment. He also checked the box for bed wetting. The doctor looked over the form and then asked him, what about this bed wetting? Doug truthfully answered that his bunk had been wet when he woke up two weeks previously, and the doctor then made his decision. Doug was deemed too risky to be sent to Viet Nam to shoot at people and was given a medical exemption. Doug's story gave me food for thought as I finished my last term in college; I had been plagued by that problem as a youth, and this vagary of the induction process turned out to be a heaven sent reprieve in my case. When the time came I was not forced to choose between military service, prison, or exile in Canada.. Our friend Kim, interestingly, merely pretended to be gay, acting embarrassed and ashamed, laughingly telling me afterwards how the people at the induction center expressed open revulsion at his confession of moral turpitude. Of course it must be remembered that few individuals were brave enough or foolish enough to be openly gay in those days, as it* was generally thought of as a moral failing, with some people having very strong feelings on the subject. Having grown up back east however, Kim was relatively urbane and sophisticated, and had no difficulty pulling off his charade. I remember meeting many guys on my various hitch-hiking jaunts who were facing the same dilemma, one of whom told me of a friend who deliberately had a loaded pallet of concrete mix dropped on his foot to get a 4-F classification [a medical exemption for the draft]. Although this story has all the hallmarks of an urban myth, it is significant that such a story was told at all. By the mid '60s it was common for any cop who apprehended a young male hitchhiking to request to see his draft card, and I imagine that many cops resented the fact that with their II-S deferment, college boys were not drafted, while working class guys had to face it at age 19. Some of my high school acquaintances joined the Air Force or Navy for four years (rather than the approximately 2 1/2 year hitch for those who were drafted) in order to have a relative guarantee of coming home in one piece, and a few of course headed north to Canada. I probably could have gotten into the Navy reserves like my brother, and not gotten shot at too much, but based on my experiences in high school Sea Cadets and my brother's first hand descriptions of his hitch in SE Asia, I regarded military service as the next thing to being in jail. It was abundantly clear that once in, one would be scarcely better off than a slave doing forced labor with overseers who were not as smart as you and clearly did not have your own best interests at heart. But the fundamental sticking point was the basic wrongness of the war, which made us deeply resent having at best years of our lives stolen from us, and for what? I still have not come up with a good answer to this question.

*Letter- no postmark- January 28, 1969, Bellingham, Washington*

---

Hobo Dan, It is very cold here today and for the past week we have had snow almost every day with about a foot on the ground now. The temperature has been down around 5 above, much like when you were here during Christmas.

Doug is down at Fort Lewis now; he was here in Bellingham the Friday before he went in and we hitched together down to Seattle late

Friday. He left on the 20th. I plan to bring the his sailboat (actually it belongs to Kim C.) up to Bellingham in another month. I see Kim quite often at school and he is ready to go on some trips around the Bellingham area and perhaps later out to the San Juan Islands.

I went up to Vancouver over the weekend to learn more about the shipping and fishing there. There are about 50 freighters in port during the weekend, many of them from Japan. I also saw several Russian ships, and a few from Norway, Sweden, Germany, and Holland. I took the old Dodge up and there was no problem at the border getting across as I thought there might be. I got a room right next to the docks a few blocks east of Granville Street for $1 a night, so the trip wasn't too much except for the gas. I want to go up and see Leo [a former student at Western who had worked on Sourdough Mt. Lookout in 1967] soon and talk to him about Simon Fraser University, and also about moving to Canada. Vancouver is really beginning to attract me and for that matter Canada in general. There are a number of people here at Western who were good friends of Leo's last year who are planning to move to Canada or who have 4-F's. At any rate you are probably writing to Leo now, but when I see him I'll find out all I can and send you word. It might be possible for you to continue studying in Canada next year as Leo is doing now. (But we have already discussed all this.) The thing about Vancouver is that it is so international, and to get back to Japan from there would be no problem on one of the many Japanese freighters that are there each week. I want to get back again to Norway one of these years, soon, too, and eastern Canada would be as good as any place to leave from (Halifax for example). Even though I have this property here in Bellingham I could sell it within a month's notice, or for that matter I could just keep it and fish this next summer and own it in full. I intend now to stick around Western at least until June, fish the summer and do some travelling around Canada during the late summer. Sometimes however I ask myself just what I am doing in school getting a second-hand education, &c.

I've been reading Jack Kerouac lately again, along with Emerson and Whitman for a class in American Literature. I've been doing more sketches as of late. There is so much to draw around Bellingham, the train yards and fishing harbor and even some of the old homes in south Bellingham. The time to gather up materials and learn about different methods of ink and pencil sketching is now during this cold spell, and it is really enjoyable working with various media. I'm including a couple of some earlier ones this quarter. *[Enclosed were an ink sketch of a conifer branch and historic era Indian plank houses.]* I've got a set of Speedball pens and several dark pencils. It takes a long time to develop a style and to form the drifts of hues and proportions in a suitable fashion. But more than that, some of the delicate interplay of nature becomes increasingly more apparent while drawing. I'd like eventually to work out some type of story told through the media of sketches and written expression of days spent on the freights and the growths into the natural world through the train-mountain-and-sea milieu.

...The pragmatic application of words and careful detail concerning the revolving perspectives of a short story or sketch will have to be worked with and formed and re-formed (The various views, the shifting scene from the boxcar and in the mountains or along the coast). It seems that every trip taken becomes more significant and the solid images of the natural interplay of the experience take on a deeper association with not only the reflective past but projection into the future. Each trip is like a well-shot image or group of images into the mind; they form the basis for a continuation of adherence to the open road.

I'll hope to hear from you, and goodbye for now.
Steve

*Writing fragment-no date*

---

We both sat in opposite corners of the room, she in the front and I in the back. She would smile occasionally and I would attempt on more occasions than not to return her glancing friendliness. I did not know her name nor she mine, and it wasn't as if we felt any mysterious force drawing within each other. She had wide brown eyes that she would open and gently receive my drifts of glance, and then her head would shift down again to her work with bits of colored paper and paint. I

Sketch of Ozette village by Steve, no date. Courtesy Daryl Hoyt.

*The Letters of Steve Hoyt* 197

would work quietly, usually not saying anything to others in the class, and eventually they would feel uneasy about my reserved nature.

My hair was long, and I wore a small pack for my art supplies and books, yearning constantly to be gone on the road and away from these confining walls of higher learning. My thoughts were of riding trains for I had in my years just following secondary school, traveled somewhat, working and riding a bike from place to place. I had on longer sojourns loaded myself in an empty and floated across the broad reaches of the land. My favorite poets were those who sang songs of the Open Road. I had wanted to be immersed in the ties and rails of physical being, to roam as a free vagabond forever...

*Letter- no postmark- Bellingham, Washington, March 4, 1969*

---

Dear Dan, Thanks so much for your last letter. Much has been happening lately. Doug is working in Everett on a fishing boat. I haven't seen him for several weeks now, since he has been fishing most of the time. I am planning to go fishing in about two weeks if things go as planned. I want to fish this next quarter and then in the summer my brother and I will be able to build the cabin we had planned on the property here in Bellingham. I'll probably go to summer school, but if the draft does not require it by that time I'll probably just build and work through most of the summer and take a few trips, sailing. I'm working now on a small Penguin boat and may take it down to Kirkland to let my brother Daryl finish building it if I'm unable to finish it by the time I start fishing.

The boy I'm living with now is leaving in about two weeks to go around the States by freight train. He does a lot of drawing and plans to head south to LA, across to New Orleans and up through New England to Nova Scotia and then across Canada and down to St. Paul, through to Seattle. If it wasn't for the land that I'm buying now I think I'd go with him. But it will be nice to have a place here in Bellingham to come back to and I guess for the present, things will work out so that by next year we will be free to come and go, &c.

After taking this next quarter off I may decide to return to school and eventually work for the Peace Corps after graduating next year, but right now, as always, I'm thinking only in the immediate present and the fishing opportunities here along the west coast. I guess you will be out here in another month and a half. There is an outside chance that I may decide to go to school this next quarter and then work during the summer and if so, we will be able to do the sailing we had planned, &c. School is out in another two weeks here and spring quarter starts near the end of March. I developed those pictures that we took out on the beach at Ozette and as soon as I get some prints made I'll send some along to you. My brothers Daryl and Russ rode the trains from Chehalis to south Seattle several weeks ago so we have some new members for the club. Russ even wrote a story about his trip which was pretty good. I rode down to Kirkland from Sumas several weeks ago and the train stopped in Kirkland, so the service is improving all the time. I'll include a poem that I wrote several weeks ago while heading home on the train.

In the GN road
light
from within the walls of Bethlehem steel
filtered hints of corner edges.
Southbound train, at night
lights with town
advance-recede
Pragmatic gondola box along night's random drift
light
circling receptive to variegated veins of pounding inner iron.

I begin the poem with "In" because I wanted to convey the feeling of the rider being in between the two outer rails as compared with the conventional "On". This is only one of many drifts of expression that could deal with the train experience. I've been working with some ideas concerning the reflection of shadows, like our trip at Christmas time to Bellingham and how the sun would throw our shadows across the snow and then onto the alder trees and then back again onto the snow, extending and filtering with the drifts of the open road. Write, write, write, is all that one can do to come up with something. Let me know how things are going.

Steve

*Letter- no postmark- Bellingham, Washington, March 16, 1969*

---

Dear Dan, Thanks so much for your last letter. I've heard from some friends at school that there is a small community out on the San Juan Islands that is farming and fishing and perhaps the girl you know at Beloit would be interested in living there and farming. I would think that living alone up past the Nesset's farm would be first impractical and secondly too difficult to be done in a legal manner. It would be a nice place to have a small community of farming and logging, but to live there alone (and especially if the girl has never been exposed for long periods of time in the mountains and woods) would be difficult. At any rate you might tell her about the communities along the west coast where groups of people are farming and working with their hands. [Diana, my girlfriend at Beloit, had expressed an interest in living in a rural area and raising sheep. No doubt Steve's letters to me during the bleak winter season of the upper Midwest excited the both of us to dream of heading out to the Northwest and finding our place in it.]

School is over for this quarter and I'm going down to Everett tomorrow to find some work on a dragger until it is time to leave in April for halibut fishing. I'll probably work for over a month down here in the Sound, and then head north about the 20th of next month. I'm going to apply for a C.O. [conscientious objector] before I go north and I may talk to the Norwegian consulate in Seattle about citizenship papers and such if I decide to go back again to Norway this next fall. My plans are to fish at least until June and most likely throughout the summer. My induction, if I do so, will not be until Oct., so I'll have some time to think things over and generally decide the course of the next few years. There are many times when I wish that I had stayed in Norway the first time I was there in '65 but things will iron themselves

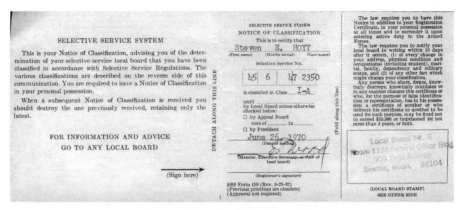

Steve's draft card (unsigned). Courtesy Daryl Hoyt.

out better spending these next few months at sea and if the season is good I'll have enough to consider moving back across the Atlantic. I'll probably sell the land I have here now and use that money to buy a small farm along the western coast over there. At any rate these are my latest thoughts and I'll resolve myself by this summer as to what appears to be the best thing to do. Hopefully, if I fish through the next 5 months I'll be able to earn at least a couple thousand which would help if I do finally decide to move back to the old country.

I've been plowing up part of the field this week here in Bellingham and if I do decide to remain here next year at least we'll have some vegetables to keep the food bill down for the winter. My brother Daryl may be here next year so he'll be able to live and go to school reasonably. I may decide myself after several months out on the open sea to return again to Western, but right now I'm tired of all this bullshit and the open road (Whitman's Song of the Open Road) is an extremely meaningful poem at this time. I've been reading more lately: some Hesse, Gide, Dostoyevsky, Kafka, Updike, and Thoreau. The mountains are just beautiful now on many of the clear March days that we have been having thus far. I went down to Kirkland last week on the Sumas to Woodinville train and the trip back up on the GN was really something, racing by all the beachcombers between Seattle and Everett. I went with a girl who I've gotten to know this quarter and she really enjoyed the trip. She is from Illinois and came out here to go to school and be close to the mountains. There are really many fine people here at Western, some from all over the States who have come to get a chance to do some climbing, &c., in their spare time.

You can write to my home address in Kirkland as I'll probably be there once or twice this next month. I'm wondering just what you are planning after Beloit and hope we can do some hiking together when you are out here. Keep hitting the ground running.

Vice President of the Road, Steve

*Letter fragment to Steve's family, April 4, 1969:*

We are in Neah Bay today. The weather has been bad and fishing slow so we probably won't be back to Seattle for at least another week. We fished up along the western coast of Vancouver Island late last week but now we are down along the Washington coast between Cape Flattery and Cape Alava. Hopefully we will have better weather tomorrow and run into some fish soon.

*I finished my studies at Beloit in early May and drove out to Seattle in a driveaway car, taking about 40 hours to get there, driving non-stop. Diana had come with me and we spent a few days camping out on the southern tip of Whidbey Island, walking miles of beaches without encountering a single other person. From the point at Scatchet Head, huge cliffs rose above our camping spot with eagles soaring along the cliff tops. We could look east across Saratoga Passage towards Edmonds and see the occasional freight train, looking like a string of colored beads crawling slowly along the beach on the way to Seattle or Everett. To the west, tugboats pulled huge red barges full of wood chips up Admiralty Inlet on their way north to the pulp mills in Canada, and as they did I wondered what it would be like to stow away on one of them and see where it would end up. Even in the midst of paradise I felt the tug of the open road. After our idyllic campout we got in touch with Doug and drove up to Saxon. After visiting with Tom and George at the Nesset farm we walked up an old logging road to show Diana the abandoned Overby place which I had thought might be a good place* to re-inhabit. Part of me longed for the road, but another part wanted to find a rural place with less noise and pollution to build a home and settle down with Diana. It was years before I was able to resolve these conflicting desires.

Although I was itching to head north, maybe to Southeast Alaska or somewhere north of Vancouver on the west coast, there were a number of things keeping me in limbo as spring turned into summer. Most importantly, I had to take my draft physical and learn whether I would be drafted or given a medical exemption. If found fit to serve, I would then have to decide whether to join the Navy or head for Canada. As well, I still had one last exam to take in order to complete my graduation requirements, and I had been planning a climb in the north Cascades with Ralph, my fellow student at Waseda University. Later in the summer we planned to take his father's 26' sloop for a cruise on Lake Huron, so I would be able to get in a little traveling riding the high line out to the upper Midwest. My draft physical was in late June, and a day or two after being found unfit for duty due to "chronic intermittent enuresis during adolescence" I climbed Mt. Sahale near Cascade Pass with Steve, my brother Dave, Steve's friend Tim, and Milo. Milo was the only close friend of mine from high school who chose to join the military, and was on a 30 day leave after finishing a year's deployment in Germany. As he was about to be shipped out to Vietnam, he found the climb good mental therapy. I was of course greatly relieved to have been found unfit to kill Vietnamese and climbing Sahale only added to my elation. Getting back up into the pristine high country was a tonic to my soul, which had been languishing during my exile in the flatlands of the Midwest.

Excerpts from my journal:

20 June 1969-

***

Up the dusty, bumpy Cascade River road to the trailhead: a huge snowbank which hadn't melted yet. A couple more hours up to the pass,... We got there early in the afternoon, set up camp and ate, and then just sat around all afternoon. The view was fantastic, including the Johannesberg Massif,

At Cascade Pass- Milo, Dave, myself, and Steve. Photo courtesy C. Milo McLeod.

On the summit of Sahale- Steve, myself and Milo. Photo courtesy C. Milo McLeod.

Magic, and a few other peaks to the east and west. The climb the next day was beyond description; as we gained altitude on Sahale Arm, more and more of the mountains towards the Glacier Peak area became visible. At the summit ridge we suddenly came face to face with Boston, Formidable, and a gaping cliff; the latter unnerved Milo and me, the last two up. We sat on top for over an hour under sunny-hazy blue skies. I could even see the south side of Jack Mountain, Sourdough, and way off to the north through all the haze, Hozomeen. [These were mountains near my old fire lookout on Desolation Peak.] We plunge stepped and glissaded part of the way down, trotted down the Sahale Arm trail, and broke camp after a short rest.

27 June 1969-At Steve's cabin

---

I left for Bellingham catching one ride from Mountlake Terrace right up to the Value Mart Shopping Center near Steve's cabin. I went over to his Granny's place and met Daryl, and we sat and talked. Steve later showed up, but was planning to go down to Seattle early so I walked over to the cabin with him and stayed with him and a few other guys. Steve got up early and left to work on a boat; the rest of us slept in till about 10. Steve had been telling me wild tales about wine, women, and song down at the cabin, but it seemed to be rather peaceful when I got there. Quite a few self-done drawings and paintings hung on the walls. Also a couple of signs: "STUDENT/SEATTLE", "STUDENT/BELLINGHAM". A couple of mattresses on the floor with old boots and blankets intermingled, about 9 or 10 apple boxes full of paperbacks on academic subjects and a few good authors, old bottles which once held burning candles now holding dried weeds, hats, coats, canteens hung on nails. A wood stove covered over the top with spices, straw matting on the floor. We sat around in the morning playing guitars and talking, then into town looking for work at the cannery, and then back to the cabin.

---

I went out to the Lummi Stomish [canoe races and slahal (the "bone game"), a carney, &c., sort of a coastal pow-wow] the next day with Steve's brother Daryl. We got back in the afternoon in time to play softball, playing until after sunset. Steve, who had been quite an athlete in high school, kept knocking them out of the ballpark (the pasture where his garden was located). I hung out there another day or two, sitting in on classes that Steve's friends were taking at Western for both entertainment and educational value, and then hitched back to Farmer Brown's Corner. I worked on making pottery at home, took my area exam, attempted a climb of Whatcom Peak on the edge of the Picket Range, and spent an itchy couple of weeks installing insulation in Bremerton navy housing in order to pick up a few bucks. With my wages I bought a small Honda 65 motorbike, spent a little time learning to ride it and made a few repairs on it as well. In early August I called Steve up in Kirkland and we decided to visit the Nessets, using my motor bike as transportation. Although Steve and I were a lot skinnier in those days, our combined weight had to be well over 300#. Steve had a small pack as well, but we miraculously made it up State Route 9 to Saxon on the Honda, not being in too much of a hurry so as to go easy on the motorbike. Wanting Steve's opinion about the possibility of living there, I suggested that we visit the abandoned homestead a mile or two up the old logging road beyond the Nessets' place. But I learned that it was now owned by one of the big timber companies, and the last thing they would want would be some hippies living in the woods where their timber was waiting to be harvested. We visited with Steve's cousins, Tom and George (true Norwegian bachelor farmers) and their sister "Johnnie", who told us about the early days on the farm when Steve's great grandfather had come over from Norway, and then continued our journey to Steve's cabin in Bellingham. In late August I hopped a freight out to the Midwest and went sailing with Ralph on upper Lake Huron for a week, and then hitch-hiked home in time to see Diana off to Japan where she would be studying for the coming year.

After fishing in Alaska for a few months, Doug had remained there a while longer, working with an old socialist radical log cabin builder near Palmer, and returning only when his draft induction notice came late in 1968. His stories about that part of Alaska made me want to see the place for myself. Visiting Leo up at SFU, I met another bush hippie who told me about the Fairbanks area and how people could live there in the bush on little money if they were willing to live simply and were into hunting and fishing. I finally packed up and headed north, catching a freight up to Prince

George and then hitch-hiking the Alcan the rest of the way to Fairbanks around mid September.

The trip north was of course the beginning of the real adventure for me; I was finally heading to Alaska, not for a week or a month, but maybe for the rest of my life. A solid week of seeing nothing but mountains and rivers without end impressed me deeply as I rolled up the Fraser Canyon and hitched along the Liard River, past Teslin and the upper Yukon River, on and on, the wilderness surrounding the narrow ribbon of highway seemed endless. When I arrived in Fairbanks, the weather was crisp and clear, pleasantly warm during the days, but decidedly nippy at night. The first thing I did after thanking my last ride into town was to purchase a USGS topographic map of the area, and then I began searching for work, asking everyone I met about any leads they might know about. I spent a week doing odd jobs, camped out in an old school bus and older cabin, and then met what I can only refer to as a character, a carpenter in his 50s, short, stocky and bearded who introduced himself as the "world's greatest carpenter". Howard offered me the use of his small travel trailer while I continued to look for work and I eventually ended up living in what locals called a "wanagan", an addition to an otherwise beautifully built log cabin where he lived at the bottom of Chena Ridge near the University. As the days became shorter the temperature was dropping noticeably and I considered myself fortunate to have found a warm place to live until breakup. I worked at a few more short term jobs until Rodger, another friend from high school who had flown in from Kirkland (also looking for work) tipped me off that the Caterpillar warehouse just northeast of town was looking for a warehouseman. I hitched out there the next day and filled out a job application, only putting down two years of college on the form as I didn't want them to think I was too educated to stick with a blue collar job. My next concern was to find some kind of vehicle to get me to work, but by this time I knew that I would make it through the winter. I bought an old '54 Ford pickup at an auction that still had river silt in the glove box from the flood in 1968 and a friend from Beloit I had run into over at the university helped me get it running. After a few trips to the surplus stores for winter gear I felt ready for the extreme winter I had heard so much about.

I had initially used my USGS map to decide which part of the Fairbanks *area to concentrate on when looking for a place to live. I was lucky to have decided on the Chena Ridge/University of Alaska area west of town, as it was there that I met Niilo Koponen, who offered me the opportunity to build a cabin down in the woods on his 160 acre homestead on Chena Ridge. Niilo was clerk of the Friends (Quakers) Meeting and I began attending Sunday mornings. He also had a weekly sauna at his house where I met many of the local freethinkers, pretty much the polar opposites of the folks who drove skimobiles through the woods and shot at anything furry that moved. After Friends Meeting on Sunday morning we would adjourn to someone's house for tea and conversation, so I even had a social life of sorts, but I longed for spring when Diana could join me and together we would begin building the cabin. I spent the winter working steadily and banking every penny I didn't need for books, groceries, and keeping my old pickup running. In my spare time I built a rugged sled from a pair of old wooden skis, planning to use it to move a few thousand board feet of rough cut lumber from the top of the ridge down to the cabin site. After a few months, my job at the warehouse felt a bit like being in jail; although the work was at times challenging, especially digging the giant tracks of a D9 bulldozer out of a snowbank at 50 below, I didn't really feel like it mattered. At times I also felt some guilt because I was basically working for the people who were doing their damndest to promote the proposed oil pipeline from Prudhoe Bay which I was not in favor of. As the days imperceptibly began to lengthen I found myself counting the days until I could quit and begin building the cabin that I would live in.*

*All through my college years, while receiving Steve's letters from Norway and later from the Pacific Northwest, I had continually told myself, "I'll just get my degree, and then I'll do what I want." After four years of book learning, I did not want to defer my desires for "doing my own thing" as the phrase went in those days, but within a few months of arriving in Alaska I had signed myself up to get into the carpenters' union in Fairbanks, thinking how I would then be able to find good paying work wherever I went. But I found myself once again saying, "I'll just get my union card, and then I'll do what I want." I had put myself back inside of a cage, and I soon realized that I felt uneasy about my plans, logical and prudent as they seemed. Perhaps Steve's letters from Bellingham gave me the impetus to break out of my cage and decide instead to build my own log cabin, rather than putting my nose to the grindstone, with the carrot of a union card and a high wage job dangling ahead of me, and the dream of doing what I really wanted remaining always just out of reach. One thing that I knew for sure, after four years of what Steve called "four walls education", I now wanted to work with my hands. I called the carpenters' union hall and told them I would not be entering their program. When I left Beloit the previous spring I had felt the same way about the idea of attending grad school; my reaction was pretty much the same as the song: "No thanks, Omaha, thanks a lot."*

*Writing fragment—no date*

Economy and Thoughts

The world in which I live is filled with those who are caught in the never ending pattern of getting and spending. I see men who work merely for the money they can acquire. Their lives are unhappy because nothing in their lives is satisfying or lasting. Their material wealth leads them only to momentary happiness. They impress others only when their pocket book is full. Every man likes to impress others, if he thinks only of himself. Those who think not of their own lives never need or have use for material wealth. That sort of wealth is a changing whim. Down through the ages men have placed values on different articles. The values change was the society's changes. Something that men strived for a hundred years past may be not recognized as having value today. Life becomes more empty when one fills it with more things. There are thousands of living examples in our society today.

The simpler one makes his life, the more readily he can develop wants that pertain to the happy joys and basic fulfillment of life. No one can ever fulfill his life unless he simplifies it and experiments with it. Life is an experiment. The test tubes are filled by our day by day living. The experimenter mixes and stirs and if the colors are still true after all the mixing and stirring the experiment is complete and death washes the earth with our colors, making it a little better place.

*Before I left for Alaska, I remember Steve turning me on to the poetry of Walt Whitman, particularly the* Song of the Open Road, *and the* Song of the Rolling Earth. *Steve had taken to heart the admonition of his creative writing teacher who had encouraged his students to "listen to the sound of the words you write". As Whitman was the first poet to eschew the use of both end-rhyme and meter, his anarchistic style may have particularly appealed to Steve. I felt that Whitman's style definitely influenced Steve's writing, and I later learned that during his time in Bellingham he had, like Kerouac, experimented with what might be termed "automatic writing" or "stream of consciousness" writing. Samples of those experiments seem more like the chanting of mantras than the development or elucidation of specific ideas, as if he were attempting to plumb the depths of a mystical relationship with the environment, and there are tinges of this style in his later letters to me. In many of these writings he repeated the phrase "the rolling of the earth", along with numerous other organic metaphors, indicating strong feelings of connection to the natural landscape that he experienced wherever he traveled. From about this time I noticed Steve's use of terms such as "filtering", "drifts", "drifting", and "blendings" in contexts which seemed to indicate an attempt to formulate a new vocabulary of a person's relationship to the natural world. Because these contexts in most cases do not indicate specific, objective meanings I was (and still am) only able to wonder about what transcendental concepts he was struggling to express.*

*In spite of owning two acres of land in Bellingham, there was no structure on the property, and although he lived there in a tent at times, after he dropped out of college Steve spent time alternately "couch surfing" with various friends and occasionally sleeping in his brother's dorm room at Western. By early 1972 he was staying in a cabin on nearby Lummi Island while diving for urchins and trying to establish a garden there. As in many other parts of America, at this time there were a number of communes in the Bellingham area, with many aspiring members of the counter-culture trying to find or found the perfect commune, a place where everybody could do their own thing and not be involved in activities that were harming the environment. Steve's desire to help create such a community in the San Juan Islands paralleled my own hopes of finding like minded people in*

*Alaska as the decade of the '60s ended. After a couple of winters in central Alaska however, I realized that I was much more likely to feel at home with boat people on the coast than with the bush hippies of the Alaskan Interior. My encounter with the vastness of Alaska and its wilderness areas made me want to find a place on the northwest coast that was less civilized than the Bellingham area, and thus I had applied for landed immigrant status in Canada, hoping to somehow find a place to live and work on the wilder parts of the coast, well north of the last road. I believe that Steve's strong dedication to simple living at least partly hampered him from achieving his stated goals of boatbuilding and gardening. He never earned enough money to build a place to live in or, like Doug, a boat to live on, yet he still chose not to compromise his commitment to simplicity. Similar to my own decision to skip the union card, for Steve, finding a steady, high paying job, even for just a year or two, making enough money to buy a plot of land or build a boat big enough to live on, was not his way. Perhaps he felt that if he made the kind of individually focused commitment involved with a steady job or "career path", by the time he had made his stake, he would have forgotten the original reason he wanted the money. His previous experience fishing in Alaska with its extreme focus on making money on the part of most fishermen had perhaps soured him on this option and he did not return for another season there, even though he would likely have made as much or more as he had in 1968. Working on fishing boats locally however, seemed to bolster his connection to the waters of Puget Sound in a way that working toward a degree in marine biology could not, but he only worked for short periods before returning to Bellingham to pursue his boatbuilding and gardening projects and his involvement in environmental issues. Although not financially remunerative, I believe Steve chose these activities both for their communitarian value and (paradoxically) so he could "do his own thing".*

*Some comments made by Doug in 2011:*

---

I think Steve was out with me on another bigger dragger briefly in the summer. He did not like the heavy equipment and wasting of fish [by-catch] on dragger style fishery. But I do remember conversations with him when both of us were tied up alongside during storm days at Neah Bay. I was working during the winter, spring, and summer aboard a small Everett based dragger. Because it was the smallest of the fleet there were only myself and the owner/captain working. This made quiet time for me aboard, working the decks and reading inside while the captain was steering. I still remember the heightened awareness, a revelation of personal fulfillment, the sensation of the perfect moment. These sensations were what Steve tried to hold onto as well, working at sea, with fish and mountains in view, making a living as well, but in a time honored, simple, outdoor profession, with enough leisure time to reflect. A complete sensory and intellectual realization: "I am doing the right thing, in the right place, surrounded by beauty, and making a simple living with my hands, unencumbered by noises, busy people and distractions other than natural challenges."

*From my journal, Fairbanks, Alaska:*

---

*I go through a letter [which I have since lost] from Steve and note a feeling of despair. His [draft] lottery number is 114 and he says nothing about going to Canada, quoting two fragments of poems by Gary Snyder:*

> *I cannot remember things I once read*
> *A few friends, but they are in cities.*
> *Drinking cold snow –water from a tin cup*
> *Looking down for miles*
> *Through high still air.*

> ————————————-

> *Caught more on this land-rock, tree and man,*
> *Awake, than ever before, yet ready to leave.*
> *Damned memories,*
> *Whole wasted theories, failures and worse success,*
> *Schools, girls, deals, try to get in*
> *To make this poem a froth, a pity,*
> *A dead fiddle for lost good jobs.*

Steve signed his letter "A friend left in the city".

A copy of a letter sent to Steve in early January 1970:

Dear Steve: I suspect that I read my own feelings of despair and stagnation into your letter: "Damned wasted theories, schools, deals, lost jobs, &c., &c.,..." And in contrast:

> How still it is here in my lovely hut!
> Before me and behind-untouched and unstirred-
> Blue misted mountains, cloaked with forest, dark and wild,
> Mass themselves and pack;
> Folding me in their somber might.
> Above my head to east and west
> Fair clouds, far lifted, float and sleep,
> And cover me with their softness.
> Should human footsteps pass this way,
> My being would be a thing unknown,
> Encircled in unfathomable solitude.
> —Ryokwan of Echigo

I get the feeling that you are not particularly satisfied with things- I imagine your draft lottery number has something to do with it. I wonder if you feel that you are stuck back in the city and I am out here in the open, free wildness of Alaska. I'm not. I'm stuck in the city too.

Well, I imagine that the above must come as a surprise. I should add in all honesty that I am enjoying my free time a great deal, but I wonder about the validity of saving up some more, for the future. And try to learn a trade, join a union without involving yourself in some hassles. (I don't know- maybe you're really digging auto-tech. school, but why not pick up a '50 Ford and head for Baja California learning auto mechanics as you go?) I am joining the carpenter's union this March in order to learn to build houses and to make some money. I expect to turn down the chance to go on an archaeological dig up in the Brooks Range this summer. I will have to wait until I quit working to have the time to have a *garden, build a potter's wheel, a kiln, learn how to spin and weave wool, bake sourdough bread,... But I keep telling myself that it takes money to do all these things, that one needs a few acres of land as a base for his wandering, that it costs money to go to Japan to study Rock Gardening, &c., &c.,... The letter I sent in October or November was a pretty empty statement I think, just something to let you know where I was. I really hadn't spent enough time here to have anything to say. So it's good that my letter didn't reach you until just recently. Although I probably have read things into your letter that really aren't there, receiving it has been more fruitful that way. I have been meeting some very interesting people who are doing interesting things, and I have pretty definite plans to "stop working and start living" once I have my union card and maybe some land up here. I remember the trip you, I, and Daryl took just a year ago out to Lake Ozette and the Pacific shore, and I wonder if one couldn't spend one's whole life like that... What good will money be when this country falls apart in 20 years? I don't know- maybe you're envying me going to saunas through the woods on skis at night- moonlight on the birches at 40 below... I sure do miss the ocean and plan on heading down to Kenai in a year or two at the latest. As for what I am doing, I work 5 or 6 days a week driving a fork lift which has the exhaust coming right into the cab and no door. Heaving around 3 and 4 hundred pound D9 rollers, idlers, sprockets, &c. Unloading Sealand vans, working stock inside. It was OK for a month or two, but less so now. In my free time, I ski, hike out in the woods where I live, go to Friends Meeting, saunas, read in the evenings, sew, &c. I also have my guitar here now. I guess I'll have to return to Kirkland to get some of the stuff I left there, but I doubt that will be before 1971. I really like Alaska but I have no idea whether I'll stay here for good. I kinda want to spend a few years traveling, kicking around with no obligations or pressure to be somewhere at a particular time, &c. I'd like to work myself from place to place, hike the Appalachian Trail from Georgia to Maine. I'd like to study pottery, build a cabin on a beautiful cliff somewhere in the Cascades, maybe on one of the cliffs of Hells Gorge, live on wild food and food stamps, let my hair grow righteously long... Maybe we can get together in Southeastern or the Anchorage area or even up here sometime this spring. My brother plans on coming up here this summer. Have you seen Snyder's*

*Earth House Hold? Pretty good stuff in it. Let me know your reactions to the above. Later, Dan*

---

*Once his draft status had been resolved, Doug no longer felt the need to remain in college. He had gone to work on a small dragger, the* Maria, *out of Seattle, and in about a year he saved enough to buy a 28' Monk Sloop which he named* Grebe. *He lived aboard while moored at various marinas, working on other boats after leaving the* Maria, *and in the spring of 1971 he prepared for a summer trolling for Salmon. By living on board, he was able to have a low or no rent place to live for the next few years as he gradually made the transition from fishing to working as a boatbuilder and shipwright in marinas around Puget Sound. During a trip south from Alaska, Diana and I spent a couple of days sailing up Puget Sound with him on the* Grebe *before hitch-hiking back to Farmer Browns Corner near Kirkland. Doug continued up into the Gulf Islands on the Canadian side of the border for a shakedown cruise. Steve joined him that summer for a few days of sailing in the San Juan Islands, and in August, Steve and Doug spent about a week together trolling around Neah Bay. Many of Doug's log entries indicate that he was as much interested in the aesthetics of sailing a small craft as he was in catching fish. Moored at Reid Harbor he noted,* "This place is a panacea for all ills", *off Matia Island,* "tranquility impressions", *and coming into Anacortes,* "Smooth transition to Civilization." *Once he began fishing commercially, he caught three fish on his first day and noted* "best of spirits". *About a week later, catching about ten times (by weight) of salmon, his log noted,* "Such a beautiful night, I would like to stay out here all night. I'm all by myself & in complete comfort." *A few days later,* "Don't remember too well now, lost track of days—the time goes so quickly. I'm out there 16 hours a day and as far as my time consciousness goes it seems like less than an 8 hour day—It's so great out there I hate to come in." *The next day:* "Been sitting out a storm, so I approached the ocean cautiously. It was a big storm, a tuna boat said there were 50' swells in close. I ran up the line from Tatoosh to the Whistler and saw the waves making surf all down the line. I turned around and decided to go around the Whistler where the bottom is deeper and shouldn't break the swells. I went out more for adventure than anything else. The rough swells smoothed out, but if it blew up I would have my hands full." *By late August he was learning to troll under sail:* "After a couple of hours and no fish with increasing wind I decided to put up full sail and experiment sailing and trolling. It worked out well, I could watch the line and maintain speed. The wind was right and I could troll downwind at the right speed. After several hours my intuition told me it was going to blow harder so I took down the mainsail and found I could go well with just the jib downwind. It feels so good to sail and troll—my grandest expectations." *At the end of the season he noted:* "I said goodbye to a good summer and now am thinking of what directions to sail this winter. The long trip back inside frames the mind to thoughts of future plans." *He spent a few months with Sequim Bay as a home port and then sailed back to Seattle in January.* "I got up at 7:00 AM. It was blowing hard all night and I could see small whitecaps from the marina, but I wasn't going to wait any more to get to Seattle. I headed out and found the whitecaps weren't small, but after blowing all night it was rough for Puget Sound. The waves were about 4 feet and all whitecapping and surfing. The boat and I got soaked every 15 seconds. The man who was with me had sailed all over the world on ships and traveled on his small boat in Puget Sound. He said the night before that he had never been seasick and figured it was all psychosomatic. Well, half way to Seattle he hollered—'Hand down the bucket!'". *Doug sailed back to Kirkland, luffing right up to the dock without touching, stepping off to tie up. His last log entry describes sailing back to Shilshole Bay:* "Now I can no longer put off selling the boat—It's going to be hard".

*Once he had his land in Bellingham, Steve earned money by occasional work on fishing boats, spending more and more time concentrating on learning how to build wooden boats and about the ecology of Puget Sound and the San Juan Island area. He also got involved in the CO-OP gardening project as his last letters describe. By the early 70s, he would quaff the occasional beer or take a toke on a joint, and he had also become more open to spending time with like minded young women. Steve developed no serious long term relationship however, probably due to his fairly extreme* voluntary poverty and love of the road. He took up playing the fiddle at this time, and as a token of his time spent in Norway, began signing his letters "Sven". Sometime after June 1970 he finally managed to resolve his draft status, apparently finding a sympathetic anti-war doctor in Bellingham who helped him get classified as physically unfit for service due to a childhood injury. Although a close friend once encountered Steve chanting and dancing with a group of Hare Krishnas in front of the Student Union at Western, he was more likely to be spending time with Joe Bertero, of Joe's Garden, one of the larger nurseries in the Bellingham area. Steve was focused on learning the basics of growing food, and specifically how to start and transplant the various crops that were later to be cultivated in the CO-OP garden.

I had spent the winter of 1969-70 working in Fairbanks, saving what I could to buy the lumber for my log cabin. Just before break-up (the short period between winter and summer when the ice melts and the rivers begin to flow) I hitched the Alcan highway south while waiting for the ground to thaw out so I could begin building. From Seattle I traveled back east by freight and hitch-hiking to visit friends in Philadelphia and then returned to the Seattle area. Just before returning to Alaska in mid-May, a couple of friends and I hopped a freight up to Bellingham where we found Steve driving an old panel truck boldly painted in stars and stripes, red, white and blue. We had shared a bottle of "dago red" as we rolled north in the boxcar and by the time we met Steve we were feeling no pain; it was an exuberant reunion, hanging out with a friend of his on a good sized sailboat, the Fred Free.

Back in Alaska, I spent the summer and fall of 1970 building the log cabin with Diana, who had returned from Japan. We got our cabin closed in and weatherized, and after freeze-up we flew into a remote lake on the south slope of the Brooks Range where we were cabin-sitters that winter, our nearest neighbors being about 50 miles to the south.

Steve and friend in
Bellingham, early
70s. Photo courtesy
Daryl Hoyt.

Steve and Doug,
ca. 1970

*Letter to a female friend- Bellingham-Jan 22/1971 [This may have been a copy, or a letter that was not mailed, as it was with Steve's effects when he died.]*

Dear M___, I came home early tonight after working with the boatbuilding to get another letter off. I'm still looking for a buyer for the first boat that I built, but thus far nothing definite. Several people whom I've been in contact with are planning to come and look at it later this week, so I'm keeping my hopes up that it will be sold soon.

In the mean time I'm working on No. 2, but soon I'll need to have the other one sold to finish buying the materials for the next several boats.

It has been enjoyable just working with the wood, gathering all the materials, learning just how to save when buying parts, and the final test of sailing the boat is certainly what I'm looking forward to this next month.

We have had mild weather now, days of scattered rain. I've been doing more reading with various types of science studies, and doing some work with sketches.

Today I went down to Samish Is. with my friend John who is from Waldron Is. And we talked with several boat builders there who are building the small version of the boat I'm working with this year. A beautiful clear day with miles of blue western Washington sky, the birds flying on Samish Flats, the wind in the Sound, Lummi Is., Chuckanut Drive.

I'm really trying to get it together, so to speak, through the boatbuilding. More people come to visit each day and there are a number of Fairhaven students who are interested in the possibility of sailing and teaching sailing in the future. It, sailing, has started to grow with each day spent getting the boats together. I mean a growth within, a new tapping of creative blendings that allow for a variety of new expressions and changes. The days are passing very quickly, a week is gone in no time and I keep missing you, but I'm glad for your teaching opportunity.

Of real concern to me are my thoughts about traveling again in

March, so I find myself busy 20 hours a day, just working along; rest several hours in the afternoons and late in the evenings. But time will certainly tell me the best and complete answer about plans for the coming months.

I guess there is a good chance that you may decide to come home after March, but both of us have plenty to do, so basically I'm going to try to not think into the future as much as I have, and only make each of these days count, just getting everything together, and keeping plans moving. The fishing boats are coming in off and on, so periodically I'm down on the docks, speaking Norwegian with some of my friends from Ballard.

I'm going to include some more pictures, they really can explain perhaps better just how I feel now, and it also lets you know about my surroundings.

Huxley College is a busy place, with discussions on biochemistry, genetics, and a group of students are working on the local Bellingham area to try and develop some new park areas, less pollution and a greater awareness of the interdependence of man and his environment. The campus is growing and growing and it borders your old house on 25th now. They are going to build a new part of the college in the fields just north of College Parkway. My building shed looks right over onto the new building and Fairhaven College.

I heard on the radio that England is having a postal strike, so I guess that Scotland is affected too. Hopefully my last letter reached you just before the strike began. It is Sunday morning now, raining quite hard. I plan to continue with building today, and then do some studying later in the day.

I started reading Irving Stone's *Lust for Life*, a story dealing with Van Gogh. I've read some of Stone's other books and enjoy his style, vocab., and just the general drift of his work with artistic exposure through the development of the character of Van Gogh.

I'm sitting in a log cabin just near to where I'm building. My friend Paul, John's brother, lives in a nice little cabin near Fairhaven College, perhaps you have seen the cabin before when you were living on 25th and walking to school. It really is nice staying here during the evenings.

Paul is the one who is good with water colors and sculpture. He has a lot of old furniture here, some from Waldron, so the room pervades with a good feeling, a variety of shadows from the lamps and stove fire.

If you do decide to return to Washington in the spring, by then I'll be well into boat building, sailing, and the development of an understanding of ecology. I'd like to start a variety of associations with sailing, my friends Paul and John have a cabin on Orcas and that would be a nice place to stay for some time after I finish with the work here in Bellingham. We have friends on Waldron too, so it would be possible to live there, perhaps even to buy some land, as I would have some money with the boat building for several acres. Fishing along the coasts of Vancouver Is. like I did last year would be another possibility and then perhaps teaching, in the future. But as far as a job at present there is enough interest in the sailboats that I'll be able to make my way with the boats. So if you did return I would be able to take care of you, or perhaps it would be better to say vice-versa. Especially if you think you would like to be in the San Juan Is. area again. The small community on Waldron has a school, good garden areas, a beach around the entire island, warm summers, no electricity, sailing and fishing in the Sound, a life close to nature, it would be a new extension. With love, Sven

_That spring (1971) Diana and I flew to Seattle and then rode freight trains as far as Chicago on our way to visit her family on the east coast. While she returned to our cabin near Fairbanks, I once more got a job on a fire lookout for the summer, this time in western Montana near Whitefish. I was conveniently able to ride a freight there from Seattle, and when I wasn't scanning the ridge tops for smoke my major project that season was writing the first draft of a book on riding freight trains. At the end of fire season I stopped in Bellingham to visit Steve, and then returned to Alaska. By this time I was less interested in the existential questions that I had pondered while in college; I was pretty much finished with psychedelics and more concerned with what to do with the rest of my life. I still wanted_

# Grow Up for the Co-op
## by sven hoyt

Community gardens are beginning this year in Bellingham. The concept that we are using is to blend garden areas right into the city so that all can begin to relate to the significance of total seasonal changes. Already in Ann Arbor, Michigan Food Co-op gardens have been successful. We are planning to develop many areas in south Bellingham, by using Joe's gardens as a link into the wild and natural plant communities that still exist in the south Bellingham area. The basic plan related to the garden development is that small and community plots of land along with many unchanged areas need to exist throughout the entire town, internal combustion transportation needs to be lessened as soon as possible. People will then be able to develop communities like the one that is developing in Ann Arbor; the slow, gradual blending of life into a total organic environment, that allows peace and understanding to replace noise and confusion. A synthesis of Indian and Chinese cultural values with the positiveness of western culture, ecological change, poetry techniques.

The evolution of the garden must include the entire city into cooperative efforts. At present the Food Co-op is working on a very limited funding and manpower, but more people are becoming involved and the changes are gathering - ebb lines - the yaqui way of knowledge. We are gathering mulching material this week and more manure. We will start plowing in another week, April 4-12. We are in need of a tractor and rotavator and plenty of people to help planting which starts between the 4th and 10th. At present we have over 10,000 starter plants, and we plan to buy a number of seeds this week to plant in the coming month. Anyone with a good source of chicken or cow manure should bring some into the Co-op.

We also need grass and hay for mulching. Come down to the Co-op, bring planting tools and everyone can become involved. We need several innovators that can concentrate on managing various aspects of the gardens. This is a good chance toward positive political change, Tom Hayden, Renie Davis, Rodale float in the early spring days of this land. Charles Reich's "Greening of America" - Counter Culture Roszak threads. We'll gather a feeling for the soil floating through time on Spaceship Earth.

Article from *Northwest Passage*, ca. 1972

to live close to nature but since homesteading was no longer permitted in Alaska it was clear that the only way to live in a wild place would be to buy a piece of land, a very unlikely option for me if I remained in Alaska unless I changed my tack and spent a few years with my nose to the grindstone working at a high paying job. After spending a winter in the very remote Brooks Range of northern Alaska and talking with Alaskans who were interested in wilderness living it was clear that I had missed my opportunity of homesteading or even buying cheap land by a few short years. Likewise, my observation of those who had homesteaded was that all of them still needed at least some cash income to survive on their land, even at a fairly primitive level. And the more remote and wild it was, the more difficult it was to live there without having to return to civilization, to make yet another stake, in order to once again return to their homestead—a vicious circle. I could see that finding that special place would take some time and effort but the letters I received from Steve made me feel that the search would be worthwhile. I was still unwilling to join the carpenter's union. Rather than having to pay a bush pilot to fly me into and out of a remote spot in the interior of Alaska, I reasoned that having my own boat would give me much more control over the necessity of moving between a wild homestead on the coast and the civilization where I would inevitably need to earn at least some money to keep the homestead functioning. At this time I had come to think that the coast of British Columbia might be worth checking out; maybe I could build a sailboat on Vancouver Island and then sail north to find my dreamed of place in the wilderness.

*Letter- no postmark- May 1971*

---

Dear Dan, I'm still settled in south Bellingham, but I plan to start moving around some in the next few weeks to see about other working situations. There is a chance that I'll start herring fishing, for about a month. I find myself more or less strung out at the moment, and I want to start saving some funds so that by next spring I'll be ready to travel to Sweden. If I don't start fishing right away, I plan to visit with Doug. He is over in Sequim working with oysters and other marine life. He is living on the boat and keeping it in the bay near Sequim. We might get together this winter, work various jobs along the coast and spend some time sailing through Puget Sound. The main idea would be to become more familiar with the towns around the Sound, and to plan for trips later on in the year and next spring.

I've been reading more of Gary Snyder lately, mostly from *Earth Household* and some Alan Watts, along with several books dealing with the ocean and sailing. I can really understand Snyder's writing about <u>Tribes</u> and another essay entitled <u>Poetry and the Primitive</u>. When we are sailing on Puget Sound and living exclusively from the sea, the integration of animal senses is more complete and one is able to link the understanding of books with the variety of the natural world. I hope to evolve in the future as a sailor, writer, traveler, so at this point I have to get involved more with the international situation, and to work toward an involvement with ecological concerns and the environment here in America. We have potential in America to become more involved with the values that will link people back into the earth, and at the same time allow them to not become overcrowded and polluted. The main concern will be to find new, clean power sources, and to encourage more people to ride bicycles and live in cluster communities where they won't have to travel great distances. Also to develop an adequate rapid transit system so America will be a mature part of the world. The country now is just emerging, and after it has been finally settled for more than a generation, the concerns now are to develop those potentials, weaving it into the international community. Snyder's book hints at some of these thoughts and William O. Douglas' book *International Dissent* is another that provides new direction for this country. With effort the great task will continue to be one of gathering all the countries together in peace. With China now in the UN, perhaps this will start to happen. At least more cultural exchange is needed and I hope to become involved in this aspect of the future by travelling more this next year. It seems amazing to me that in this country few programs of education are geared now toward international understanding. So much of American's free time appears to be spent with activities that ignore the international community. At any rate on most campuses now, more concern appears to be focusing on improved relationships with China and Russia, and hopefully these concerns will reach the majority of the American public in the future. At Western there has been more speculation about students travelling to China in the coming years, and the hope is now to set up exchange programs with China like the Canadians have at present. [At that time it was all but impossible for an American citizen to visit China.] Groups of students from UBC are travelling there almost 2 or 3 times a year. China should be developed as our mutual friend. Then we can develop better ecological practices here and spend time relating in a constructive manner with all the countries of the world. Slowly and silently this appears to be the gathering trend among students here today, and for more Americans if Nixon's trip to China is a significant one. The latest word on Vietnam is that the troops will be home mostly by after Christmas and then the majority by this June. There is going to have to be some delicate and peaceful moves in the near future but we are all pressing toward peace, and hopefully the US will slowly (in realistic terms) fade out the military in this decade. Then we will be ready to emerge as part of the peaceful world ecological tribe, that will link both the primitive and the modern as Snyder discusses in his *Earth Household*.

I imagine that you are settled back into life in Alaska. Being that I am oriented to Alaska after working there in '68 there is a good chance I'll be fishing up that way again. Doug has been talking about fishing in southeast [Alaska] this next summer. I may very well go with him if I decide not to go to Sweden just yet.

The violin is sounding better, and I've been learning many new songs from the local people that play at Toad Hall [a hippie venue in old Fairhaven, on the south side of Bellingham]. I've also found a book of old Norske tunes and a bluegrass tune book so I have lots of music material to work on these next few months. I hope to get better on the clarinet too, so I'll be able to play a variety of woodwind and string tunes. Your autoharp was very interesting, and I think about you playing it when you were in Bellingham. If I ever spend a lot of time in one place, like you have done there in Alaska, that would be the best way to get into a lot of music and play for people in the community like we are doing at Toad Hall now. Lately Toad Hall has been a gathering spot for many music people and more people are coming all the time to listen and dance. I find myself linking many images written by Snyder with the people that live in the south Bellingham community. There is Chuckanut Mt., the gardens, the vacant lots, the fruit trees, blackberries, the bay, Toad Hall, and the old buildings of south Bellingham, the food co-op; that is really going well now. There are so many small stories, events, poems, floating through the milieu that link back to the poems found in *Riprap* and *Mountains and Rivers without End*. I think about Snyder's written material often and especially now *Earth Household*. One of the most important parts of his writings is his blending of East and West, and the concept of modern tribes, the link of the primitive and the modern, taking the better elements of both to form the new Dharma culture.

I've been reading more about oceanography and marine biology at the U of W library for the last few days. There is such a variety of materials there for all aspects of study in all the oceans of the world, many books in Russian, Swedish and Norske too. I plan to go back again today, to look over several thousand more and talk with a friend who I worked with in Norway in '67; he is doing research on the Amchitka blast [a subterranean H-bomb test on a small Aleutian island conducted in November of 1971] and plans to fly there at the end of this week. The University of Washington has been working with much of the research for the blast and also the follow-up.

I guess your brother is planning to climb the highest mountain yet to be climbed in the world. He is going with some other local climbers; it was in the *Seattle Times* several days ago.

It seems like such a long time since I was last in the mountains. But the sea really is much more of a home now. I plan to continue with some studies of the ocean and have been looking into some of the studies offered at the U of W. The best way to do that would be to live on a boat since the marine studies are right down on the water. Doug might be interested in going there too. But we will have to talk it over. There are some real advantages in using the materials at the U. A good deal of my time spent here in the Puget Sound area will be for understanding more about marine animals and the farming of the sea. Near Bellingham there is a group of Indians who are farming the sea, growing oysters and fish like the Japanese are doing at present.

The entire coast could start to develop this way if we do away with the local polluting industries and link the primitive with the modern, but using our knowledge of the sea to our advantage in growing and harvesting marine life. The U of W is working on some of these projects at present. There are so many new ideas at the U that need to be applied to the society as a whole. In many respects the U and Colleges hold the essence of a new ecological community, in the respect that the area reflects both the modern and the primitive (the primitive being the surrounding of trees, leaves, and grass). In other words, the U reflects man and his integration into the natural world in a social setting, and a place for new and meaningful change. We are planning to have a large vegetable and berry garden at Western in the future, the idea being that people will be able to relate to the local environment, obtain a variety of fresh food, and learn about all the qualities of plant growth, both wild and cultivated, here in western Washington. Then the colleges will be one step further along as they develop as ecological communities. Write soon. Sven

*Writing fragment—no date*

---

I met a man today, who others called very old. But to me he was just a lad. He was a salty fellow, said he'd been a sea captain, but that was some years back. When I told of my plans to sail the high seas, he told me it wasn't an easy life, but he said he would have lived no other way. He'd settled down to a coastal town and married a woman young enough to be his child. And all the city women and dandies gossip about how out of taste the match is. How terrible it would be for his two young boys, to have a father old enough to be their grandfather. But I thought to myself, how lucky those boys are, for they have a father who has the wisdom of a young lad. He was only old because of the years he'd lived. And to me he is younger than all those who talked and gossiped their lives away.

It was 1971 and Steve had a problem—where to store his and Daryl's 12' Penguin sailboat? Welcoming beachfront property households dwindled for the boat and the accompanying motley sailing crews dressed in worn clothing with long hair and beards. How about my parent's place on Whidbey Island? Not having any way to haul it, Steve and I took the more adventurous route, sailing the 60 miles from Bellingham to Coupeville. We left Chuckanut Bay, passed Dot Island and stopped to explore grassy lanes on Sinclair Island. We sailed to the northwest side of Guemes Island, swam in the sea, basked by a fire and slept on the beach.

In the morning, we set out again, and we soon learned about tidal currents which pushed us back towards Bellingham, even while rowing. Back to land we went until at dusk the breeze filled the sails. Sitting astern, we sailed into the light of the western sky, feeling content and alive.

Our next choice was whether to row through Swinomish Slough "on the inside" or sail around the west side of Fidalgo Island and through Deception Pass "on the outside". The wind was perfect for continuing on the outside so we sailed past Anacortes. The wind calmed as we neared Burroughs and Allen Islands and the sky darkened.

Steve rowed towards a boat with a light and asked the folks aboard about possible campsites. They directed us to an Allen Island beach a few hundred yards away. With no flashlights we rowed through eerie black air-and-sea until near the island the phosphorescence dripped exquisitely from the oars, sparkling liquid silver, gold, and green. When an oar clunked on a rocky island cliff, we pushed away to continue south and westward past the cliffs into a sandy cove and the safety of land. We pulled the Penguin above the high water mark, wrapped ourselves in an old brown comforter, and slept soundly. The next morning we blithely sailed on to Deception Pass.

Our "solid" plan (or seemingly so for immortal-feeling 21 and 23 year olds) was to sail to the pass to learn if it was safe to enter. If conditions were unfavorable we would sail across the pass to the south and wait on the beach for the tide to turn. This was a bad idea. As we neared the western entrance, the current simply swept the 12' Penguin around the corner and along the steep cliffs directly into the pass. There were no floatation devices built into the boat, only weather-beaten lifejackets on board that we did not bother to wear.

At first there was only a light chop and no wind. Steve took down the sail and began rowing. I sat astern, next to the rudder, terrified, as the turbulence increased. At this point Steve began rowing, smiled at my terror and said at one point, "You look like a very worried lady!" On he rowed, happy and calm, no doubt enjoying memories of sailing rougher seas along the coast of Norway and the Shetland Islands. People on the bridge above waved to us, not realizing my own deep consternation. As we passed under the bridge we encountered huge boils interspersed with smooth, flat patches caused by the upwelling currents. Then we hit more chop before finally drifting eastward toward Hope Island. Later, looking at a chart, we figured that we rode the current over five miles through the pass.

More excitement occurred later that day when two fishing boats changed course towards us, continuing under full throttle, with each one passing closely on opposite sides of our tiny boat, almost swamping us. As if to balance the scale, a few hours later a large and sturdy sailboat came alongside and the crew kindly offered us a tow to Long Point, east of Coupeville, where my parents lived. The couple told us tales of sailing in Puget Sound while we stood on deck with them watching the Penguin bobbing along behind.

Before hitchhiking to Seattle, Steve regaled my parents with an account of our trip. I remember saying something about how clean we felt from swimming in Puget Sound. My dad thought otherwise, noting how "fragrant" we were. The next day a 30-foot fishing boat went down in the currents of Deception Pass, losing all crewmembers.

*In the fall of '71 I had returned from my fire lookout in Montana but had to remain in the Seattle area for about six weeks to get some dental work done. I spent a few days at the folk's house, which was about to be sold, so I had to gather up all of the stuff I had left there when I left home, sorting everything into two piles—keep and give away. As soon as I had tidied up my affairs I hitched up to Canada, visiting Victoria to do research on wild and remote land on the BC coast, then over to the west coast of Vancouver Island to see the end of the hippie encampment on Long Beach that summer. The Canadian government had automatically evicted everyone by creating a national park (Pacific Rim National Park Reserve) once the presence of vast hordes of hippies brought the natural beauty of the area to the government's attention. I had organized a couple of classes in the free universities in Vancouver and Seattle, mainly to see if I could find other people who wanted to move to a remote place and try to create some kind of community there. On the way to and from these places and activities I stopped in Bellingham where Steve and I talked about our plans and I gave a presentation on the technical aspects of hopping freight trains at Toad Hall one evening. By late October I had a new gold tooth in my mouth (20% of my summer's wages) and I was on my way back to the cabin on Chena Ridge. Back in Fairbanks I soon got a job working as a teachers' aide at a local elementary school while Diana took classes at the University of Alaska.*

*Postcard- postmark BELLINGHAM- DEC 16 1971*

---

Dear Dan, I hope you received the letter I sent. I'm still in Bellingham, studying about life in China, working with fishing boats.

I plan to spend most of the next several months fishing and then start sailing later this summer. Doug and I plan to sail some in the summer. I'm still working on the small sailboats. Doug may plan to sail up to Alaska this summer; I'll find that out when I see him again in two weeks.

If I work for the next 5 months I may decide to start travelling by late this summer, maybe sailing with Doug or over to Europe and on around the world. My brother Daryl will be there in Sweden this next summer too. I'll write a longer letter explaining more. Sven

Hobo Dan, I remember when I used to write to you from Norway and we were both hoboes bumming around the land, in college, on the lookout, at sea, and I feel as if threads are coming together between us more, ecological threads, land, clouds, Why Tribe.

I'm living on Lummi Is. now with a dharma friend; we have a farm with small cabins, and we are diving here for sea urchin earning about $30 a day. The experience here has been Richard Alpert, Watts, Snyder, Kesey, *Between Pacific Tides* and natural history studies of the land and sea. We have some small cabins in a 40 acre field. I'm spending some of my time in Bellingham too, going to land use hearings. And I have been working on a sketched journal of NW impressionism; the land, the people, trees, forest, field, sea, tide, field, life of the mind. *Sometimes a Great Notion.*

We are scuba diving for urchins, collecting them to sell to the Japanese. The urchins eat the kelp and subsequently the small fishes don't have a place to hide and spawn. The sea otters used to eat the urchins, but now with them depleted the urchins are abundant. We have been doing a survey of the shorelines here and have found a bad case of marine pollution along the eastern shore of Lummi Is. We are working along with the Lummi Aquaculture and Dept. of Fisheries to attempt to bring pressure on the Intalco Aluminum plant, Mobil in Ferndale, and Georgia Pacific in Bellingham to get them to clean up or shut down. Several weeks ago three mills in Everett and Tacoma were forced to shut down, so things are happening here. Nixon goes to China in less than a month. The dharma culture starts along the west coast in small farms, communities, the colleges change, but to be more realistic, Nixon lets Amchitka go, and it seems as if the changes are slow, freeways in rat-tail patterns on the ground, back and forth the crazy commuter. Here we are playing the violin and guitar, banjo, Crosby, Stills and Nash, Carole King, Lost City Ramblers, music festival at Toad Hall, music until late at night, 200 people dancing, drinking tea, long hair, dresses, some smoke in the air, but lots of fresh smiles, the Food Co-op in south B'ham, gardens, the book store.

Yes, I can see your point about hunting and gathering, and that is basically what we are into here, along with some gardening. [I had expressed some ideas picked up from friends who had homesteaded in the Brooks Range, later made into a film: *The Year of the Caribou*. They felt that hunting and gathering was a much purer, more direct way to interact with one's environment, compared to what they characterized as the more artificial, one step further removed experience of gardening.] We are living more and more off the wild plants here, rose hips, scallops, fish, apples, vegetables, nuts. You have to have gardening in sound ecological balance with land use. As soon as western culture evolves out of its involvement in the ignorant destruction of the land we can start to form a culture, Dharma Now Age, on the earth. Slow threads in Snyder's Why Tribe, Poetry and the Primitive, Buddhism and the Coming Revolution.

Music keeps us together, some chickens, a couple of goats, Lummi Is. farm floats in mid-January snow, cold, pressing on the ground, silver maple, dogs barking, I have a poem here:

Thomas and I live in a cabin 40 acre field, smoke strings on
sourdough bread, big maple, cluster of alder, Wyeth would enjoy it
here living in isolation, dropping out of –into reality.
Our two dogs Partner and Sillivan, their bodies active in the dry snow.
Roszak and McHarg some where between here and nowhere, be here
    now,
now here be, be nowhere, here now be.
Ladies in long dresses, men working naked, sailing with clusters of
birds-tribes of America, it may happen, ecological poetry technique.
From pages to grasses, from symbol to mind sets, man the floating
symbol of nature.
Deep song voice late at night invites a new yoga age, the age into
the mind slowly, gathering speckled chemistry of body mind.
Yellow, red, green, brown tapestry, winter blending twigs, day after day
along the road, with light field hay-sharp-in the contrast web
like comrades.

I begin to see much of our present life style was determined by the fact that we did so much mountain climbing in our junior high-high school days. That basic experience of living with a pack in the wilderness has been the prime motivation in what I'm involved with now. I think it is important to reflect back on a variety of mountain-freight hopping experiences to decide just how your present day attitudes have formed. With me it was that basic healthy contact with nature, expressed in the days at Kelly Butte or on the chip car we rode over to Wenatchee. Now the San Juan Islands seem to be my home, working with marine studies, sailing, gardening, and the essence of all this involvement is to define an ecological life style which neither of us had in Kirkland. In other words, one has to examine just how much rearrangement of nature man can afford before we start moving toward harm to the natural earth systems of water, wind, sun, and land. We have to look at ourselves as animals who must limit our numbers, and it is difficult to do that since we tend to be the most sexual animals on this earth. But in our evolution, basic numbers will have to be a determining factor in how we plan for the future.

Population growth is still going to be a big problem in the future. And unless numbers are limited soon, I think the government is going to step in and demand a program that makes it difficult to have any more than two children. What has been found to be a battle, basically one of education, new ecological education that seems to be a keynote now here along this coast. Sailing fits into this realm of ecological thinking. We are attempting to start a sailing culture here in Puget Sound, a culture that will be involved with marine awareness, aquaculture, and water quality. I plan to work hard in the area of marine pollution. We have such a wealth here in Puget Sound, scallops, clams, oysters, urchins, fish, and to see these destroyed by heavy industry just cannot be allowed to happen. The waters must be kept clear and natural. Here in the next 20 years we should see an increase in earth ecological planning, and soon several new marine organisms can interact with the water environment, so this seems to be an important field to continue with in terms of long range studies.

All involvement with Puget Sound by man will have to be

reconsidered; sailing should become increasingly more popular, sailing, diving, collecting marine food, and stopping the pollution that affects life along the shores. A new clean power source needs to be invented to limit our present wastage of fossil fuels.

We have had a cold winter here, snow for over two weeks; at least cold for here, and I'm looking forward to spring so we can plant our garden, continue more extensively with sailing and diving. In another month warming trends should set in, we have so much to gather together, basically in an attempt to develop a good farm here in Lummi and to start several in South Bellingham too. I feel very much into the land here, living on the earth, building our sailboats. Tom and I plan to build more boats this spring, so if you plan to have a sailboat in the future maybe we can get together when you are here in the fall. I really think I'll be settled here for a while since the situation is such a good one. Thanks again for your letter and I'll write again sooner.  Hobo, Sven

*Postcard- dated Thursday, 10th of Feb. (1972) to a female friend:*

---

I'm on my way back to Lummi today to continue diving. Tom and I have his car almost together. We are planning to continue our diving research, and finish the car this weekend.

I'm becoming increasingly involved with the environmental protection research here. Tom and I are collecting information about marine intertidal relationships, and we are working with several state agencies to give them some of the information they need to assist them in shoreline management.

The sun is full today, warm February, we are collecting gardening tools and seeds for starter plants. We plan to have berries and more fruit trees, several goats. The winds are gathering for some spring sailing. I really want to take you sailing, and we could get into free diving (without tanks) or scuba with tanks.

It appears now that we will have to wait several weeks until our market is secured in Japan before we go into any extensive urchin diving. If we get a good market there I'll be able to live on Lummi during the spring, collecting urchins, and have enough funds to build up some travelling money- $40-$50 a day. We have a really good chance to contribute to significant studies that are being conducted here by the EPA. I'll see you in Oregon soon, this coming week. Much love and warmth. Sven

---

*In the spring of '72 I left Alaska for good, planning to move to British Columbia after my summer job on the fire lookout. I stopped in Bellingham to visit Steve again where I found him busy with his food CO-OP and garden projects. I remember seeing south Bellingham at that time as "a focal point of hip culture", with the old brick buildings at Fairhaven bustling with the combined activities of numerous hippie entrepreneurs. Along with most of the people making up this vibrant community, I was completely unaware that a developer had been buying up many of these old buildings and adjacent lots with an eye to rehabilitating the neighborhood and it would soon be transformed into a facsimile of Disneyland's Main Street, a beautiful group of refurbished buildings saved at the cost of the community that had sprung up there precisely because it was a low rent district, forgotten and ignored after the local pulp mill had closed. After bidding Steve goodbye I headed east to Whitefish for my last season as a fire lookout. It was while I was on the lookout tower that I learned of Steve's death.*

*Letter- no postmark- late spring 1972*

---

Hobo Dan, In south Bellingham. Planting large Food Co-op Gardens. We are forming a community here of alternative life style, the tribe Snyder's *Earth Household*, and everything is going well. Time passes so quickly, I think about you all the time in the context of our days as Dharma Bums. And I've been seriously thinking about writing a novel- short sketched stories dealing with some of the changes that we have gone through relative to the mainstream of American culture. Charles Reich's book *The Greening of America*, here in Bellingham, with efforts to stop the new freeway. And we are planting large areas with vegeta- bles. The Food Co-op. I've been reading Snyder, Kesey, social change,

Pencil sketch of
Johnson Peak LO
by Daniel Leen

writing for the *Northwest Passage* [the local counter-culture newspaper, also sold in Seattle and Vancouver], and in the evening working on another sailboat. We have a sawmill out by the Nessets' place to cut wood for larger sailboats now and a number of us are planning to build wooden 17 ft to 24 ft. boats in the next 6 months. Plans are really coming together here and I think your plans for a commune, building boats, co-op would certainly be realized here. Tom Blume and I have a 40 acre farm on Lummi Is. that we are leasing. I spent the winter there, but now I'm back in Bellingham organizing the Food Co-op Gardens and selling some sailboats that I built last spring. We plan to cut wood in Van Zandt and build in our barn on Lummi, gardens, fruit trees, berries, and with good efforts, in the fall we'll be on our way with several boats. I'll probably sell the land in south B'ham, take the money and use it to buy a boat, or the wood to build one. The Nessets will let us have some of their wood and we plan to build Norwegian type double-enders. On Lummi we have hens and a goat, so everything is coming together. This operation seems to be just what you would want to build your own boat, to wander in the Sound and up along the BC coast. My thoughts are there too, and my efforts are totally into sailing and the gardens right now. We have yards of sail cloth here in B'ham that we are planning to use in making sails. The desire is to develop a large sailing culture in the Sound that uses smaller amounts of natural resources and is ecologically-minded, marine studies orientation. I've been able to get into diving with scuba gear this winter too, collecting sea urchins in the Lummi area.

The south B'ham community is really coming together, a lot more music, pottery, weaving alternatives, and now with the large Co-op gardens we are developing a new mentality for the entire town and the college. I guess you will be coming down soon. Montana and then I hope here. Doug is trying to sell his boat in Seattle, his father is going out of business and Doug has been there for several months in Juanita. The freight train still runs through Wickersham. I was out to see the Nessets the other day and there it was, gliding across the open fields and in between the trees. The contact with the freights has been vital for me. America is still so confused with the auto industry; if only we could turn some heads around to freight travel, it is such a viable alternative to the present corporate mess. We are fighting Arco and Mobil here in Whatcom County. They are polluting Puget Sound. Carbon monoxide America- wooden ship alternative, I feel that unless people look for alternatives, America is going to soon be a total ecological disaster, but the birth rate is going down, people are all riding bikes here in B'ham and the greening is here. Be Here Now. Brother Sven

---

*Early on June 4, 1972 a minor oil spill occurred at the Cherry Point refinery, located about midway between Bellingham and the US-Canadian border. Equipment failure on a Liberian oil tanker was the immediate cause of the spill and a protective boom which was supposed to be surrounding the discharge operation had not been deployed, thus allowing 4,000–12,000 gal-*

lons of Persian Gulf crude oil to "smear... 14 miles of beaches" in Canada as a two knot current set to the north. This incident resulted in both a political scramble for cover by US politicians and considerable outrage on the part of Canadian citizens who mobilized to protect their local beaches. Steve and a fellow Northwest Passage writer were given a bale of oil-soaked hay from the beach cleanup effort which they then passed on to Jack Racine, the ARCO refinery manager, who was purportedly too busy to be interviewed by Northwest Passage at the time. Although quite distressed by the damage to the environment, Steve was probably not involved in the delivery of another gift of oil—the dumping of a few gallons of crankcase oil on the refinery manager's front porch a few days after the spill with an accompanying note: "Jack- Do Unto Others as You Would Have Them Do Unto You" and signed: "Canadian Friends". While Steve had many friends and associates who were involved in such eco-guerilla tactics, no one I later spoke with thought Steve had abandoned his essentially pacifistic approach to environmental justice.

Steve's final letter seems the least linear in style, a collection of phrases indicating the things on his mind that he didn't want to expound on more formally, its form probably influenced by the poetry of Whitman and Snyder. Of course all of us who knew him will wonder how his thinking and his life would have evolved had it not been cut so short.

Letter- no postmark- June 1972

---

Hobo Dan,  Time floats, I start to really find myself getting into planting Co-op gardens here in south Bellingham. Starting the Co-op commune farms in the south of B'ham, with help from many other people. The Greening of America, my brother Dharma- I salute you- Gary Snyder in the mind, our karma starts to flow out over the earth. We are here Now- the earth is rich with life- the patterns of spring- I'm thinking about living on Lummi this summer- Doing a big garden, several acres and putting my entire energies- hours a day in organizing people to redirect their flow into the gardens- Maybe travel on the freight and see you in Montana- I hope you can come to Lummi- We have a saw mill- plenty of potential for building a boat- tools, land,

trees, and wood on the beach- wilderness- we start planting vegetables
, 2 acres of Lummi- 5 in south B'ham- Start the mellowed out Dharma-
rucksack rev-eco-lution, Amazingly after all these years- the earth
rolls- passage into a greater love for Zen point- spot- high mountain
poems in brother mind- Kelly Butte days- brother John- Daryl in
Sydney, Australia, Doug sailin' Puget Sound, soon to Lummi, Sven
plantin' cabbage- our small world- the vast rim of mankind- we look
around – blend- strivings of Thoreau mixed with a bit of sorrel- Making
love to a woman I get high in the mind- my arms around you- in south
B'ham along the street- playing the violin now- patterns of music- we
could live together and direct our energies into music, sailing Lummi-
harvest home, writing- Lao- subverting- rearrangement into the slow
culture- the Dharma Bums float in patterns grouping arrangements-
many people in Vancouver, the flow of the city- passage into the
gathered life of personal hints. Poems start to flow- piecing together
the groupings of Ken Kesey- Watts- Lorca- Yevtuchenko- the poet
float time space.

Take care, Sven

---

*Steve died doing what he loved, marching to the beat of his own distant
drummer. He had become interested in diving as a means of understanding
the ecological complexities of Puget Sound, and had found work diving
to harvest sea urchins on Lummi Island. On the day he died however, he
was working on the island to set the anchors for the reef nets used by the
Lummi Indians. His scuba tank was an older model, given to him by Doug,
who had warned him that it had no reserve air designed into it, and when
breathing began to become even slightly difficult it meant that it was time
to surface, immediately. Apparently Steve also put his weight belt on first
that day, forgetting that the straps securing the scuba tank would prevent
an emergency release of the weight belt as the scuba tank straps held it onto
his body. As well, Steve had once suffered from a collapsed lung, and this
has also been suggested as a possible reason he was unable to get back to
the surface in time to catch his breath. Another factor which may have been
involved is that he had recently had the flu or a bad cold, and was perhaps*

not entirely recovered. He was diving alone, not with a diving buddy as is now considered standard safety practice. He ran out of air, made it to the surface, but almost immediately sank again. There was no other diver there to bring him back to the surface until it was much too late.

Soon after Steve's death one of the gardens he had helped to create in Fairhaven was named the Sven Hoyt Memorial (CO-OP) Garden. It too would be gone before the end of the year. Along with the continuing evictions of many of the denizens of the Fairhaven community, five months after Steve's death this garden, located directly across the street from the food CO-OP, was bulldozed without warning. The developer who owned the lot had blandly reassured one and all at a public meeting only two days before, stating: "You really don't have anything to worry about". A brief standoff occurred when the gardeners stood in front of the bulldozer, one individual frantically scooping topsoil into a wheelbarrow and racing down the street to another nearby garden while the rest waited for the cops to show up with their brand new riot gear. Later dubbed the Fairhaven Eight, a number of protesters were arrested for trespassing and later fined.

To many this event symbolized the end of their community; it seems that penniless hippies were no match for American capitalism. The buildings were saved, but a community of young and idealistic individuals was obliterated in the process. Virtually all the hippie run businesses were soon gone, as exemplified by Toad Hall, the coffee house where families had gathered to enjoy music, food, and community. It closed the following February, the proprietor given a smile and some John Birch literature by the developer when his lease was terminated. Having run Toad Hall for a few years, working long hours for what amounted to minimum wage, the proprietor was later quoted in a 2008 interview: "...it's funny because one day the hippie movement just ended. It was very weird. Suddenly there was a ...values shift—people wanted to make money and get on with their lives."

Although not occurring in as dramatic a fashion, the slow degradation of the natural environment has also been mirrored by a similar process of those in positions of wealth and power casually dismissing public concerns regarding access to places of natural beauty, reminding me of the rare privilege that my generation had to experience some of these places before they were destroyed or public access was otherwise barred. A recent trip to southern Whidbey Island to revisit the beach and cliffs of Scatchet Head proved to be a disappointment. Now large beachfront houses stand where we once walked the beaches, feeling at least an illusion freedom in a place of beauty. My quest for renewal came to an abrupt end when I encountered signs stating that access points to the miles of beaches on both sides of the point are now privately owned, for members only.

We can at least take a small amount of solace that the environmental awareness of the average citizen today is fundamentally different than it was in 1972. People like Steve made that happen. When I think back to those days, especially when I think of Steve, I am reminded of that other youthful dreamer of dreams, Henry David Thoreau. I imagine how he might react to our situation today, the endless pressure to speed up, speed up, work harder, run, run, run on the hamster wheel just to stay in place, more, more,... I wonder if Henry would see us as the fabled cooking pot full of frogs, the heat being turned up gradually so that very few of us have the sense or can see a way to jump out of our metaphorical stew. So we stew in our own juices, the madness of crowds, evolving into...what? During the 60s and 70s, the legal requirement that all able bodied young men must join the military and go to Vietnam if so ordered, to participate in meaningless slaughter of a people whose political destiny we had no right to dictate, all this amplified by the growing demand for civil rights and economic justice at home, resulted in a mass movement which toppled a president and shook the nation. Today it seems that the powers that be have learned an important lesson—don't awaken the slumbering beast... so we stew gradually in a pressure cooker of our own devising while our so called leaders feather their own nests, throwing a few crumbs from the table to the rest of us when necessary, most of them only bit players, dancing pathetically to the tune of the highest bidder, fiddling while Rome burns. I think of Henry's call, "Simplify, simplify!" I think of the naïve wisdom in Steve's letters, "...there is a lot of truth to be found in the rolling of the earth."

*If when we die we go somewhere*
*I'll bet you a dollar he's ramblin' there*

—Tom Paxton

# Afterword

**E**ACH generation and each individual who struggles to find his own identity as he comes of age has to make its/his own mistakes. Our generation, the fabled Baby Boom generation, was the first one where most of us, if we wished to, were relatively free to find our calling. We didn't feel the desperate need to take the first job we could get, any job, in order to have the security that was so rare for our parents' generation during the great depression. So I was doubly lucky, to have been born at a particular time, a time that allowed those of my generation to reach beyond the limits imposed on earlier generations, and also to have known a young man like Steve, who spurred me to take seriously my own search for my place in the world. I have tried to keep from making this into a hagiography, but perhaps I have to some extent, wanting to remember the optimism of youth rather than any false steps we might have made. Certainly, due to Steve's premature death it is easier to see the positive aspects of his hopes and aspirations without any negative adumbration of these resulting from the human limitations we all face as we mature. At the time he died, Steve was still struggling with the kind of practical realities that we all confront as we trade the idealism of youth for the more attenuated but actual, material rewards of our adult lives. Steve exemplified an individual who strove to experience as much of the world as he could, physically and intellectually, and was willing to pay the price exacted by a life of voluntary poverty in order to do so. In the physical sphere, like Doug and me, he preferred moving across the surface of the earth at a rate that his senses could instinctively comprehend. Thus he preferred walking to riding in vehicles, sailboats to power craft, and he didn't like to fly at all if there was an alternative. Intellectually, he enjoyed discussing ideas with those he met, he wanted to visit other lands and meet and work alongside individuals of different cultures. He devoured literature of all kinds in his search for understanding of the world around him. Both his experiences on the road and the ideas he sought out in books and discussions generated the kind of reflections that eventually mature into self knowledge. Although the ideas that Steve struggled to express are inchoate at times, when I reread his letters to me, I am continually struck with the depth of poetic power in his prose. It is these reflections that have made Steve's letters so meaningful to me, even at the remove of more than 40 years, still striving to attain that elusive goal of self knowledge.

It's quiet up here now
The wind is gently blowin'
It whirls around a bloom and bends it slightly earthward
And then gently lets it go and moves on to another
There's the little burbling brook that flows because
some snow high up hasn't had enough sun
I can hear the brook, sometimes, when the sun
peeks out and changes the ice to water
Not far down in the valley a goat is telling
his master where he's strayed to
He rings his bell with every move he makes
There's something more though, I can only hear it
When it's very still. It's those hills across the valley
They are singing, yes they are singing. It is a beautiful
tune. One I haven't heard for many days
I listen and softly sing back to them
There's a blending and we sing to the world
O, listen world.

# Acknowledgments

**I** WOULD like to express my thanks to members of Steve's family: Russ and Cindy Pfeiffer-Hoyt and Krista Thie and Daryl Hoyt for their help and cooperation with this project including their memories, photographs, and writings of Steve's. Douglas Wilde was generous with his time and memories, helping me to reconstruct some of the details of our adventures with Steve, providing me with additional letters written by Steve and documents and photographs from that time. Another old friend, C. Milo McLeod also offered the use of his photographs as well as helping me to remember the details of events described in this book. Jon Låte very generously sent me a photograph of Steve taken when he visited Jon in Odda in 1966 and also contributed his thoughts quoted from a letter written at that time. Jeff Kronenberg spent an afternoon sharing his memories of the time he spent with Steve creating the CO-OP garden in Bellingham and related activities in the early '70s. I would also like to thank Neelie Nelson for her advice on locating sources of information on this period of Bellingham history. David Buerge, Seattle area writer and teacher generously gave his time to read and critique the manuscript, saving me from the more extreme lapses in the continuity of this narrative. Any errors that remain are my own. Further, a number of friends too numerous to mention individually have graciously taken the time to read and comment on earlier versions of the manuscript as I continually revised it. To all of you I extend my heartfelt thanks.

Daniel has built a log cabin, a 32' sailboat, and a house. He has also worked as an archaeologist, documenting prehistoric petroglyphs and pictographs in the Pacific Northwest, and has published scientific papers on rock art as well as a book on traveling by freight trains. He now makes and sells northwest coast style jewelry at Seattle's Pike Place Market.

Doug has spent a number of years traveling the Pacific, working as a fisherman in Alaska and a boatbuilder around the Pacific Rim, including California, Alaska, Japan, the Marquesas, and Palau. He now lives and works in Thailand.